GẸLẸDẸ

TRADITIONAL ARTS OF AFRICA

Editors
Paula Ben-Amos, Roy Sieber, Robert Farris Thompson

Ọrọ Ẹfẹ sways slowly, majestically swinging horsetail whisks as
he sings throughout the night, commenting on all aspects of society. His special status is mirrored in his elegant red appliquéd
costume with a reptile embroidered on the bodice, the whisks,
and an elaborately carved headdress with a stark white face and
a multicolored superstructure. Igbogila, 1978.

Gẹlẹdẹ

Art and Female Power
among the Yoruba

HENRY JOHN DREWAL AND
MARGARET THOMPSON DREWAL

INDIANA UNIVERSITY PRESS

Bloomington

Publication of this book was assisted by a grant from the Publications
Program of the National Endowment for the Humanities, an independent federal agency.

Manufactured in the United States of America

Library of Congress Cataloging in Publication Data

Drewal, Henry John.
  Gelede: art and female power among the Yoruba.

  (Traditional arts of Africa)
  Bibliography: p. oo
  Includes index.
    1. Yorubas—Rites and ceremonies. 2. Women, Yoruba.
3. Yorubas—Religion. I. Drewal, Margaret Thompson.
II. Title.   III. Series.
DT515.45.Y67D73   1983   306'.089963   82-48388
ISBN 0-253-32569-2
1 2 3 4 5 87 86 85 84 83

To our mothers and fathers

contents

COLOR PLATES

Unless otherwise noted, all photographs are by the authors.

Ọrọ Ẹfẹ in performance, Igbogila.   Frontispiece.

Between pages 8 and 9.

PLATES

PREFACE

Gèlèdé masquerades are lavish spectacles of carved wooden headpieces, cloth costumes, dances, songs, and drumming found principally among western Yorùbá peoples in Nigeria and Benin (see map, p. xxiv). According to tradition, Gẹlẹdẹ began in the latter part of the eighteenth century among the Ketu Yoruba, spreading rapidly to other Yoruba groups and, as a consequence of the nineteenth-century Atlantic slave trade, to the dispersed Yoruba of Sierra Leone, Cuba, and Brazil. Gẹlẹdẹ's fame is proverbial. Yoruba say, "The eyes that have seen Gẹlẹdẹ have seen the ultimate spectacle." Such spectacles occur annually when the first rains fall and in times of communal distress, such as famine, or as funeral commemorations, occasions when communities entertain and pay homage to the forces operating in the Yoruba cosmos.

The etymology of the word *Gẹlẹdẹ* reveals its central concerns and its ultimate significance. *Gè* means "to soothe, to placate, to pet or coddle"; *ẹlẹ* refers to a woman's private parts, those that symbolize women's secrets and their life-giving powers; and *dẹ* connotes "to soften with care or gentleness." Together these ideas convey the significance of Gẹlẹdẹ, performances carefully conceived and executed to pay homage to women so that the community may partake of their innate power for its benefit.

Consisting of nighttime (Èfè) and daytime (Gẹlẹdẹ) performances, these masquerades represent a highly visible, artistic expression of a pan-Yoruba belief: that women, primarily elderly women, possess certain extraordinary power equal to or greater than that of the gods and ancestors, a view that is reflected in praises acknowledging them as "our mothers," "the gods of society," and "the owners of the world." With this power, the "mothers" can be either beneficent or destructive. They can bring health, wealth, and fertility to the land and its people, or they can bring disaster—epidemic, drought, pestilence.

As a phenomenon that essentially belongs to the mothers, Gẹlẹdẹ provides an elaborate aesthetic and symbolic system within which to explore and evaluate the concepts and images of women in an African society and women's spiritual and social roles in Yoruba culture. Scholars have presented two perspectives about women in Yoruba society: One involves woman's social role in the home and in the market (Marshall 1962; Sudarkasa 1973; Lloyd 1963); the other deals primarily with "witchcraft" (Prince 1961; Morton-Williams 1956, 1964; Hoch-Smith 1978). The first view neglects the relationship between beliefs about women's spiritual power and their social roles. The second focuses narrowly on witchcraft, or rather on negative aspects of female power, thus leaving the impression that Yoruba women who are perceived to be powerful are necessarily regarded as antisocial. With the exception of Pierre Verger (1965) and Rowland Abiọdun (1976, 1981), who examine images of women's spiritual power in oral tradition and in art, the literature on the roles and images of women in Yoruba culture does not provide a viewpoint adequate for understanding the Gẹlẹdẹ phenomenon.

With the sanction of the mothers, Gẹlẹdẹ has the performative power to marshall the forces in the Yoruba cosmos for society's well-being. It is at once spectacle and ritual. It is entertaining and it is efficacious. But it is perceived to be more than a mode of persuasion. It is an instrument with which the "gods of society" maintain social control.

Gẹlẹdẹ spectacle thus exhibits social concerns and brings society's desires into actual existence through lavish visual and musical assertions. With the mothers' concurrence, it comments on male and female roles in society, on traditional and contemporary fashions, and on innovations and achievements. It likewise criticizes antisocial individuals and deeds. The art forms that constitute Gẹlẹdẹ comment on society both independently and collectively to produce a complex multifaceted phenomenon. A performance involves space as well as time, and seeing as well as hearing, in addition to the other senses. To understand the content of Gẹlẹdẹ performance, that is, the ideas it affirms, is to understand its creative capacity to shape the world in which it periodically exists.

Much research has been done on performance in the area of the verbal arts (cf. Ben-Amos and Goldstein 1975, Bauman 1977, and LaPin 1977), but those who study the visual arts in Africa tend merely to describe performance as a background against which to study sculpture. This volume, rather than viewing performance as the context of art, views the whole as a text of which art objects are but one element; it examines the art forms of Gẹlẹdẹ both independently and collectively.

After attending and documenting our first few Gẹlẹdẹ performances, we became aware that conventional practices of surveying and generalizing about performances were inadequate. Types of masqueraders differ from town to town, particularly the night masqueraders; there also is variation in costuming styles, dance styles, performance formats, and among the deities associated with Gẹlẹdẹ. While generalizations may provide an overview of the Gẹlẹdẹ phenomenon in broad cultural terms, they leave a number of questions unanswered. How does the researcher reconcile all the elements that do not fit the generality? How does one account for diversity? And, equally important, how do Yoruba themselves regard different ways of performing the same ritual? We set out in search of the norm and instead we were struck by the diversity.

In response to the complexity of the situation, we devised a methodology at once synchronic and diachronic. In addition to a systematic analysis of the constituent media that make up Gẹlẹdẹ performance throughout western Yorubaland, we also collected historical material on Gẹlẹdẹ societies, families, and towns. Concentrating on case studies, we documented oral traditions and personal histories in order to determine the source of these variations. We found, for example, that the area of Yorubaland known as Ègbádò is made up of peoples who trace their origins at various historical periods to Kétu, Ọ̀yọ́, Ọ̀hòrì, and even Nupe and Ègùn countries. The traditions of Ẹgbado reflect these many origins. From quarter to quarter within a town and even from compound to compound, the deities worshipped vary significantly. Case studies of the smallest social unit, the family or lineage, reveal great diversity of origins and intermingling of traditions that often defy broad generalizations and structuralist explanations.

Furthermore, kinship, inheritance, and divination play important roles in shaping ritual practice. Inheritance provides continuity, but divination opens the system to possibilities outside lineage traditions. In addition, such events in individuals' lives as chronic illness, special births, and accidents require adjustments and adaptations in patterns of worship.

Frequently researchers hear from the people they study, "We must do the ritual as our ancestors did it." They often take the statement as evidence of the static nature of African cultures and art. But when considered in light of individual case studies and the diversity that, in fact, exists, the statement suddenly takes on another dimension. One's own ancestors, after all, were different people from almost everybody else's. The Yoruba family, like every family the world over, is the product of numerous personalities, some more dominant than others, and their cumulative experiences and accomplishments. Each family is unique. Each bears the identity of its own particular past, and it is this unique identity that is lauded and asserted at virtually every celebration in Yoruba society. It emerges in praise poetry of lineages and their forebears and in songs, dances, music, and masquerades that not only affirm appropriate social behavior but, perhaps more important, are testaments of individuality, creativity, status, and personal achievement. Thus, men and women are as much creators of culture as they are products of it. Historically, traditions are formulated on the basis of self-interest as much as on sanctioned social norms and social structure.

Our ultimate goals in writing this book are: (1) to examine Gẹlẹdẹ performance, analyzing its constituent media in detail as a means of perceiving the artistic and communicative value of the whole; (2) to set

Gẹlẹdẹ into its larger cultural and historical context; (3) to provide an integrated view of women's social and spiritual roles; and (4) as a balance to the dominant cultural and social perspective present in the literature on art and ritual, to investigate the relationship of Gẹlẹdẹ to individuals, families, and individual communities. It is at this fourth level of analysis, within the context of the specific and the individual, that performance becomes creative and, as a consequence, that Gẹlẹdẹ achieves variety and diversity throughout western Yorubaland. We are, therefore, interested in Gẹlẹdẹ not only as a product of Yoruba culture but also as a forum for individual, familial, and communal self-expression and creativity.

Notes on Sources and Methodology

In our research we utilized numerous written sources, published and unpublished, by various individuals who have researched Gẹlẹdẹ in different areas of western Yorubaland. The Nigerian National Museum archives contain much information on specific towns, most of it collected from the field by the late K. C. Murray between the 1930s and the 1950s. Murray generously provided us with two letters from Reverend A. F. Beyioku, former Osunba of the Ẹgbado Gẹlẹdẹ society, dated 1943 and 1946, containing details of Gẹlẹdẹ history and performance in Lagos. The oral history and practice of Gẹlẹdẹ in Ketu and nearby towns were documented by Father Thomas Moulero, who permitted us to take notes on a handwritten manuscript he had prepared for *Études Dahoméennes*. It never appeared in print because the journal ceased publication. Father Moulero has since died and the whereabouts of the manuscript is unknown. Chapter 7, which considers Gẹlẹdẹ history, draws on these sources in particular.

In addition to these data, comparative material is cited on Gẹlẹdẹ performances witnessed by several scholars in various places. Ulli Beier (1958) provides an account of Gẹlẹdẹ in Ketu and Porto Novo, while Peggy Harper (1970) details Gẹlẹdẹ in the town of Ìjìó. Harper's study accompanies a film by Frank Speed entitled *Gẹlẹdẹ: A Yoruba Masquerade* (1968). A. Olabimtan (1970) offers some useful information on Gẹlẹdẹ in Ìlàró, and Robert F. Thompson (1971; 1974a) describes performances in Ajílété and Ìsàlẹ Èkó respectively. In her cultural history of a Yoruba kingdom in Benin (R.P.B.), Monserrat Palau-Marti (1979:934–938) characterizes Gẹlẹdẹ in Ṣábẹ̆.

Data for a historical perspective of Gẹlẹdẹ derive in large part from oral tradition. The writings of Morton-Williams (1964a), Parrinder (1967), Fọlayan (1967), Law (1977), and Adamu (1978), among others, provide historical reconstructions of western Yorubaland; these too are based largely on oral tradition, but as Robin Law (1977:24) points out, "Oral traditions no less than written sources can be subjected to rational appraisal, and made to yield information of value to the historian." Much research remains to be done, particularly in collecting detailed lineage histories of Gẹlẹdẹ members throughout western Yorubaland.

The field data upon which this study is based come from several types of sources: participant/observation, visual art and dance, vernacular oral literature, and interviews with participants. The vast majority of interviews were with those who could provide a historical perspective and special knowledge concerning Gẹlẹdẹ by virtue of their seniority and participation. Topics covered included town, lineage, and Gẹlẹdẹ history; beliefs associated with Gẹlẹdẹ; and matters of performance. Interviews were not fixed, rather a list of topics served as a framework within which informants were allowed to elaborate upon aspects of special interest to them or about which they were particularly knowledgeable (for example, composers discussed songs and drummers discussed dance rhythms).

Further, we witnessed as many Gẹlẹdẹ performances as we could and collected information from participants, recording their descriptions of what happens during a Gẹlẹdẹ festival and their views and interpretations of different aspects of performance. We were thus able to document to a certain extent performances in places where we were unable to view them firsthand. Fortunately, over the years we have witnessed numerous Gẹlẹdẹ performances—in some cases more than one per town.

We filmed many of the performances and now have approximately 85 minutes of dance footage representing about 40 danced segments from seven ceremonies in various places. We photographed masks, costumes, and dances; and we taped songs and drumming. During interviews or at festivals, we collected Ẹfẹ songs and verbalized rhythms, and we transcribed them in Yoruba with both word-for-word and colloquial translation into English. Explanatory notes provided by the informant usually accompanied them.

Sites where we have observed and documented Gẹlẹdẹ include Ketu and the nearby towns of Idahin and Idofa; Ketì in Ọhọri country; Igbogìlá, Ṣawonjo, Jọga, Igan-Okoto, Imaṣai, Ilaro, and Emàdò Quarter in Aiyétòrò, and Ibarà Quarter in Abẹokùtá, all of which consider themselves Ẹgbado; Ipokia among the Ànàgó; and Isalẹ-Eko in Lagos. In addition to conducting interviews in these places, we also interviewed Gẹlẹdẹ participants on matters of performance and on local traditions and histories, collected Ẹfẹ songs, and photographed masks in the towns of Ofia, Ilara, Ijale-Ketu, and Ika in the Ketu vicinity; Iwoyé, Isaba, Igbẹmè-Ile, Ohumbe, and Ibaiyún among the Ọhọri; the Anago towns of Pobẹ and Agoṣaṣa; the Àwórì towns of Ọta and Igbèsà; and among the

Ẹgbado in the towns of Imalá, Ilogun, Kesan, Ṣala, Ibòrò, Ibeṣé, Ajilete, and Ìlóbì and in individual quarters of Aiyetoro—Aibo, Idofoi, Ilogun, and Ketu—where there are separate societies. We also photographed Gẹlẹdẹ masks in 45 museums in the United States, Europe, Nigeria, and Benin.

Acknowledgments

During twelve years of research on Gẹlẹdẹ, we have benefited enormously from the assistance of numerous institutions and the encouragement, counsel, and wisdom of many friends and colleagues. We are pleased to acknowledge the Institute of African Studies, Columbia University, for a grant in 1970; the Institute for Intercultural Studies, Inc., for grants in 1970, 1973, and 1975; Cleveland State University for faculty research grants in 1974, 1975, 1980, and 1981; and the National Endowment for the Humanities for a Fellowship for Independent Study and Research in 1977–78 (Grant F77-42) and for a Basic Research Grant in 1981 (Grant RO-20072-81-2184). We wish to thank the Institutes of African Studies of the universities of Ifẹ̀ and Ìbàdàn for research affiliations during the periods of our work in Nigeria and Benin.

Of the countless individuals who have contributed to this work, we wish to express our gratitude to Paula Ben-Amos, Douglas Fraser, Dierdre LaPin, Margaret Mead, Melvin Peters, and Robert Farris Thompson for reading earlier versions of this work and contributing valuable editorial suggestions. We are also grateful to Ekpo Eyo, Robert G. Armstrong, S. O. Biobaku, J. R. O. Ojo, Babatunde Lawal, 'Bisi Afọlayan, Howard Wildman, Lamidi Ṣofẹnwa, Laurier Nadeau, Ron Howarth, Frank Speed, and Solomon Wangboje for encouraging and facilitating our research in Africa and to Didi and Juana dos Santos for assistance with Gẹlẹdẹ research in Brazil. We also wish to thank Louise Boston and Edward McNeely of Cleveland State University's Computer Center for advice in preparing the manuscript and Ganiyu Sanni and Kolawole Ọṣitọla for checking the Yoruba orthography. For research assistance in the field, we gratefully acknowledge Samuel Akinfenwa and Raimi Akaki Taiwo. And, especially, to Kọlawọle Ọṣitọla and Rowland Abiọdun, we wish to express our deep appreciation for many enlightening conversations on Yoruba art and culture. They, together with Foluṣọ and Carole Longe and Lea Abiọdun, have been unfailing in their friendship, hospitality, and generosity. Finally, we wish to thank all those— many of whom are cited in the text—who contribute to the richness of Gẹlẹdẹ and who were willing to share their knowledge and experience with us.

NOTE ON ORTHOGRAPHY

Tone marks are given the first time a Yoruba word is cited and also throughout Yoruba texts, whether songs, proverbs, or verbal drum rhythms. The Yoruba orthography used generally follows that of Abraham (1958), which is based on the Ọyọ dialect. However, texts collected in Ẹgbado, Ketu, Ọhọri, and Anago are presented in their original dialectic form. The translations of these data are based upon the explanations and interpretations of those who provided them.

GẸLẸDẸ

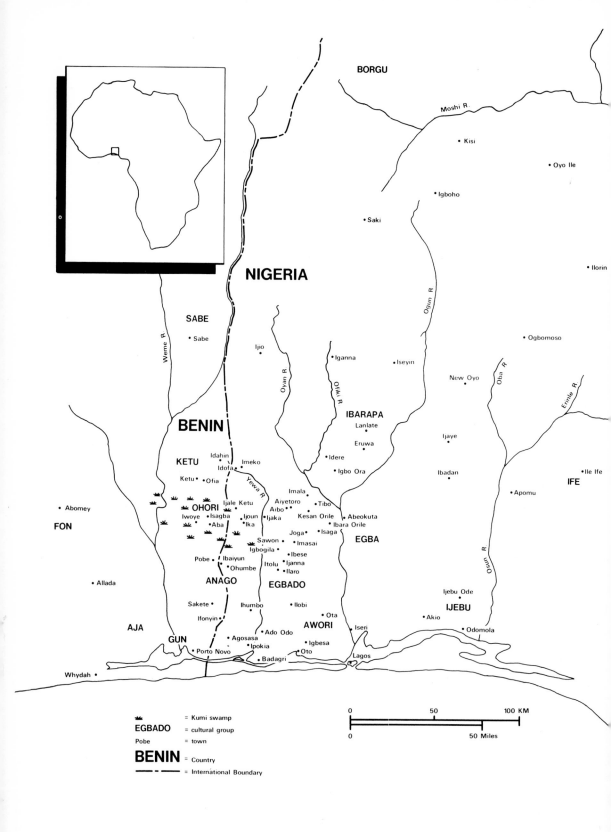

BORGU

Moshi R.

• Kisi

• Oyo Ile

• Igboho

• Saki

NIGERIA

• Ilorin

SABE

• Sabe

• Ogbomoso

Ijio

• Iganna

• Iseyin

New Oyo

IBARAPA

• Ijaye

BENIN

Lanlate

KETU

Idahin

Imeko

Eruwa

• Ile Ife

Ketu • Ofia

Idofa

• Idere

Ibadan

IFE

Imala

• Igbo Ora

• Apomu

OHORI

Ijale Ketu

Aiyetoro

Iwoye • Isagba

Aibo

• Tibo

Abomey

Ika

Ijoun

Ijaka

Kesan Orile

Abeokuta

FON

• Aba

Joga

Isaga

• Ibara Orile

Sawon

Imasai

EGBA

Pobe

Igbogila

• Ibese

• Allada

Ibaiyun

Itolu

• Ijanna

Ohumbe

• Ilaro

ANAGO

EGBADO

Ijebu Ode

Sakete •

Ihumbo

• Ilobi

• Akio

IJEBU

Ifonyin •

• Ota

AWORI

Iseri

Odomola

AJA

Ado Odo

GUN

Agosasa

• Ipokia

• Igbesa

• Oto

Lagos

Porto Novo

• Badagri

Whydah •

Weme R.

Oyan R.

Ofiki R.

Yewa R.

Ogun R.

Oba R.

Erinle R.

Osun R.

= Kumi swamp

EGBADO = cultural group

Pobe = town

BENIN = Country

— · — · — = International Boundary

0   50   100 KM

0   50 Miles

1
Yoruba Spectacle

The eyes that have seen Gẹlẹdẹ
have seen the ultimate spectacle.
Ojú to ba rí Gẹ̀lẹ̀dẹ̀ ti de òpin ìrọn.

This saying, well known even in parts of Yorubaland where Gẹlẹdẹ does not exist, suggests something of Gẹlẹdẹ's widespread reputation and its impact on spectators. But what do Yoruba mean by spectacle *(ìrọn)*? In its broadest sense, spectacle is a fleeting, transitory phenomenon. It may be a display or performance for the gods, ancestors, or the mothers; but it may also refer to mental images. Thus, the Yoruba word for spectacle is the same word used to speak of a mystical vision *(ojúùrọn* or *ojúù ìrọn)* or the power of visions *(irûrọn,* literally "act of seeing visions") (Abraham 1958:317). Similarly, *ìrọn* is used in referring to a remembrance *(inûrọn,* "a mental recollection"). It is perhaps partially in this sense that certain kinds of narratives *(àló)* are considered spectacles, for storytelling creates "the illusion of actualized events" (LaPin 1980:2). A story is a spectacle in the sense that it is visible through the storyteller's dramatization, and the spectator visualizes it further in his mind's eye. Thus Dierdre LaPin's informants referred to certain types of narrative as pictures *(àwòrọń* or *à wò ìrọn)*, images to be looked at.

As a vision, as a remembrance, as a narrative, or as a festival or a display for the gods, ancestors, or the mothers—these various usages of the term *ìrọn* have something in common: they imply, as LaPin says (1980:7–8), "a mysterious, permanent dimension of reality which, until revealed, is shut off from human view." They are otherworldly phenomena whose worldly manifestations are temporary and periodically reintroduced or regenerated.

1

Perhaps for this reason the term *irọn* also is used to designate "a generation." A generation consists of the members of a lineage *(ìdílé)* who are born into the world at approximately the same time, whose children would make up the next generation. Implicit in a generation is the collectivity of people required to formulate it. A spectacle, by definition, likewise implies a collectivity of participant/spectators and a multiplicity of images and ideas converging in the same time frame. The cumulation of all generations constitutes a lineage, that is, both the living and the departed who trace their origins to a common progenitor. Continuity or regeneration is implicit in the concept of lineage; a generation represents one of its diachronic units. Thus the notion of continuity within a lineage is expressed *l'ìrọn d'ìrọn,* "from generation to generation." A generation is the worldly manifestation of a lineage, just as spectacle is the worldly manifestation of a permanent otherworldly reality. Like spectacle, a generation is temporary, transitory, and cyclical.

The transitory nature of existence in the world is expressed in the Yoruba proverb "The world is a market, the otherworld is home" *(Aiyé l'ọjà, ọrun n'ilé).* The market as a metaphor for the world evokes an image of a place one merely visits, whereas home or the afterworld is a permanent residence. The notion that spectacles are temporary, worldly manifestations of permanent, metaphysical realities can be demonstrated in a number of specific contexts. The most explicit example is possession trance, when during ceremonies the gods become manifest in the world in the bodies of their devotees. Other examples of temporary manifestations of the supernatural occur in the masquerade performances of ancestral spirits, Egúngún, and in Gẹlẹdẹ.

Evidence of the otherworldliness of Yoruba spectacle, whether it is a masquerade display, a festival for the gods, or a narrative performance, is to be found in its clearly demarcated openings and closings, which bring it into the world and return it or "carry it away" again, i.e., back to the otherworld *(ọ̀run).* Hence, Egungun society members explained that their own masquerade spectacle opens at night when all nonmembers lock themselves in their houses. At that time, in the center of the town, a spirit known as Agan, who must not be seen by anyone, brings the festival into the world. The chants that accompany Agan's coming hint at the spirit's elusive, otherworldly entry into the world by making an analogy to the way rain falls on the earth:

> I come *weréweré* [small, quick, light, i.e., drizzling] like the early night
> rain
> *Màrìwòoo! Àgànóoo!*
> I come *kutukutu* [forceful and quick, i.e., pouring] like the early
> morning rain

Màrìwòoo! Àgànóoo!
I come *pápàpá* [large, heavy sporadic drops] like the rain at sunrise
Màrìwòoo! Àgànóoo!
The eyes of the blacksmith cannot see underneath the ground of his
  shed
Màrìwòoo! Àgànóoo!
The eyes of the potter cannot see the inside of clay
Màrìwòoo! Àgànóoo!
Mèmèmè cries the female goat
Bòbò cries the female sheep
Màrìwòoo! Àgànóoo!
I get up early in the morning
I bring dew from the otherworld to earth
I descend *rùrùrùrù* [the sound of walking through wet grasses]
Màrìwòoo! Àgànóoo!
I come with cudgels, a sheath, a sword
Màrìwòoo! Àgànóoo!
Grasp it! Nothing's there!
Grasp it! Nothing!
Grasp it! Nothing!
Amamamamamamama!
Be looking! We are looking!
Be looking! We are looking!
Be looking! We are looking!

Mo dé weréweré bi ejí orì alé
Màrìwòoo! Àgànóoo!
Mo dé kùtùkùtù bi ejí àwúrò
Màrìwòoo! Àgànóoo!
Mo dé pápàpá bi ejí ìyalèta
Màrìwòoo! Àgànóoo!
Ojú alâgbèdè ko to'lè arọ
Ojú amọkòkò ko to'lè amò
Mèmèmè nigbe ewúré
Màrìwòoo! Àgànóoo!
Bòbò nigbe àgùtàn
Màrìwòoo! Àgànóoo!
Mojí lóròru kùtùkùtù
Mogbé enìni òrun w'aiyé
Mo wò rùrùrùrù
Màrìwòoo! Àgànóoo!
Mo dé t'ogbó t'ògọ t'àkò t'idà
Màrìwòoo! Àgànóoo!
Gbámù! Òfó!
Gbámù! Òfó!
Gbámù! Òfó!
Ámamamamamamama!

Ẹmá wá! Anwá!
Ẹmá wá! Anwá!
Ẹmá wá! Anwá!

[Collected in Ilaro, 1977]

This invocation makes use of idiophonic language to simulate actual dynamic qualities, qualities likened to the way rain falls. But, according to Yoruba thought, its role is not merely poetic or symbolic; rather it invokes or brings the spirit into existence at the threshold of the phenomenal world. Agan enters at the center of the town, but in Yoruba thought the center is the place where the material and the spiritual realms intersect (cf. M. T. Drewal 1975 and Abiọdun 1980b); it is the crossroads, *oríta (orí ìta)*, literally "the head or the point of intersection." Its entry is elusive and enigmatic, like sudden rain. This elusiveness is highlighted by the fact that no one must see Agan; it comes only after the townspeople, for fear of death, lock themselves inside. Its presence is made known through sounds rather than sights. Finally, at the close of the festival, another spirit, called Aránta or Olọdúngbọ́dún (literally "The-Owner-of-the-Festival-Takes-the-Festival") carries the spectacle back to the otherworld.

The spiritual transcendence of Yoruba spectacle is also implied in the generic name given to the first rhythms played by the *bàtá* drum ensemble during Egungun displays or festivals for Ṣàngó, Ọya, and other deities. These introductory rhythms are called *alùwási,* a contraction of the phrase *a lù wá si aiyé* (literally "drums come into the world"). A sacrifice is performed before the festival begins to put the drums into a ritually transcendent state, and at the close a "cooling" rite *(ètùtù)* is performed to restore them to normalcy.

LaPin (1980:12–14) has recorded opening and closing formulas of a similar nature in storytelling.[1] She notes that

> The metaphorical assertion that *àlọ́* is like a jinn (spirit, dead person) is given further weight in the formulaic verses that open and close many performances. . . . Introductory formulas to the *àlọ́* develop the notion that the mode is a separate ontological entity that undergoes transformation and rebirth in the body of the performer. [An introductory formula] acts in an incantatory sense as a catalyst which dislodges the *àlọ́* from its home in an upper region, somewhere between heaven and earth. Thus shaken out of its slumbering state, the *àlọ́* suddenly lurches into action.

Such opening and closing conventions confirm that spectacle is perceived to be a transitory, worldly manifestation of an otherworldly reality, just as a generation is the worldly manifestation of the Yoruba lineage, which is eternal.

As an otherworldly phenomenon, spectacle partakes of a dynamic force that makes it not merely affecting but also efficacious, not merely symbolic or metaphorical but instrumental (cf. Ray 1973). It possesses the performative power of *àṣẹ*, the power to bring things into actual existence.[2] This concept is fundamental to Yoruba thought. Variously defined as "power, authority, command" (Abraham 1958:71), "a coming to pass . . . effect; imprecation" (Crowther 1852:47), *aṣẹ* has important metaphysical dimensions but no moral connotations. It is neither positive nor negative, neither good nor bad, but rather is an activating force or energy. *Aṣẹ* encompasses both the expression *áàṣẹ*, which follows prayers and invocations and affirms "so be it, may it come to pass," as well as *aṣẹ̀*, "shrine," the site of concentrated substances containing vital force—herbs, foods, blood of animals—which attract and stimulate a god's power. *Aṣẹ* is absolute power and potential present in all things—rocks, hills, streams, mountains, leaves, animals, sculpture, ancestors, and gods—and in utterances—prayers, songs, curses, and even everyday speech.

Utterances, as expressions of the spiritual inner self of an individual, possess *aṣẹ*, the power to bring things into actual existence. This belief is apparently ancient, for a number of Ife terra cotta heads depict sacrificial victims who are gagged to prevent them from uttering a fatal curse upon their executioners (Willett 1967:49; Awolalu 1973:88).[3] As Ulli Beier (1970:49) explains,

> Yoruba believe strongly in the power of the word, or rather in a mysterious force called ashe . . . that quality in a man's personality which makes his words—once uttered—come true.

Raymond Prince (1960:66) confirms,

> It would appear that their background conception is that to utter the name of something may draw that something into actual existence . . . not only within the mind and body of he who utters and he who hears the word, but also in the physical world as well.

And according to J. A. A. Ayoade (1979:51),

> The second and more difficult level [in evoking spirit forces] is that in which the spirit forces still remain dormant until they are called forth through the utterance of words of power. The knowledge of the secret names of these spirits and of incantations is of special importance in concretizing the inner essence of an object.[4]

In this way, the spirit Agan is invoked to bring the Egungun festival into the world. Similarly, in Yoruba incantations *(ọfọ̀)* chanted during the preparation or application of medicines *(oògùn)* to invoke the dynamic essences of all their ingredients, a monosyllabic action verb drawn from each ingredient's name is pronounced following that name to set the ingredient into action (Verger 1976).

Words possess a dynamic unleashed in the act of pronouncing, thus activating latent forces through effective patterns of stresses—the combination of tone, duration of syllables, and vocal force. This power is especially evident in the voicing of idiophonic words, or what S. A. Babalọla (1966:67–68) calls "word-pictures," words that by their very sound and intensity evoke mental pictures, such as those cited above to invoke the Egungun spirit Agan. Thus, words and phrases not only carry meaning through their definitions and relationships to each other, but may carry extraordinary power in their performance, that is, in the dynamics of the act of pronouncing. By this means, latent forces, or rather forces residing in the otherworld, may be brought into existence, into the phenomenal world. This power is most obvious in incantations and invocations, but it is also explicit in a variety of other verbal arts performances, including those of Ęfę night.

The spoken word carries the power to bring things into being, especially when uttered by the *aláàṣẹ,* "one who has and uses *aṣẹ,*" during invocations and sacrifices. Blood also contains *aṣẹ.* The shedding of blood in ritual sacrifices, which precedes ceremonies for the gods, ancestors, or the mothers, releases a vital force that is transferred to the god or spirit to renew his or her *aṣẹ* for the purpose of benefiting the devotees. Blood or *aṣẹ* is also poured on ritual objects associated with a deity to infuse them with power. The act of sacrifice is a reciprocal affair between man and the gods in which the devotee nurtures the spirit of the divinity in exchange for increased protection and blessing (cf. Awolalu 1979:134–142).

All sacrifice, however, need not be bloody. When prescribed by a diviner, performance is sacrifice, for it requires great expense on the part of the supplicants. Thus, a diviner may instruct a client to sacrifice by giving a cloth to Egungun in order to conceive a child. In effect, the individual must create a masquerade and perform with the Egungun society during its festivities. Likewise, the community may be told to sacrifice in order to appeal to the spiritually powerful women, and this obligation will be met by performing Gęlędę. Art is sacrifice, and artistic displays carry the sacred power to bring things into existence.

The fundamental concept of life force—that it exists in many forms and manifestations and in varying amounts—is at the foundation of Yoruba philosophy and social organization (cf. Drewal and Drewal 1980). The system acknowledges innate individual power and potential. Similarly, the concept of *aṣẹ* is basic to the structure of the arts, whether verbal or visual, a structure in which the units of the whole are discrete and share equal value and importance with the other units and in which the autonomous segments evoke, and often invoke and activate, diverse forces. So far, this concept has been demonstrated in the opening and closing segments, which bring spectacle "into the world" from its other-worldly realm and carry it away again. This type of organization or compositional style is seriate.[5]

Seriality is a fundamental organizing principle in Yoruba spectacle as well as in praise poetry, invocations, incantations, textile designs, body tattoos, and sculpture (cf. H. J. Drewal 1977b:6–8; Drewal and Drewal 1980). Attention to the discrete units of the whole in any medium produces an overall form that tends to be multifocal, often characterized by a shifting perspective. Its outer features—whether its units are arranged spatially or temporally—include clearly demarcated openings and closings, segmentation, discontinuity, free rhythm, repetition, and density of meaning.[6] Other concepts of performance will become evident as we examine Gẹlẹdẹ as the "ultimate" in spectacle.

The Spectacle of Gẹlẹdẹ

Gẹlẹdẹ, found principally among western Yoruba peoples (including those of Ketu, Ọhọri, Anago, Ifọnyin, Awori, Ẹgbado, Ibarapa, and Ṣabe), varies greatly as a result of historical factors and inherited and acquired worship patterns within lineages. In each town, it is generally associated with a deified founding foremother, either an earth or a water deity, and a deified forefather. Other gods, such as Ògún and Èṣù/Ẹlẹgbá, may also be honored, and individual Gẹlẹdẹ families additionally sacrifice to their own lineage gods. Despite local variations, the fundamental purpose of Gẹlẹdẹ spectacle is to pay tribute to and therefore to derive benefit from female mystical power. An elderly participant (Ogundipẹ 1971) points out:

> The gods of Gẹlẹdẹ are so called "the great ancestral mothers". . . . The power of The Great Mother is manifold. The ancestors, when they had a problem, would assemble to determine the cause and the remedy . . . and, if it is found that Gẹlẹdẹ should be done to bring about rain or the birth of children, it should be done and it will be so. The Great Mother has power in many things. . . . [She] is the owner of everything in the world. She owns you. We must not say how the whole thing works.

The Gẹlẹdẹ spectacle honors and serves spiritually powerful

elders, ancestors, and deities. Thus, "the Gẹlẹdẹ which we
for our great grandmothers whom we call òrìṣa ẹgbẹ́ [gods of
o have a collective name" (Babalọla 1971). The term ẹgbẹ refers
Yoruba society as a whole and the secret society of powerful old
who can transform themselves into birds at night and hold meet-
the forest.[7] These women are commonly known as "our mothers"
(áwọn ìyá wa), an endearment that recognizes that "we all came out of a
woman's body" (Ayodele 1971). As one Gẹlẹdẹ elder points out (Ogundipẹ 1971), they can be destructive, "but we must not call them that. We
call them mother. If they did not exist, we could not come into the
world." These statements imply something much more fundamental
than female fertility and fecundity. They claim that women possess the
secret of life itself, the knowledge and special power to bring human
beings into the world and to remove them. This knowledge applies not
only to gestation and childbirth but also to longevity. It is a sign of
women's power that they live to be very old, often outliving men. Their
knowledge of life and death demands that Yoruba herbalists in preparing medicines seek their support. A priestess (Ẹdun 1975) comments,

> If the mothers are annoyed, they can turn the world upside down.
> When an herbalist goes to collect a root at the foot of a tree, the
> mothers put it up. And when he climbs up for a leaf, the mothers put it
> down.

The power of the mothers is equal or superior to that of the gods,
for, as a number of informants suggest, the mothers own and control the
gods. As the king of a small Ẹgbado town (Adelẹyẹ 1971) comments in
English:

> Our mothers will not come out openly and say, I want so and so from
> you. They may be worrying someone until that person goes to a di-
> viner, when it will come out that it is a witch that is worrying the
> person. Then the oracle will prescribe so many things. . . . They
> [diviners] have certain means to do sacrifice. If they [the mothers] are
> worrying somebody, they can hide under an idol. So when someone
> goes to the oracle—it may be [to] Ṣango or Ọya—it means that the
> woman is fighting the patient through Ṣango or Ọya. Then if some-
> thing is offered through that idol, the woman will be satisfied.

Another elder explains further (Babalọla 1971):

> If there is an epidemic, we sacrifice to all the gods of the town. We try
> to conciliate them. All the mothers are the owners of all these gods.
> After making sacrifices to the gods, the mothers would know that we
> have begged them. After giving them something to eat there will be no
> more trouble.

1. Recreating Ọrunmila's mythic journey into the realm of the mothers, the Gẹlẹdẹ performer dances with a mask, head ties, and leg rattles. Ilaro, 1978.

2. Ọrọ Efẹ wears a headdress, a veil, cloth panels, and a hunter's jerkin, and he flashes his whisks, blessing the spectators as he sings. Ṣawonjo, 1978.

3. The back view of Ọrọ Efẹ's costume reveals appliquéd cloth panels and, on his headdress, a carved leather panel. At his feet, hunters load their guns for a salute. Ṣawonjo, 1978.

4. Layers of women's head ties fly outward as the dancer turns
rapidly. Ilaro, 1977.

5. In the Ketu region, masqueraders often incorporate elaborately embroidered and appliquéd cloth panels into their costumes. Idahin, 1971.

6. This embroidered, appliquéd wrapper shows several horizontal registers of images, including soldiers, colonial officials, hunters, people shaking rattles, and bicyclists. Ṣawonjo, 1978.

7. A Ketu male Gẹlẹdẹ wears a large bamboo hoop around his chest covered with women's head ties, thus creating a massive cylinder of cloth. Idahin, 1971.

8. An Ẹgbado male Gẹlẹdẹ combines remnants of worn-out appliquéd panels from an old costume, a long-sleeved jacket, and a mass of knotted head ties. Ṣawonjo, 1978.

9. The biplane is a technological innovation that hints at the spiritual potential of Europeans and exemplifies the constructive use of power. Lagos, 1978.

10. On this mask, a large snake encircles a priestess and other worshippers. Such superstructures can be interchanged; compare this mask and the one in plate 111. Ṣawonjo, 1978.

11. During performance, the masquerader uses a long strip of cloth to balance a large superstructure (side view of masquerader in plate 10).

12. Gẹlẹdẹ patrons in some regions prefer traditional pigments made of various organic substances, including eggs. Lagos, 1978.

13. Although it is fairly uncommon, verisimilitude seems to be a concern in these masks, painted in brown tones to approximate skin color. Lagos, 1978.

And as a female Gẹlẹdẹ cult leader told Beier (1958:7):

> No orisha [god] can do good, without the mothers. The mothers could spoil any good action if they wanted to. Therefore Sango himself cannot help his worshippers without permission of the mothers. The prophesies of the Babalawo [diviner] will come to naught, if he has not appeased the mothers. Oro and Egun cannot kill without the mothers.

A priestess confirms (Ẹdun 1975):

> Ifa is senior to them [the mothers] *(alágbára wọn)*, but aside from Ifá, nothing is elder to them. . . . They are more powerful than any deity.

These comments by western Yoruba peoples are not Gẹlẹdẹ-centric, for Verger (1965) collected a number of detailed divination verses, primarily from the Oṣogbo area, that attest to female suzerainty at the very creation of the world. In one of these myths from *ọsa méjì* (1965:204), Òlódùmarè gave woman (Odù) control over the gods on the condition that she use her enormous power with care, calm, and discretion *(máa rọra lọ rèélò agbára)*. When she abused this power Olodumare gave it to Òriṣánlá, her male companion, decreeing that he would exercise it but that the woman would retain control over it (Verger 1965:142). In southeastern Yorubaland, an Ijẹbu diviner (Oṣitọla 1982) explains that it was Odu, a wife of the first diviner, who loved her husband Ọrúnmìlà so much that she revealed to him the knowledge of divination so that man could communicate with the spirit realm. And Rowland Abiọdun (1976:1), relying primarily on central and eastern Yoruba sources, writes

> It is believed that from the beginning, the creator-God put women in charge of all the good things on earth. Without their sanction, no healing can take place, rain cannot fall, plants cannot bear fruits and children cannot come into the world.

Because of the mystical power of women, devotees of the gods and ancestors seek them out and encourage them to attend rituals. Their very presence is efficacious. *Àjẹ́*—a generally perjorative term—is used rarely and with caution. No one would address a woman suspected of possessing such power as *ajẹ*, not just out of fear but because such women also work positive wonders. Therefore they are called "our mothers" *(awọn iya wa)* and are addressed personally with "my mother" *(ìyámì)* or "old and wise one" *(iyá àgbà)* in recognition of their positive dimension as protective progenitors, healers (MacLean 1969:37), and guardians of morality, social order, and the just apportionment of power, wealth, and prestige (Verger 1965:159). It is in this last capacity, as guardians of society, that the mothers are central to Gẹlẹdẹ spectacle.

The otherworldliness of the Gęlędę spectacle is evident in its place and time settings. Gęlędę performance takes place in the main marketplace—a setting that is significant for several reasons. The marketplace is a metaphor for the world. Existence on earth is like coming to the market to do business before returning to the realm of the ancestors (Lindfors and Owomoyela 1973:23). The marketplace itself symbolizes Gęlędę's transitory, worldly manifestation, while at the same time it represents its otherwordly dimension, for the market is a liminal place, where spirits intermingle with human beings. It is often situated at the center of the town, at a crossroads where one finds the shrine for the deity in charge of the crossroads, Eṣu/Ęlęgba.

Numerous stories involve the marketplace: Hunters' tales describe the way animals in the bush remove their skins, transform themselves into human beings, and go shopping on market days. Other stories tell of spirits in human form who frequent the marketplace, marry mortals, and bear their children, only to disappear one day, taking the children with them. The intermingling of mortals and spirits in the marketplace during Gęlędę is suggested by an Ęgbado king (Bakare 1971), who contended that when Gęlędę is a success, spirits known euphemistically as "strangers" visit the performance. They appear as mortals and are identifiable by the fact that they are unknown to the community. When many strangers are in attendance, it is felt that the community has been successful through performance in communicating with the supernatural realm. As Bakare explained, "We realize our prayers have been answered when strangers visit in the night. Young children, grownups, and old people come and then disappear at daybreak."[8]

It is not inconsequential that the market is a major setting of social and economic activity involving primarily women. Trading is probably the most common profession among women in Yoruba society. Indeed the market is controlled by women; its administrative head, the Ìyálòde, holds a position on the king's council of chiefs. Women are economically independent, and through trading they can acquire greater wealth and higher status than their husbands (Lloyd 1963:39; 1974:38). By bringing the spectacle into the market, the Gęlędę society introduces it directly into women's realm, the place where their collective social power is most consciously felt. The marketplace is thus a most appropriate setting for a ritual that seeks to gather all segments of the society in order to pay homage to the special power of women and to partake of their influence.

The market is a transient place, at once the domain of women and the worldly domain of spirits, the place where they enter "the world" to mingle freely with mortals. "The mothers," by definition, also have this ability; they are mortals who have access to the otherworld. It is in their supernatural capacity, reflected in the power of transformation, that women are considered the "owners of two bodies" *(abâra méjì)* and the "owners of the world" *(oní l'oní aiyé).* They control the world; they control the market. Indeed the market is a microcosm of the world, for the Yoruba concept of *aiye* implies the phenomenal world that any number of spirits, by assuming human or animal form, can penetrate.

Another important and very popular element of Yoruba spectacle is the nighttime ceremony. Thus spectacles such as Gẹlẹdẹ, Egungun, and festivals for the gods often open around midnight and end at sunrise. Informants offer several explanations for nocturnal performances, or *àìsùn* ("without sleep"). One is that it is cooler at night and therefore more enjoyable. Indeed, even when performances occur during the day they are generally scheduled for the late afternoon. While this explanation and others[9] may account in part for the prevalence of night ceremonies, they are not entirely adequate.

Normally nights are devoted to rest after long, hot hours of physical and mental activity. Thus to set aside such time for participation in some ritual activity lasting eight hours or more is to demonstrate a certain and unusual devotional commitment. The tradition of the "wake-keeping," or "vigil," however, is an integral part of Yoruba religious life. The funeral rites of almost all individuals include a sleepless night during which the family and friends of the departed remain vigilant to ensure the safe and proper transfer of the deceased's spiritual essence to the afterworld, *ọrun.* The same principle seems to operate in the openings and closings of rituals to the ancestors and gods, when the supernatural forces inhabiting *ọrun* are coaxed into *aiye,* the phenomenal world, by humans. These difficult and critical occasions involving the interpenetration of realms are most appropriate at night, when spirits are thought to be most atten-tive (Ọṣitọla 1982). Darkness is the natural abode of the mothers and the creatures most often associated with them, such as birds, bats, rats, and reptiles. The obscurity of the night adds to their awesome, unknowable qualities. If the market is the place inside the community where spirits are most likely to mingle with humans, then the most likely time for intermingling is at night in the market.

Another distinctive feature of Gẹlẹdẹ spectacle that perhaps alludes to its otherworldliness is the theme of doubling. The spectacle itself is in two parts—the nighttime Ẹfẹ performance and the daytime Gẹlẹdẹ dance—and informants stress that one cannot take place without the other. Within the Ẹfẹ rites, the singing male masquerader, Ọrọ̀ Èfẹ̀, must be preceded by a partner, either male or female, who is viewed as a companion, wife, or twin. And in Gẹlẹdẹ, masqueraders traditionally perform in identical pairs.

Inherent in the pairing of masks, costumes, and movement, like the ultimate creation of the mothers—twins—is the concept of elaboration.

Automatically the pageantry and energy are doubled as each masquerader dances toward the drum ensemble, individually interpreting the intricate verbal/rhythmic percussive messages. The observer is surrounded by a wealth of artistic display as each performer emerges, dazzles, and quickly disappears only to be followed by another spectacle.

The Gelede spectacle is a lavish two-part multimedia production created by singers, dancers, carvers, drummers, and spectators. It appeals to the senses through a brilliant array of sounds, sights, and energy. The impact is immediate and striking yet enduring, as evidenced by the easy recall of songs and spectacles that occurred in the distant past. Gelede has been called "the ultimate spectacle" for its ability to shape society and to create a lasting impression by means of an absorbing multimedia experience.

The first part of the spectacle, Efe, is a night of songs. Many of the performers are dramatically attired and are constantly in motion. The senses are activated not only by sound but also by sight and energy made visible. Each performer is an entity unto himself. With each successive entrant, the crowd becomes increasingly excited, and the emotion reaches its peak with Oro Efe's gradual emergence. The undulating melody of his songs are made visible in the sweeping, curving, and spiraling movement of his arms and in the complex circular/spiraling forms of his mask. He begins to move through the performance area, orally and physically carrying his words to the crowd. Stateliness and grandeur characterize his moving image, for Oro Efe's appearance and manner communicate overt masculine power and authority, the authority that comes from the mothers' support. Oro Efe, the "voice of Efe," who can utter his thoughts on any topic, is a monarch of the night, immune to all attacks, responsible for the well-being of his "subjects." As he moves through the darkness, appearing and disappearing, his words are now clear and loud, now muffled and distant. The total illusion is both mystical and immediate, just as the songs themselves deal with both spiritual powers and human society. Oro Efe is transcendental voice, powerful man, and servant of the mothers.

The dramatic flow of Efe night mirrors the serial structure of the spectacle. The tension builds with each performer; a lull follows until the next one appears. Excitement peaks at the most dramatic moment—Oro Efe's entrance—and remains sustained yet diminishing during the remainder of the night while songs are sung. Like the masqueraders themselves, songs follow one another in serial fashion, yet their concerns are different and often unrelated.

Power made visible is essential to the second part of the spectacle, the afternoon Gelede performance. Yet this spectacle is not created by movement alone, but by the integration of masks, costumes, music, and dance.

Here, as in Ẹfẹ night, the artistic modes create images that embellish reality. The Gẹlẹdẹ masquerades present elaborate statements of maleness and femaleness through a profusion of visual elements. Rich cloth heightens the grandeur of the figures while it reinforces and responds to the movements of the dancer. At the same time, it speaks of the support by the females in the community who have lent their head ties, which are incorporated into the costumes. In the dance, these visual, sculptural forms become kinetic. The cloth whirls; articulated superstructures move; the breasts and buttocks bob up and down, thrusting sharply into space to add force to their forms. The masks further define roles and power in society—knives, guns, and caps for the male; bowls, head wraps, and trays for the females. The elaborate form and motion of the costume and dance are echoed in often elaborate superstructures above the composed mask face. Embellished by means of attachments, forms extend beyond the physical limitations of the original wood cylinder. Elaboration and elegance are conscious goals in the masks as well as in the dance, for the curving interwoven forms recall the swinging arms and weaving trace-patterns of the dancers. And in some, stationary and moveable attachments reach down to the torso and affect the posture, position, and movement of the dancer, thus structurally unifying the image.

The relationships among the art forms are multiple and reciprocal. Upon seeing the sculptured forms representing a Muslim priest, for example, the drummers may launch spontaneously into a verbal/rhythmic text associated with this visual motif. And since the identity of the dancer is generally known, his name may be sounded and incorporated into the rhythm. And yet at the same time, the media that make up the whole may have distinct referents and meanings, giving each autonomy. Multiple images and ideas converge in time to produce a multifocal, multifaceted event. Thus, at times, the media as well as the performers vie with each other. For example, during the performance of the night mother masquerade, when the singers ask, "Mother, child who brings peace to the world. Repair the world for us," the drummers are sounding, "Mother, the one who killed her husband in order to take a title." The masquerades themselves have no thematic relationship to each other. Therefore, in Ilaro, for example, where numerous Gẹlẹdẹ rush into the performance space all at once, images compete for attention.

With its performative power, Gẹlẹdẹ thus treats numerous matters and manages them simultaneously. In the process, Gẹlẹdẹ serves a didactic function as it reinforces social values and traditions. Values are enforced with reference to particular individuals or groups, or sometimes they are asserted in general terms. These value-laden expressions can be honorific or derisive. In the very structure of the performance,

Gẹlẹdẹ asserts an egalitarian ideal, insuring that the opportunity to perform is distributed among all members (cf. Drewal and Drewal 1980). It further defines and distinguishes male and female roles and intrinsic power and also reinforces role expectations. Gẹlẹdẹ dancers externalize the inner natures of men and women, shaping as well as dramatizing their distinct inner potentials.

Performance implies a separation between actor and audience, both in distance and in distinction, maintained by means of a masquerade format. Yet in the course of Gẹlẹdẹ the lines between performer and audience blur as enthralled spectators become active participants. This process of inclusion and participation is precisely the ultimate goal and meaning of the ritual, for its fundamental purpose is to honor the mothers from whom we all come. Ọrọ Ẹfẹ speaks out, expressing the conscience of the community, voicing its hopes, fears, desires, and opinions, and stressing unity and adherence to traditions as a way to honor the mothers. The Gẹlẹdẹ dancers, representing generalized roles or groups both inside and outside the traditional society, are the "children" of the mothers. Thus Gẹlẹdẹ is all-inclusive in character, including the membership of its society, its audiences, and the themes and motifs in the songs, masks, costumes, and dances.

As a "plaything," Gẹlẹdẹ is intended to be entertaining. As one member of the Gẹlẹdẹ society explains (Legbe 1971), "We call the women together, the old women, in order that they will laugh, in order that they will have something to enjoy. If we have no food in this world, it will not be sweet." The analogy between food and Gẹlẹdẹ performance suggests that Gẹlẹdẹ is a sacrifice to these elderly women. The notion that Gẹlẹdẹ performances are sacrifices to the spiritually powerful women is alluded to by another elder, who asserts (Babalọla 1971),

> I can tell you that this Gẹlẹdẹ dance is mainly danced for them more than anybody. We dance it mostly for them. That is why we say Gẹlẹdẹ belongs to the women. . . . Our forefathers told us that these were destructive women *(ajẹ)*, that we must not look down upon them. If we despise them it means death. We must pamper *(tù)* them and live.

Tu (to pamper, literally to cool) is the root word for a type of sacrifice known as *ètùtù,* a cooling or propitiatory rite.[10] It is precisely its capacity for entertainment that enables Gẹlẹdẹ to function as an *etutu* to assuage this collectivity of powerful women, the gods of society. All the participants—dancers, singers, costumers—are performing a sacrifice when they strive to achieve perfection in performance.[11] Indeed, Gẹlẹdẹ is an expensive sacrifice that requires the combined resources of the community. Thus, a Gẹlẹdẹ elder comments (Legbe 1971):

There is no difference from the old days to the present, except that the festival is more enjoyable now than in the past when there was no money. Now there is financial power for everyone. When we prepare for the festival, we will buy clothes for all the children which we have collectively given birth to. They put on fine clothing to express that it is festival time. Many of us have money to spend; we have drinks and much food that we eat for the nine days of the festival. We eat to our full satisfaction. We rest for one year until our financial power is good so that the next festival will be better than the one before.

It is not that one must be wealthy to participate in Gẹlẹdẹ activities; rather one must be willing to commit whatever resources one has at any given time for the festival. That is the meaning of sacrifice.

As a sacrifice designed to placate the mothers, Gẹlẹdẹ advises patience and indulgence rather than confrontation and aggression. According to one devotee, "the one to sacrifice to the Great Mother must have patience." The value of patience is implicit in the masquerade images themselves. The heads of the Ẹfẹ and Gẹlẹdẹ performers are the essence of calmness and composure, while the rest of their bodies engage in powerful dance sequences. Likewise, the faces of the masks represent the idealized inner head, which must remain calm in order not to spoil the countenance, for, if the outside head displays anger, individuals risk direct confrontations, and possibly death, at the hands of others. As a Yoruba prayer states, "May my inner head not spoil the outer one." During Ẹfẹ night, Ọrọ Ẹfẹ appears only after a prescribed host of costumed performers have brought the festival into the world, preparing the ground, opening the way, and giving approval. Then and only then, with protective medicine and the approval of the female cult head, Iyalaṣẹ, does Ọrọ Ẹfẹ emerge slowly and cautiously. He prudently honors the forces in the Yoruba universe with his chants before he comments on society and individuals. Gẹlẹdẹ is thus an appeal to balance and reason.

Patience and indulgence are the requisite attitudes with which to channel the vital life force of the mothers and their "children" in the world. Patience is perceived to be inherent in femaleness. The Great Mother herself is the epitome of patience; that is, her inner head is composed. She is in control. She does not become visibly angered, but she exacts revenge covertly. These ideas about women are expressed in the channeled and controlled steps of the female Gẹlẹdẹ dances, which are powerful but restrained. The mothers, who are united with all women by the "flow of blood," embody the concept of balance, a female quality that men must understand—indeed emulate—in order to survive.

Gẹlẹdẹ thus mediates between the owners of society—those who generate, manage, control, and also punish it—and the community.

Through praise and criticism, prayers and curses, Gẹlẹdẹ spectacle carries out the perceived will of the mothers. The community is responsive,
in turn lending its support. The art forms that make up spectacle thus
become instruments for regulating society. Most important of all, perhaps, is that Gẹlẹdẹ affirms patience and indulgence, qualities thought to
be possessed innately by women, as ideal means of correcting imbalances
and maintaining peace. The arts of Gẹlẹdẹ touch upon different concerns in different ways. They constantly reinforce and revitalize each
other to reach all segments within the community.

2

Gẹlẹdẹ Performance

Prudence was the ancient wisdom of the Ẹgba
Prudence was the ancient wisdom of the Ijẹṣa
It was divined for Ọrunmila, who was going to the town of the
  owners of birds [i.e., spiritually powerful women]
That he must put on an image [mask], head ties, and leg rattles
He obeyed, he put them on, he arrived in the town of the owners of
  birds and he survived
He rejoiced in dancing and singing—
"I have covenanted with Death, I will never die
Death, worrisome Death
I have covenanted with sickness, I will never die
Death, worrisome Death"

Pẹlẹ ni nṣ'awo won lode Ẹgba
Pẹlẹ ni nṣ'awo won lode Ijẹṣa
A da f'Ọrunmila, o nṣ'awo re Ilu Ẹlẹiye
Won ni ko ru Aworan, Ọja ati Iku
O gbo, o ru, o de Ilu Ẹlẹiye, o yè bọ́
O wa nsunyẹrẹ wipe—
"Mo ba'ku mule nwo ku mọ
Iku, Iku gbọingbọin
Mo b'arun mule, nwo ku mọ
Iku, Iku gbọingbọin"

[Beyioku 1946]

This Ifa divination text from *ọsa meji,* drummed at the beginning of
Gẹlẹdẹ spectacles in Lagos as the masqueraders enter the arena to perform, recounts the mythic origin of Gẹlẹdẹ masquerading. Ifa instructed
Ọrunmila, the deity governing divination, to exercise great caution (*pèlé,*
pèlé) in entering the domain of spiritually powerful women known as
ẹlẹiye (literally "owners-of-birds") by donning a mask *(aworan),* head tie

17

(ọja), and leg rattles (iku), three essential elements found in all Ẹfẹ and Gẹlẹdẹ costumes (color plate 1). Ọrunmila did not confront these power-ful women aggressively, rather he sought to assuage them. As one elder comments, "we must pamper (tu) them [the mothers] and live" (Babalọla 1971). And, "it is the Great Mother who gave instruction saying anyone who worships her must have patience (sùúrù)" (Ogundipẹ 1971). For the mothers "from the left and from the right, from the front and from the back" are asked to descend and join the gathering; their reply comes from the trees in the form of birds' cries (Beier 1958:10). Another elder, this time a priestess, asserts (Akinwọlẹ 1971): "these masks are like the vital power (aṣẹ) that the ancients wielded in the past which they called ẹ̀ṣọ̀ [a thing done with carefulness]. . . . They must not perform it nakedly."[1] With the requisite attire and demeanor, Ọrunmila journeys safely into the midst of the owners-of-birds, where he sings and dances. Gẹlẹdẹ performances recreate this mythic journey.[2]

The Sounds and Sights of Ẹfẹ Night

As darkness approaches, the community completes its preparations for the Ẹfẹ ceremony.[3] Between 9 and 10 P.M. a large crowd gathers in the central market—men, women, children—all bringing with them lamps, mats, chairs, and food. They arrange themselves in a large circle, often sitting together in age group societies (ẹgbẹ́). The performers' entry way into the circle, known as the "mouth of authority" (ẹnuàṣẹ), orients the crowd. Families with titled elders, especially women, and other im-portant personages are given preferred positions along the edge of the performance space (fig. 1). This mass of people, sometimes numbering 1,000–1,500, includes Gẹlẹdẹ society members (actually a small percent-age of the total audience), local inhabitants of various religious faiths (Muslim, Christian, and traditional, including devotees of diverse deities), relatives of local people who live in other towns (sometimes from as far away as 150 miles), and "strangers" (a category that includes spirits as well as ọmọ ar'aiyé, "children of the world," a euphemism for evil-intentioned persons). From all parts of the town and from neighboring villages, from the otherworld, and from all age groups and all walks of life, the people assemble to see the Ẹfẹ spectacle.

The drummers arrive first and set up their ensemble within the arena just opposite the masqueraders' entrance. The ensemble of four to six drums contains two large lead drums approximately three to four feet high; the larger is called "mother drum" (ìyâlú), the other "female ómélé," or ómélé abo. The iyalu and omele abo together beat verbal messages by reproducing the rhythmic and tonal structure of spoken Yoruba. The smaller supporting drums, the omele akọ (or "male omele"), which are fixed

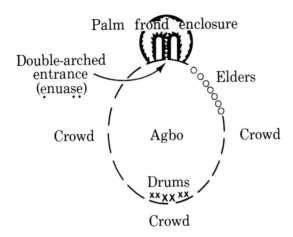

Fig. 1. Performance space, Ketu region.

at different pitches, maintain a rapid, complex polyrhythm. Over this background rhythm, the mother drum and the female *omele* weave well-known proverbs and praise the gods, ancestors, and elders while awaiting the arrival of the chorus of singers.

The singers, known collectively as "the carriers of the news" *(abanirò),* consist of male and female members of the society, called respectively *akijẹlẹ̀* and *akọdan.*[4] Upon leaving the Gẹlẹdẹ shrine, they proceed to the gathering singing a song such as the following, which announces that all are in place and ready:

It is now time to start, it is time.
Bush fowl lives in the forest, it is time.
Teak is found in the grasslands, it is time.
The lavish display is prepared, it is evening, it is time to start.

Nṣe kókò àkókò, nṣe kókò àkókò.
Àparò n'igbó, àkókó.
Ìrokò lọ l'ọ̀dàn, àkókò.
Ìdàgbà là fújà, àkókò, nṣe kókò lálẹ́ yì, àkókò.

[Collected in Ketu, 1971]

The stage is now set for a series of masqueraders to appear. All the masquerades are performed by men, but the costuming and movement may represent either males or females. First, a delightful puppet act may appear, featuring a figure on a platform called "machine magic" *(ẹ̀rọ).* From underneath the platform the performer manipulates the puppet's arms by pulling on a string, while children cheer, pushing and shoving to get a closer look at the animated figure.

After this lighthearted spectacle, Ẹfẹ night opens with a series of introductory masquerades known generically as "spirits of the earth" (òrọ ilẹ̀). The first is Ogbagba, who represents the divine mediator, Ẹṣu/Ẹlẹgba. As mediator between men and the gods, Ẹṣu/Ẹlẹgba is honored first and encouraged to "open the way" (ago l'ọna) for a successful ceremony. Crossroads, entrances, exits, and liminal or transitional sites are the abodes of the one who straddles two realms. He appears twice, first as a "young boy in a white cap and raffia skirt," as people sing, "Eshu comes with light leaves"; then as a grownup wearing banana leaves and iron anklets, as cult members sing lines such as these (Beier 1958:9):

> Ogbagba carries leaves
> On all the rubbish dumps he has picked up the *eko* leaves
> He comes carrying leaves

Ogbagba, or Ẹṣu/Ẹlẹgba, is followed by Arabi Ajigbálẹ̀. As the name suggests, Arabi is "The-One-Who-Sweeps-Every-Morning"; literally, he "sweeps" and thus clears and cleanses the marketplace (pl. 1). His costume of shredded palm leaves (*mariwò*) and his clearing actions allude to Ogun, the god of iron (cf. Barnes 1980:38–40), for both he and Ẹṣu/Ẹlẹgba serve to "open the way" for all men's communications with supernatural forces (Beyioku 1946; Osubi 1973). At his appearance people may sing (Moulero 1970:44):

> Arabi, The-One-Who-Sweeps-Every-Morning
> The cloth of another is good for sweeping
>
> *Arabi Ajigbalẹ*
> *Aṣọ alaṣọ dun igbalẹ*

Fire is the focus of the next masquerade pair. The first—Agbéná, or Fire Carrier—appears with either a mass of blazing grasses or a pot of fire balanced on his head and a costume of white cloth. The performer moves quickly through the space as sparks fly, forcing the crowd backward as it sings (Moulero 1970:46):

> The fire in the bush starts without warning
> Farmers with fields near the bush, beware
>
> *Ko pa ina njako*
> *Oloko l'adugbo*

PLATE 1. Wearing the cloths of the iron deity, Ogun, Arabi Ajigbalẹ sweeps the market to clear the way for the masqueraders that follow. Lagos, 1978.

These series of masquerades ritually reenact the steps taken in establishing a shrine, a house, or a settlement, actions of entry, clearing, and finally burning off the remains, actions presided over by Ẹṣu and Ogun. As the god of iron and the one who clears the way, Ogun in particular is regarded as the tutelary deity of this process. Agbena, disappearing as quickly as he appeared, may be immediately followed by Apana, the "Fire Extinguisher" (Beier 1958:9–10):

> Owner of fire, kill your fire!
> The hoopoe [a bird with decurved bill] is coming
> Put down your load,
> Because one does not light fires
> To regard the bird of the night

The performance enters a new phase now that the marketplace has been ritually prepared. All lights are extinguished as the impending "bird of the night," the most sacred of Ẹfẹ and Gẹlẹdẹ forms, the Great Mother, Ìyánlá, appears either as a bearded woman (pl. 2) or as a bird called Ẹyẹ Òrọ̀, Spirit Bird, or Ẹyẹ Òru, Bird of the Night (pl. 3). In the darkness the Great Mother comes trailing a white cloth. While she performs, all lights must be extinguished. As she moves in a gentle, slow dance (ijó jẹ́jẹ́), matching her steps with the drum rhythms, the elders of the Gẹlẹdẹ cult flock around her limiting the audience's view of the headdress.[5] The headdress, worn almost horizontally, is fastened to a long white cloth that often trails on the ground. Emphasizing the horizontality of the mask, the performer plunges his torso forward and maintains a crouched position throughout the performance; his elbows and knees are bent and spread laterally to evoke hoary age. Ankle rattles echo the Gẹlẹdẹ drum rhythms as the mother masquerade slowly advances and then retreats using small-amplitude jumps that barely leave the ground. The Great Mother does not speak. A series of songs and drum rhythms accompany her, creating layers of messages. If the masquerade represents Spirit Bird, the chorus and crowd sing:

> Spirit Bird is coming
> Spirit Bird is coming
> Ososobi o, Spirit Bird is coming
> The one who brings the festival today
> Tomorrow is the day when devotees of the gods will worship
> You are the one who brought us to this place
> It is your influence that we are using
> Ososobi o, Spirit Bird is coming
>
> *Ẹyẹ Òrọ̀ mbọ̀*
> *Ẹyẹ Òrọ̀ mbọ̀*

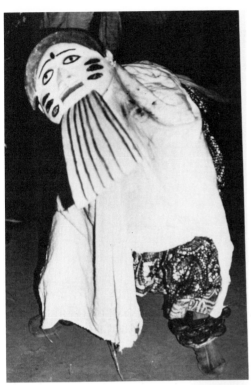

PLATE 2. The bearded Great Mother, Iyanla, bent with age, trails white cloth on the ground. Photograph by Edna Bay in Cove, Benin, 1972.

PLATE 3. Spirit Bird with blood-red beak hastens through the marketplace and disappears into the darkness. Ilaro, 1978.

Òsòsòbí o, Ęyę Òrǫ́ mbǫ̀
Eni l'olòdùngbòdùn
Ola lolò'sà mbǫ̀ òrìṣà
Iwo lokowa délè̩ yi
Ola rè̩ lawa nje
Òsòsòbí o, Ęyę Òrǫ̀ mbǫ̀

[Recorded in Ilaro, 1978]

If, on the other hand, the masquerader appears as bearded mother, the community offers the following:

Iyanla come into the world, our mother
Kind one will not die like the evil one
Ososomu come into the world
Our mother the kind one will not die like the evil one

Ìyánlá è̩ sò w'aiyé o, Ìyá wa
Olóòré ka kú sipo [ikà]
Òsòsòmú è̩ sò w'aiyé o
Ìyá wa olóòré ka kú sipo

And:

Ososomu e e e
Honored ancestor *apake e e e*
Mother, Mother, child who brings peace to the world
Repair the world for us
Iyanla, child who brings peace to the world o e

Òsòsòmú e e e
Ọlájogún àpàké e e e
Ìyá, Ìyá, ọmọ atún aiyé ṣe
Ba wa tún aiyé ṣe
Ìyanlá, ọmọ atún aiyé o e

[Collected in Ibaiyun, 1975]

As the songs praise the Mother, the drums approximate the tonal patterns of Yoruba speech and simultaneously offer another message:

Mother, Mother, the one who killed her husband in order to take a
    title
Come and dance, the one who killed her husband in order to take a
    title, come and dance
Stand up, stand, come and dance
One who killed her husband in order to take a title, come and
    dance. . . .
Honored ancestor *apake,* come and dance
Come home immediately
One who killed her husband in order to take a title, come home
    immediately

One who has given birth to many children, come home immediately,
   come home now
I made a sacrifice, I received glory, the day is proper
I sacrificed, I sacrificed, I sacrificed, I sacrificed
A woman will not describe what happened during travel
A woman will not tell what we have done
A woman cannot have Ajanọn [title] in Oro
In this world, in this world, in this world

Yé yé, Apọkọdọsù
Wá ka jó, Apọkọdọsù, wá ka jó
Nde, nde, wá ka jó
Apọkọdọsù, wá ka jó. . . .
Ọlájogún apake, wá ka jó
Wanle wara, wara, wara
Apọkọdọsù, wanle wara, wara, wara, wanle wara
Abiamọ didé, wanle wara, wara, wara, wanle wara
Mọsẹbọ, mogbaiyin, ọjọ́pé
Mọsẹbọ, mọsẹbọ, mọsẹbọ, mọsẹbọ
Obìnrin kì royìn ajo
Obìnrin kì sọ ohun wà ṣè
Obìnrin kì jẹ́ Ajanòn Òrò
L'aiyé, l'aiyé, l'aiyé

                                    [Collected in Ibaiyun, 1975]

In darkness and completely surrounded, Iyanla circles the performance area and quickly returns to the shrine, where the mask, wrapped or draped with white cloth, serves as the focus of worship for society elders.

    With the departure of Iyanla, the first singing mask arrives. It is known in some places as Tetede (The-One-Who-Comes-in-Good-Time), in others as Aiyé Tùtù (Cool World) (pl. 4). The role of this masquerader is to prepare the way for Ọrọ Ẹfẹ with chants (*ijúbà*) that honor the mothers, the gods, and the assembled elders and then to call Ọrọ Ẹfẹ, ensuring that he may safely begin his night-long solo performance (Moulero 1970:51):

Amulohun, if I call you the first time and you don't answer
You will become an anthill
If I call you a second time and you don't answer
You will become a piece of wood
If I call you the third time and you don't answer
You will become a savage beast

Amulohun, ō bi mo ba pe ô l'ẹkini o jẹ
Ẹ di igbodi pẹtẹ
Bi mo ba pe ọ l'ẹkeji ō jẹ
O di kukubọlẹ
Bi mo ba pe ọ l'ẹkẹta ō jẹ
Ẹ di ẹran oko igbe

PLATE 4. Tetede, "The-One-
Who-Comes-in-Good-Time,"
appears with a tray of ritual
containers to sing the praises of the
supernatural forces and to call Ọrọ
Ẹfẹ to begin his performance.
Ṣawonjo, 1978.

With the call of this introductory singing masquerader, two attendants of Ọrọ Ẹfẹ come into the area and kneel before the entry way, or
"the mouth of authority." They carry special medicines to protect Ọrọ
Ẹfẹ throughout his performance. From the area in front of the entrance,
the female cult head and her assistant, both dressed all in white in honor
of the cool, or "white," deities (òrìṣà funfun) and Òduà, the Great Mother,
strike sacred four-sphered bells. They ritually call Ọrọ Ẹfẹ to the world,
announce his coming, and insure that he is protected. Next a flute player
appears. His short bursts of music praise Ọrọ Ẹfẹ, call him by name, and
silence the crowd. The slow, insistent beat of Ọrọ Ẹfẹ's leg rattles announces his coming, as he appears in the "mouth of authority." He sways
slowly, majestically swinging horsetail whisks in each hand (frontispiece).
With his first high, piercing note, the flute ceases and the crowd becomes
quiet. With everything readied and ripples of expectation and excitement
running through the crowd, the drums fall silent, and Ọrọ Ẹfẹ, accompanied by the flute (fèrè), replies to the first singing masquerader (Moulero 1970:53):

When you called me the first time,
I had been doing a task for the *apa* tree.
When you called me the second time,
I was providing service for the *iroko* tree.[6]
But when you called me the third time, I answered in a clear,
    resounding voice.
Now that you have finished calling me, go home.

Nigba t'o pe mi l'ẹkini
Apa l'o ran mi l'iṣẹ
Nigba l'o pe mi l'ẹkeji
Iroko l'o be mi l'ọwẹ
Nigba l'o pe mi l'ẹkẹta
Mo je fun rerere apela l'ai p'agba
Bi o ba pe mi tan mā lọ

All attention now focuses on Ọrọ Ẹfẹ's words, as the performer carefully begins to honor deities, ancestors, the mothers, and elders. His sharply inclined torso and slow, methodic stamping express reverence to these spiritual powers. All the while, men in the hunters' society shout and fire their guns, the loud reports echoing in the night, punctuating the honorific incantations of Ọrọ Ẹfẹ. When he has completed this important devotion, he emerges fully from the entry way, rises to full stature, and moves toward the center of the performance space, where he delivers a song of self-assertion (pl. 5). His majestic costuming reinforces the extraordinary quality of his tense, piercing voice, which must project well, for high volume and vocal clarity are essential qualities by which Ọrọ Ẹfẹ's performance is judged. He paces up and down the arena while singing, flashing the whisks as a way of greeting and blessing the assembled community.

The performance continues throughout the night with only brief interludes, during which the drum ensemble offers a variety of praise poems, proverbs, jokes, and riddles. As dawn approaches, a stilted masquerader in the form of a hyena *(kòrikò)* (pl. 6) enters the marketplace to divert the attention of the crowd. His appearance allows Ọrọ Ẹfẹ to reenter the "mouth of authority," signaling the conclusion of Ẹfẹ night. People collect their belongings and slowly disperse to their homes to rest. They will return in late afternoon for the next spectacle—Gẹlẹdẹ.

The Daylight Dances of Gẹlẹdẹ

After the night's Ẹfẹ performance, the town is unusually quiet for most of the day, but as the shadows lengthen and the heat diminishes, the afternoon Gẹlẹdẹ dances build like a gathering thunderstorm. The drummers arrive and position themselves opposite the masqueraders' entry way. The audience gathers slowly. First come the children, curious

PLATE 5. In a headdress adorned with woodpeckers, snakes, and
a leopard and in a costume covered with geometric and
representational images, Ọrọ Ẹfẹ moves through the
performance area guided by his attendants. Igbogila, 1978.

PLATE 6. The gaping jaws of a Hyena headdress divert the attention of the crowd, allowing Ọrọ Ẹfẹ to disappear, thus ending the night ceremony. Kẹsan Ọrile, 1971.

to watch the musicians' preparations. Then the teenagers and adults begin to appear. The elders, especially the elderly women, fill their places on the perimeter of the performance space. The ever-increasing crowd listens to the stirring rhythms of the drummers while awaiting the appearance of the first masqueraders, who are preparing themselves in their compounds or at the Gẹlẹdẹ shrine. Crowd controllers—male Gẹlẹdẹ cult members aided by hunters—move back and forth across the marketplace; with large sticks or palm branches, they attempt to keep back the accumulating mass of people in order to maintain a large performance area between the entrance and the drummers.

PLATE 7. A partially costumed Gẹlẹdẹ-to-be holding an old
broken mask on his head marks the drum beats with persistent,
if unsteady, stamps. Ilaro, 1978.

PLATE 8. An older child with a more complete costume dances under the critical eye of his instructor. Ilaro, 1978.

The format of the Gẹlẹdẹ spectacle, no matter what the occasion, is serial, and the masqueraders usually make their appearances in order of age—the youngest appearing first. As the drums launch into their dance rhythms, a small, partially costumed "Gẹlẹdẹ-to-be" wearing an old mask marks the beats with persistent if unsteady stamps (pl. 7). Lacking the finesse of his seniors, he must hold the mask with his hands to balance it on his head. Older children follow, more daring in their kinetic offerings (pl. 8). The crowd greets these youngsters with great enthusiasm and amusement. Some shout encouragement, while others rush forward to reward their efforts with small coins. These first awkward attempts are

PLATE 9. Stronger, self-assured teenagers provide a relatively accomplished performance as their dance master watches. Ilaro, 1978.

PLATE 10. An identical pair of master dancers match each other's intricate dance patterns, as the crowd strains to see the action. Ketu, 1971.

followed by stronger, more self-assured teenagers (pl. 9). Often a teenager is accompanied by his mentor, who stands over him and watches every detail of his performance, sometimes tapping out the rhythms visually or verbally in order to assist the teenager and to keep him on the right track, sometimes to shout out instructions or to correct him if he makes a mistake (pls. 8, 9).

These preliminary performances heighten the crowd's anticipation, for they herald the imminent appearance of the master dancers, elegantly attired in elaborately carved headdresses and a profusion of cloth. The tone becomes more serious and the critical evaluations of the performance more exacting. The crowd strains to see a pair of dancers in front of the drums as they match each other's steps (pl. 10). The crowd controllers make a conscientious but futile effort to keep the crowd from pressing forward. Moving back and forth along the perimeter of the performance space, they lash the ground with their switches just at the toes of the spectators, forcing them to retreat. Masqueraders perform in quick succession, each striving to outdo the others in his mastery of

PLATE 11. As enthusiasm mounts, spectators spur the
masquerader on to greater choreographic heights. Ilaro, 1978.

PLATE 12. A crowd controller rushes into the arena to perform with a masquerader. Ṣawonjo, 1978.

PLATE 13. At the close of the afternoon dance, the deified
ancestral priestess, dressed in white, comes to bless the
community. Imaṣai, 1971.

increasingly complex rhythmic patterns. As enthusiasm mounts, crowd controllers and cult elders—men and women—rush into the performance area to accompany their family's masqueraders and spur them on to greater choreographic heights (pl. 11). In the dimming light of dusk the last Gẹlẹdẹ perform (pl. 12), and the spectacle usually closes with a special masquerader representing the deified ancestress of the community (pl. 13). Her appearance reassures the crowd of the mother's blessings and signals the conclusion of a successful festival as all reluctantly disperse to their compounds.

By examining the content of the various art forms that constitute Gẹlẹdẹ performance, it is possible to understand its social concerns and the way these concerns are expressed both verbally and nonverbally. It is also possible to perceive how Yoruba spectacle operates, communicating discrete bits of information simultaneously through the use of multimedia.

3
Ẹ̀fẹ̀ Songs—Voicing Power

The term *ẹfẹ* literally means "joking," and many informants explain it as a "play," "buffoonery," "something to laugh at." The humorous side of Ẹ̀fẹ̀ night is apparent in numerous songs ridiculing or mocking foolish or antisocial behavior. Yet its very serious side will become evident as we examine the repertoire of Ọ̀rọ Ẹ̀fẹ̀, for Ọ̀rọ Ẹ̀fẹ̀'s words have the power of *aṣẹ,* the power to make his assertions, with communal assent, come to pass. This force is alluded to by an elderly Ẹ̀fẹ̀ singer and priest of Ifa (Legbe 1971):

> The Ifa Oracle is a seer. If something bad were going to happen and the Ifa Oracle sees it and tells us that, today, he wants us to celebrate Ẹ̀fẹ̀, it should be done. After doing it, the bad thing which was to happen would be sent away. . . . What prevents the happening from coming to pass is that what Ifa predicts is wind [*èfúfù*] and the Ẹ̀fẹ̀ that we do is also wind.[1]

A deep philosophical concept is embedded in these words. Although Ẹ̀fẹ̀ contains humorous anecdotes and satire, they are only a superficial aspect. Ẹ̀fẹ̀ songs possess vital power *(aṣẹ),* which is activated in the pronouncing of the words of all Ẹ̀fẹ̀ songs regardless of subject matter. Ẹ̀fẹ̀ is, in effect, the public equivalent of private invocations that occur during sacrificial ceremonies, Ifa divinations, and in each individual's striving to communicate with the deities, ancestors, and the mothers. Stated another way, the voicing of an invocation to bring something to pass or to prevent something from happening is likened to "wind combatting wind" (Kilomọninṣẹ 1971).

The efficacy of the publicly spoken prayer, the voiced *aṣẹ* that constitutes Ẹ̀fẹ̀, has been attested to in numerous incidences, most clearly in the case of women who want children. They pray to the mothers or female deities of Gẹlẹdẹ in public celebrations of Ẹfẹ while all are gathered, especially old men and old women. The presence of these elders and especially their voiced "*aṣẹ*," meaning "so be it," add power and efficacy to the request for children. The voiced request is heightened, intensified, and strengthened by the *aṣẹ* of individuals within the gathering and especially those believed to have special *aṣẹ*, the elderly women. The uniting and voicing of these forces produce a request that must be fulfilled.

Likewise, the manner in which Ẹfẹ are presented adds to its powers. Ọrọ Ẹfẹ as a male elder of the cult is chosen and controlled by the female cult head, *iyalaṣẹ*, who by definition is one of the mothers.[2] He is thus sanctioned both spiritually and socially. Indeed Ọrọ Ẹfẹ is considered to be the "servant" of the mothers (Aṣiwaju 1975:203). Because of this role, he is immune to any repercussions as a result of his words and deeds. A. I. Aṣiwaju (1975:203–204) notes such incidents recalled by his informants in Mẹkọ and Ketu. One involved an Ọrọ Ẹfẹ who was released from jail on the grounds that his offensive song was authorized by *aiye*, the world (i.e., the mothers). With the sanction of the mothers, Ọrọ Ẹfẹ has complete freedom to voice his opinion on virtually every aspect of society, and those who happen to be the object of his biting criticism have no recourse.

This double sanction creates a special status for Ọrọ Ẹfẹ, which is mirrored in his song presentation and attire (frontispiece). His voice has a quality that is superhuman yet not supernatural, as are spirits associated with ancestors in the Egungun masquerades. His voice is most appropriate for one who seeks to communicate with supernatural forces, as well as with the human forces in society.

The topics of Ẹfẹ songs are all-encompassing. Ọrọ Ẹfẹ, "the king of Ẹfẹ," begins by respectfully honoring forces greater than himself. They include the deities, the ancestors, and the mothers; he appeals to them to secure their benevolent intervention in the affairs of the community. These honoring invocations (*ijúbà*) are followed by a change in attitude, intent, and direction as Ọrọ Ẹfẹ turns to other matters. He first buttresses himself as a means of protection in his temporary and vulnerable position as the verbalizer of the mothers' desires and opinions. He must not falter or stumble; he must be clear and forceful in projecting the "wind" that combats "wind." Then he devotes the remainder of his verbal program to social concerns, always mindful that the traditional attitudes and mores he reinforces are those most desired by the deities, ancestors, and the mothers. He seeks to please them by teaching these precepts and by ridiculing, condemning, and cursing all who contravene the wishes of these owners of powerful *aṣẹ*. The community, well aware of the dire consequences of wrongful actions by any of its members, adds its combined force in verbal concurrence. No transgression is left uncondemned, no contribution left unpraised, for the act of voicing communal opinion carries with it sacral power.

While Ọrọ Ẹfẹ's opening incantations of honor are based upon ancient formulas, his repertoire of social commentary songs are composed only a short time before each performance to ensure that they will be topical. The songs are composed by all the male society members who have performed Ẹfẹ in the past. As one of them explains (Ayọdele 1971),

> We will dream a situation and in our minds we will compose a song about that situation. We will meet in a private place [usually the Gẹlẹdẹ shrine], about 10 of us, and sit down and think of songs. . . . [The songs] sing about the situation presented.

Other elders, especially the women, may also offer suggestions for songs that "follow contemporary events, the happenings of the times" (Akinwọlẹ 1971).

The corpus of Ẹfẹ verbal arts may be divided into five major subject categories, with subdivisions, although some could be classified under more than one heading.[3] We shall analyze each category briefly on the basis of motivation and content and then examine specific songs in each category and subdivision.[4] The categories are:

1. Opening incantation of homage *(ijuba)*
2. Invocation
   a. Self-affirmation *(ikasẹ̀)*
   b. Prayer
   c. Curse *(èpè)*
3. Social comment
   a. Sexual behavior
      Sex roles
      Morality
   b. Politics
      External
      Internal
   c. Religion
   d. Seniority
4. History
5. Funeral commemoration

Opening Incantations

Since Ọrọ Ẹfẹ places himself in a spiritually elevated yet vulnerable position, he must protect himself from all potential detractors, whether spiritual or earthly. He does so by means of his initial chant, or, more accurately, incantation *(ijuba)*. *Ijuba,* sometimes known as *ìgèdè,* means "prayer of honor and respect." It always occurs at the outset of Ọrọ Ẹfẹ's performance and, unlike the subsequent songs, does not go through a phase of choral repetition.[5] Ọrọ Ẹfẹ directs his *ijuba* to those beings more powerful than himself—gods, ancestors, and the mothers—who could disrupt the performance or cause him harm. Performing an act of self-protection, he invokes and honors them with praises containing imagery from oral literature and myth associated with these beings. Ọrọ Ẹfẹ thus compels them to support and protect him by voicing formulas that amuse, exhalt, and flatter them.

The following *ijuba* opens with a sustained piercing note, as Ọrọ Ẹfẹ proclaims the commencement of his performance and demands the silence of the large audience. As the noise dies down, he begins the *ijuba.* The order of invoking the gods is not based on a hierarchy but on their roles in the ritual. Therefore, like the order of appearance of the night masquerades, those who "open the way," Ogun and Ẹṣu, come first.[6]

Being a "hot" god, Ogun has a strong, arrogant, aggressively masculine temperament, and the *ijuba* imagery reflects these traits. Ogun is believed to have been the king of Ire, and one of his praise names recalls this event with "Ogun Onire" (line 2) and tells of his bravery, violent temper, and thorough vengeance (lines 3–7). His manliness and virility are lauded in lines 8–10, when, with extreme audacity, he exposes himself in the presence of the king's mother, who by definition is a spiritually powerful woman (line 11).

Èṣù Laróyè is honored next. All men wishing to communicate with the deities must present a portion of their offering to Ẹṣu, for he serves as messenger to the gods. Ọrọ Ẹfẹ exalts Ẹṣu's mischievous, unpredictable nature with pungent images. Ẹṣu sheds tears of blood in mock sympathy with mourners and then succeeds in frightening a defecating man by excreting intestines rather than feces (lines 12–13). These verbal praises remind humans of the countless possibilities that can confront them when dealing with supernatural forces that are not bound by the rules of the living.

Ọrọ Ẹfẹ then honors the mothers. He calls upon them and, using their "owners of birds" imagery, talks of the sick and elderly bird that refuses to be warmed by fire or sun (lines 16–17), for the obscurity of the cool night is her abode. Lines 18 and 19 refer to the belief that the destructive mothers in concert with their male minions *(oṣó)* bury certain powerful substances in the earthen floor of their homes.[7] The singer intones her praise epithet, "my mother *ọ̀pàkẹ́*" *(iya mi ọpake),* and, playing upon the sacred and awe inspiring words, produces alliterative variations to the final poetic form (lines 18–22). Then he recalls the female mysteries of the mothers and their controlling power over human creativity in referring to the vagina and pubic hair (lines 23–24)—private parts that symbolize the secrets that women will never reveal to men. The final lines allude to the mother's spiritual eating of a victim trapped as a result of her whims.

Ọrọ Ẹfẹ thus secures the support and protection of Ogun, Ẹṣu, and the mothers by playing upon the formulas that invoke their participation. For Ogun these formulas flaunt the male ego—the strength, virility, and audacity symbolized by the lengthened penis—and invoke his overt, aggressive power, his quick vengeance.[8] Ẹṣu's power surfaces in his ability to wreak havoc. He assumes the blame for human tensions and their various kinds of social releases, alluded to in this instance with physiological acts of release. Ẹṣu, the deity at the crossroads, simultaneously offers many options and "opens the way" by forging a direct channel of communication to the spirit world and giving Ọrọ Ẹfẹ access to a vast reservoir of power. Finally, invoking female power represented by "the mothers," Ọrọ Ẹfẹ summons power that is secret, enigmatic, and covert, thus amassing spiritual support to assure that his words will take effect.

1 Honor, honor, honor today, honor to the deities
2 Honor to Ogun Onire, my husband
3 Ogun the brave one in firing, in firing
4 Ogun left [killed] his wife in the bathroom
5 Ogun killed the swordsmen
6 He destroyed them with one blow[9]
7 Ogun, I asked you to chase them, not to lick their bones
8 Honor to the one whose penis stood up to father a child in the room
9 He made his penis lengthen to father a child in the house of Ijana
10 We heard how the penis struck those in the market
11 Ogun, the one who saw the king's mother and did not cover his penis
12 Ẹṣu Laroye, the one who weeps with tears of blood
13 When one began to excrete feces, you frightened him by excreting intestines
14 Honor, ooooo [elongation of particle used in greeting to indicate respect], honor today, ooooo
15 Odulebe [destructive mother], I, I honor you today
16 Old bird did not warm herself in the fire
17 Sick bird did not warm herself in the sun
18 Something secret was buried in the mother's house
19 A secret pact with a wizard *ni jẹnnejẹnnẹ*
20 Honor, honor today, ooooo
21 Honor to my mother *ọpake na nake, nake, nake, eeeee*
22 *Ọpake na nake, nake, nake*
23 Mother whose vagina causes fear to all

24 Mother whose pubic hair bundles up in knots
25 Mother who set a trap, set a trap
26 Mother who had meat at home in lumps

1 *Ìbà ìbà ìbà l'oni ìbà òrìṣà*
2 *Ìbà Òguń o Onire ọkọ mi o*
3 *Òguń kọ́kọ́ ni muna ni muna*
4 *Òguń f'aya rẹ si bálùwẹ̀*
5 *Òguń p'oni'dà*
6 *O p'awọn bẹrẹ kojó*
7 *Òguń eri mó fún ẹ dú ngo fùn ẹ l'egungun pọ́n lá*
8 *Ìbà baba ó o ṣ'okó dòdò dòdò dòdò bi'mọ sá dòdò*
9 *Ó ṣé'pọn jannà bi'mọ ś'ile Ijana*
10 *A gbọ ṣ'okó luku ọkọ èrò ọjà*
11 *Af'ayaba ma p'okó mọ*
12 *Ẹlé kun nsún kun Láróyé a ma sún ẹ̀jẹ*
13 *B'onimi nṣú mi Láróyé a ma ṣú fùn k'ẹru bá lé ba onimi*
14 *Ìbà o ìbà loni o*
15 *Odulẹbẹ mo mọ̀ jubà ẹ loni*
16 *Arúgbo ẹyẹ ko yá'na*
17 *Òkùnrùn ẹyẹ ko yá óòrùn*
18 *Ṣà'ṣẹ́ gun'lẹ̀ ile 'ya*
19 *Ṣoṣọ mulẹ ni jẹnnẹjẹnnẹ*
20 *Ìbà o ìbà loni o*
21 *Ìbà ìyá mi òpàké na nàkénàké e*
22 *Ọ̀pàké na nakènakè*
23 *Ìyá o olòbò a o jẹ dó*
24 *Ìyá n'irun o n'irun'bẹ́ o ṣikí*
25 *Ìyá o dẹ'kùn ko dẹ polo*
26 *Ìyá ti l'ẹran okìri nle pìrìgìdì pìrìgìdì*

[Recorded in Emado Quarter, Aiyetoro, 1971[10]]

His performance safely launched with homage properly given to powerful forces, Ọrọ Ẹfẹ can now begin the repertoire of songs that will be repeated by the chorus and picked up and sung repeatedly by the audience. The form of presentation—the accompaniment, format, and song style—remains more or less constant throughout his performance.

The actual presentation of an Ẹfẹ song takes two distinct forms—the solo rendition and the choral repetition. During the entire solo, Ọrọ Ẹfẹ sings with minimal accompaniment to a relatively silent crowd, thus enhancing his presentation. He is set apart further by his distinctive costuming and physical position—in some places emerging from the "mouth of authority," in others perched on the roof of a house. His piercing voice and mode of delivery are also distinctive. In some Ẹgbado towns, where Ọrọ Ẹfẹ sings from a rooftop, he holds a broad fan near his mouth in order to deflect his words toward the masses below. His singing voice is generally high and loud, lending a somewhat tense, narrow, and piercing quality to his delivery. In other parts of western Yorubaland, where the mask and costume cover the singer's mouth, vocal quality seems more unnatural. The voice is partly muffled, and the high register is tense and thin. Ọrọ Ẹfẹ sings with high volume and good projection—essential qualities of a good performer whose voice must reach a good portion of the audience, especially the chorus. He may also embellish the song, but by using *glissando* liberally he adheres to the basic melody and rhythm. In spite of the physical handicaps of costuming and distance, Ọrọ Ẹfẹ enunciates clearly. With a subdued accompaniment, the text is easily understandable, since Yoruba is a tonal language.

Everything is set up to make sure Ọrọ Ẹfẹ's words are distinct and understandable. Nowhere is this more evident than in Ẹgbado area, where Ọrọ Ẹfẹ speaks the words before singing them, and the chorus may sing a reproach to an inexperienced Ọrọ Ẹfẹ if his song and intent are not clear:

> Ẹfẹ we would be grateful for an explanation [*bis*]
> You better explain very well so that we understand [*bis*]
> Be direct, like the penis splitting the virgin's vagina
> Ẹfẹ we would be grateful for an explanation [*bis*]
>
> *Èfè yi o káre alaye l'à nfẹ*
> *O jé láà mọlẹ gan ko ye wa sí*
> *Èlà poro lo'kó làdí ape*
> *Èfè yi o káre alaye l'a nfẹ*
>
> [Recorded at Emado Quarter, Aiyetoro, 1971]

The chorus must learn and repeat the songs. Choral repetition completes the precise transmission of the Ẹfẹ song text. At the same time it adds the combined power of the united communal voice. As one term for the chorus, *alàgbé*, implies, these voices "carry" the song to all parts of the assemblage, thus teaching it and encouraging full audience participation. After Ọrọ Ẹfẹ's solo, the chorus moves as a group through the performance area. Supported by the rhythms of the drum ensemble, the chorus sings the text through completely and repeats it as many times as is necessary for the entire audience to learn the melody and the words. Like a spokesman for the king, the chorus makes public the sacred utterances, continuing to sing until the entire audience joins in the performance in a united and spirited manner. This full participation implies acceptance of and support for the opinions expressed by Ọrọ Ẹfẹ. Some songs, of course, may be more popular than others, but nonetheless the community joins in the singing. This united expression of public opinion has the power to strengthen the communication with extraordinary beings (gods, ancestors, the mothers) as well as the practical power to compel antisocial individuals to "mend their ways" or face public ridicule, ostracism, or banishment. The weight of public opinion voiced by Ọrọ Ẹfẹ and intensified by communal assent can and does have the power to affect the future; it has the power of *aṣẹ*.

The choral phase differs from Ọrọ Ẹfẹ's solo performance in several respects. Consisting of men and women in the cult, the chorus performs as a loosely organized social unit, although choral leaders occasionally sing more loudly and with more embellishment. The degree of tonal blend depends on the amount of practice the chorus has had. The volume is high at the outset but decreases slightly as audience participation increases. The chorus takes considerable freedom with the rhythmic structure of the song, using very pronounced *glissando*. Its rhythm varies some, but generally the attacks and releases are well coordinated, although they become less so when the audience joins in. Both male and female chorus members sing above their normal speaking range, generally in the head register. But in contrast to Ọrọ Ẹfẹ, the chorus is more resonant with only intermittent tenseness and harshness. Overall, the Ẹfẹ choral performance is one of vocal unity touched with fleeting individual variations done in a joyful manner.

Most Ẹfẹ songs are simple strophes: a series of three to eight phrases that are repeated, phrase by phrase, over and over, with no insertion of new material and no change in order. Thus, the phrase structure and performance format of an Ẹfẹ song might be ABABCCDDEDED, ABABCCDDEDED, repeated until the entire audience has learned the song. Approximately half the text is repeated with little or no embellishment. Phrases range from three to seven seconds in length and have a distinctly undulating, wavelike melodic shape, which is greatly emphasized by the *glissando* of the chorus. The phrases are generally executed at a slow to medium tempo.[11]

The drum ensemble provides accompaniment when the chorus *(abaniro)* and assembled audience join in the singing. It establishes a steady, strong rhythm, which continues throughout the repetitions of each Ẹfẹ song. Despite its strength and persistence, the drum accompaniment remains subordinate to the song, which is sung by an ever-increasing number of people as it is distributed through the crowd. The tonal blend in the drum ensemble is moderate. The *iyalu* and *omele* drums are of similar construction yet differ in size, pitch, and manner of playing. The *iyalu* is played with the hands while *omele akọ* are played with thin sticks, thereby producing different tonal qualities.

There are two kinds of musical interludes between Ọrọ Ẹfẹ's song presentations: a slow, simple beat played by a gong striker *(aláago)*, which serves to announce that Ọrọ Ẹfẹ is about to begin a song, and short bursts of notes on a flute *(fere)*, that approximate the tonal pattern of Yoruba phrases, sometimes calling Ọrọ Ẹfẹ by name and praising him, sometimes instructing the audience to quiet down and listen, or sometimes imitating the first words of the singer. The gong and the flute help only to announce the beginning of the song presentation but do not continue to play once Ọrọ Ẹfẹ starts his song. The gong rhythm has little flexibility; the flute, on the other hand, has great rhythmical freedom.

Invocation

One of the first songs offered by Ọrọ Ẹfẹ is a self-assertion, or *ikasẹ*. *Ikasẹ*, literally "to step out slowly . . . with measured tread" (Abraham 1958:356), may form part of Ọrọ Ẹfẹ's opening material. It is sometimes embedded in an *ijuba*, but it is usually presented as a separate song immediately following the *ijuba*.

Both *ijuba* and *ikasẹ* serve to insure the singer's safety during his perilous performance. In the *ijuba*, Ọrọ Ẹfẹ expresses his honor and obedience to those more powerful than himself. In the *ikasẹ*, however, he directs his words to the general audience and seeks protection through self-affirmation. He asserts his right and obligation to serve as the communal voice by recalling the names of the predecessors who passed the authority to him and by boasting about his prowess as a singer and his wisdom as an elder. With these justifications, Ọrọ Ẹfẹ seeks to increase his chances for success by verbally increasing his stature and the power of his presence. He thus fixes himself at a place comparable in stature to that of supernatural forces from which he can, with impunity, ridicule and condemn important persons in the community who might otherwise attempt to destroy or diminish him physically and spiritually.

The following *ikasẹ* demonstrates self-affirmation. Ọrọ Ẹfẹ begins by challenging the audience to solve the riddles he will sing (lines 1–4) and compares himself to the *àwòko* bird, which is renowned among the Yoruba for its singing ability (line 5).[12] He asserts his wisdom in knowing the proper moment to begin his voyage (i.e., his performance) just as the boatman knows the safe time to sail (lines 6–9). He then establishes his importance in relation to the audience by using "pecking order" imagery. First, he associates himself with a rich man in relation to a pawn (*ìwọ̀fà*), a debtor who offers himself as a bondsman to his creditor. Second, using sexual imagery, he is the pointed hook that pierces and subdues his wife, the fish (line 11). Third, with political imagery, he becomes the "king of Ẹfẹ," for whom all must prostrate themselves, just as the magnificent king of Ketu recognized political domination by the white man during the Colonial era, and Agura Quarter bowed down before Ademọla, the paramount king or Alake of Abẹokuta (lines 12–14). Then, returning to his elevated status and emphasizing his royalty, he demands respect from his subjects, literally "lionizing" himself in relation to those around him.

Thus buttressed, Ọrọ Ẹfẹ can now voice his opinions with impunity, secure in his superior position and in his vital power.

1 Ayandokun, a riddle, a riddle, riddle, riddle
2 Okegbemi, a riddle, riddle, riddle, riddle
3 If I gave a riddle, who could solve it
4 I will take a song and fool you
5 The *awoko* has come from a journey, the head of the singers has come
6 I, the wise one, have come out, have come out, may my coming be good
7 When the river is in flood, the boatman sails
8 Aresa, I have come out, come out, may my coming be good
9 When the river is in flood, the boatman sails
10 A pawn never equals a man with money
11 A hook is the husband of a fish
12 The king of Ketu salutes the white man with "sir"
13 Agura Quarter prostrates before King Ademola
14 I have become the King of Ẹfẹ, all youths prostrate before me
15 A dog can never rival a leopard

1 *Ayandókun àlọ́ àlọ́ àlọ́ àlọ́*
2 *Okegbemi àlọ́ àlọ́ àlọ́ àlọ́*
3 *Bi nbá p'álọ tan l'o le m'alọ mi*
4 *Ma f'orin rẹ wọn jẹ*
5 *Àwòko t'ajo de, olóri àlaróye*
6 *Olugbọn mo d'ode, mo d'ode ode ré*
7 *B'odò kun ọlọ́kọ̀ a la ja*
8 *Aresa mo d'ode, mo d'ode ode ré*
9 *B'odò kun ọlọ́kọ̀ a la ja*
10 *Iwọfa kan ki jolowo lọ*
11 *Iwọ l'ọkọ ẹja*
12 *Ọba Alakétu mbẹ̀'ri 'Sa' f'òyinbó*
13 *Àgurá ndòbálẹ̀ bo ba f'oju k'Ademọla tan*
14 *Mo d'ọba èfẹ̀ o, majẹṣi ẹ dòbálẹ̀*
15 *Ajá ki b'ẹkùn ra gbagba*

[Recorded in Idofoi Quarter, Aiyetoro, 1971]

In a briefer self-asserting song, Ọrọ Ẹfẹ likens his dramatic performance to a blazing fire (line 1), his power to that of a leopard (line 5), and his voice to the sweetness of honey (line 7):

1 Wood is burnt to a knot
2 People of Aiyetoro, I have really come
3 Wood is burnt to a knot
4 People of Aiyetoro, I have really come
5 If a dog spies a leopard, he will tell himself to be careful

6 If a dog spies a leopard, he will tell himself to be careful
7 Eh!! Honey has come, throw away the bean cakes

1 *Igi jo ókan kókó*
2 *Ar'Aiyetoro, mo de nì ní*
3 *Igi jo ókan kókó*
4 *Ar'Aiyetoro, mo de nì ní*
5 *B'ajá ba f'oju kan ẹkùn yio sofin apẹpẹ*
6 *B'ajá ba f'oju kan ẹkùn yio sofin apẹpẹ*
7 *E!! Oyin de ẹ gbe àkàrà sọnu*

[Recorded in Emado Quarter, Aiyetoro, 1971]

Finally, before launching into songs on various topics, Ọrọ Ẹfẹ marshals his company of performers—drummers and singers—as he boasts of his retentive memory:

1 Drummers stand up! I am about to sing
2 Ọlọjẹde don't waste any more time [*bis*]
3 *Omele* drummers it is in your hands
4 *Iyalu* drummers begin to drum well
5 All who are to sing, don't be playful
6 Singers are you correct, we are correct
7 Tell Salawu that the singers should be correct
8 I, the one with endless wisdom, will recite the history including
    not only the exact day we came to settle this land, but who
    cooked and what they ate!

1 *Onilu ko nde! Ngo ṣorin kọ*
2 *Ọlọjẹde ma ma ṣafara mọ́* [*bis*]
3 *Òlòmele o má dọwọ rẹ*
4 *Oniyá'lu ko pà wọ'dà*
5 *Gbogbo ẹniti ngberin ẹ ma ṣàwada*
6 *Olorin ṣe ẹ ti pe a ti pe*
7 *Ẹ wi fun Salawu ko lorin o pe pere*
8 *Ngo pitan ọlọgbọnjọgbọn njọ t'a de 'lẹ yi ta lo se'bẹ t'a jẹ*

[Collected in Aibo Quarter, Aiyetoro, 1971]

A second type of invocation, which follows the voicing of *ikasẹ*, is the prayer for blessings on the community as a whole. Ọrọ Ẹfẹ expresses the communal longing for good fortune and fulfillment in life, which inheres in health, wealth, progeny, peace, and longevity; he appeals to the forces to hear and accept these supplications, and the people add their accord with raised voices. Sung prayers invariably recall the periodic scourge of smallpox and, more recently, of cholera. References to wealth, associated with agricultural success, appear in requests for good weather, relief from locust invasions, and profitable markets.

The request for offspring is a perennial concern among a people plagued with high rates of infant mortality. A man feels accursed if he has no children to bear his name, to work his fields, to support him in his old age, to bury him, or to keep his memory alive after death. Since the mothers control menstrual blood as well as agricultural fertility, it is not surprising to find these Ẹfẹ songs occurring frequently at annual festivals.

Ẹfẹ songs concerned with peace were prevalent during the nineteenth century, a period of intermittent warfare in many parts of Yorubaland, especially in Gẹlẹdẹ areas. Some of the oldest songs collected in Ẹgbado recall the ever-present threat of Dahomean invasion and Ẹgba encroachment. Peace was, thus, of vital importance to the relatively defenseless Gẹlẹdẹ areas of Ẹgbado, Awori, and Ketu.

A final concern is with the desire for a full and long life. The Yoruba view death at an early age as a great tragedy, especially if the deceased has no children. Such a death is often regarded as the work of an enemy, perhaps someone jealous of the person's good fortune. Death in old age, however, is regarded as a normal and joyful occurrence. The funeral of an elderly person is celebrated with happiness because long life, in and of itself, is viewed as fulfillment.

In the following Ẹfẹ song, Ọrọ Ẹfẹ asks the mothers to explain the sudden, unexpected deaths that are occurring and to bring them to an end. He reminds the mothers that he (i.e., the community) has offered certain medicinal leaves to calm their anger, but that farming and hunting accidents continue to occur (lines 1–4).[13] The references to hoe and knife accidents may mean deaths caused by Ogun, working on behalf of the destructive mothers, who "hide under all the gods" and whose vengeance is sometimes symbolized by knives. Then in an appeal to Ṣango, god of lightning and thunder, who is most angered by untruthfulness, Ọrọ Ẹfẹ insists upon his honesty (lines 3–4). He points out that a thunderbolt would never strike a young *oṣé*. The *oṣe* refers to the *oṣe Ṣango*, a double-celted wooden dance axe carried by devotees of Ṣango and placed in Ṣango shrines. The inference is that Ṣango would never destroy one of his own children. Ọrọ Ẹfẹ asks, Have you *oṣo* and *ajẹ*, who are our progenitors, forgotten us? (lines 6–11). He pleads for the mothers' forgiveness and their protection from sudden death, and calls for the support of all assembled (lines 12–16).

Throughout this request, Ọrọ Ẹfẹ exhibits sensitivity toward superior and unpredictable power. He attempts to reason with and calm the mothers in proclaiming sincerity in his concern. He pleads with them to hear his words. He even suggests that one of the society members may have "offended," and, if so, the offender alone should be made to suffer the consequences. The tone is persuasive yet respectful, far different from the self-assertive tone of the *ikasẹ*. Ọrọ Ẹfẹ must exercise caution and, above all, patience in dealing with the powerful mothers.

1 *Orijio* leaves charmed you to forgive my misdeeds [*bis*]
2 Never have we suffered death from hoes, never from knives
3 Have I lied? [*bis*]
4 Never have we seen a thunderbolt strike a young *oṣẹ́*
5 Wizard in the house were you not the one who fathered me
6 Are you not our fathers?
7 Why do you not know us any longer
8 Powerful mother in the house were you not the one who gave
    birth to us
9 Are you not our mothers?
10 Why do you not know us any longer
11 It is prohibited for a dog to devour its child [*bis*]
12 Our mother *ọpake* forgive us our misdeed
13 If a cult member has offended, expose him
14 Join us in our offer of thanksgiving to Agbojo[14]
15 Onidofoi was the one who saved us from death
16 Youths, elders, family members, visitors greet me for my
    dangerous journey

1 *Ewe orìjìó lope ẹ f'ọraro jimi* [*bis*]
2 *Ai gbọ̀kù ọkọ, mo lai gbọ̀ t'ọbe*
3 *Mo fi purọ̀ ndan* [*bis*]
4 *Ē wọ̀ arira ki p'oṣẹ́ lai gbọ*
5 *Oṣó'le ṣe be nyin lẹ̀ bi mi*
6 *Ṣe b'ẹnyin ni baba wa*
7 *Ki lo ṣe te o tun mọ wa mọ́*
8 *Àjẹ́' le ṣe bẹ̀ nyin le bi wa*
9 *Ṣe be ẹnyin ni ìyá wa*
10 *Ki lo ṣe tè o tun mọ wa mọ́*
11 *Ē wọ̀ ni àjá ki run ọmọ rẹ ko kan egun* [*bis*]
12 *Ìyá wa ọ̀pàke ẹ fori eyi ji wa*
13 *Ìyá ma ma jẹ nṣiṣe a ṣẹ́ fi sun ntọ̀mọ awo*
14 *Ẹ b'awa dupẹ lọwọ Agbojo o*
15 *Onidofoi gbàwala nbo gbawa la ni ngo ku mọ*
16 *T'ewe t'agba o, at'onile t'alejo, mo ni ẹ ma ki mi ewu*

[Collected in Idofoi Quarter, Aiyetoro, 1971]

The third category of invocation is the *epe*, or curse. Just as the *ijuba*, *ikasẹ*, and prayers invoke the forces for positive ends, so an *epe* calls upon those same forces for the destruction or diminution of an enemy. An *epe* has the same power as the other invocations with the limitation that "a curse reflects before it attacks" *(Èpèé ńrò kó tó jà)* (Abraham 1958:161). In other words, an undeserved curse cannot take effect and, in fact, may return upon the curser. Thus as Ogundipẹ, an Ọrọ Ẹfẹ from Ketu, explains, "If someone has offended society, [Ọrọ] Ẹfẹ will compose a song predicting his doom and the song will come true." There are numerous instances of curses sung as Ẹ̀fẹ̀ songs that are believed to have taken effect. For example, during World War II some soldiers camped near the town of Imaṣai began to "molest" the townspeople, so an *epe* was composed and sung requesting the deities to "remove the troublesome soldiers." Within a few days "the soldiers began to die a few at a time . . . which made the rest leave." Aṣiwaju (1975:258) also notes an Ẹ̀fẹ̀ curse that caused death from fire and one as a result of insanity. The voiced power of these songs make Ẹ̀fẹ̀ much more serious than mere "joking."

The following *epe* was sung by an Ọrọ Ẹ̀fẹ̀ whose house in Aiyetoro was burned during the political upheavals in Yorubaland in December 1965 and January 1966. Lines 5–6 offer a reproach to those who think they can hide the terrible things they have done in the past. It recalls another Ẹ̀fẹ̀ song that says character *(ìwà)* "follows you wherever you go." In lines 7–9, Ọrọ Ẹ̀fẹ̀ calls on Aibo and Idofoi Quarters of Aiyetoro to avenge him with a horrific death that implies destruction by the mothers, "with eyes plucked out like shells" (line 9).

1 Fire spread swiftly on Alapa's house
2 People of Aiyetoro you are treacherous
3 Fire spread swiftly on Alapa's house
4 People of Aiyetoro you are treacherous
5 The wickedness you seek to forget will find you
6 The wickedness you seek to forget will find you
7 Aibo is the next to avenge me
8 Idofoi, come and avenge me
9 All who set fire to my house may you die with eyes plucked out
   like shells

1 *Ina fẹ́rẹ́ ni'le Alapa*
2 *Ara Aiyetoro e kọtẹ nkun*
3 *Ina fẹ́rẹ́ ni'le Alapa*
4 *Ara Aiyetoro e kọtẹ nkun*
5 *Ìkà l'ẹ gbe sọnu, e o ri hé*
6 *Ìkà l'ẹ gbe sọnu, e o ri hé*
7 *Aibo lokú kó gbeja mi o*
8 *Idofoi ẹ wa gbeja mi o*
9 *Gbogbo ẹni sun'le mi a ku y'ọ́ju nt'òkòtó*

In another curse, Ọrọ Ẹ̀fẹ̀ attacks those who have slandered him unjustly (line 1). Calling the mothers by their praise names, *iya mi oṣorọn-ga/ṣonga* and *olòbẹ ṣonga*, "the one with knives ṣonga" (lines 3 and 4), he asks them to punish the offenders.

1 Those whom I did not offend are slandering me
2 Mother I leave it in your hands
3 My Mother Ṣonga bring trouble to him

4 Mother I leave it in your hands, The-One-With-Knives-Ṣọnga

1 *Ęniti ngò ṣẹ̀ tì nfẹjọ mi sùn*
2 *Ìyá ni ngo fi lé l'ọwọ́*
3 *Ìyá mi Ṣọ̀nga ni o gbe wàhálà bá*
4 *Ìyá ni ngo fi lé l'ọwọ́ Olọbẹ Ṣọ̀nga*
                    [Collected in Idofoi Quarter, Aiyetoro, 1971]

Social Comment

The bulk of Ọrọ Ęfę's performance consists of commentary on contemporary events that have occurred in the community since the last Gęlędę festival. The singer delves into all aspects of community life that affect its continuity and stability, especially sexual behavior, politics, religion, and competition. On these topics, Ọrọ Ęfę utilizes two methods of persuasion—positive reinforcement through praise and blessing, and negative reinforcement through ridicule, condemnation, and curse. The weight of such judgment is not Ọrọ Ęfę's alone, for in one united voice the entire audience adds its collective social pressure and power.

Criticism of improper behavior, usually between the sexes, is popular in Ęfę and Ọrọ Ęfę seems to derive as much enjoyment from such scandals as does his audience. Songs of this sort are usually in a mocking tone that highlights by exaggeration the grotesqueness of the situation. In a direct reference to a sexual scandal within the community, Ọrọ Ęfę criticizes the culprits.

> Who owns the child, who owns the pregnancy?
> Pregnancy caused a fight in the house of Ajęlę
> Who owns the child, who owns the pregnancy?
> Pregnancy caused a fight in the house of Ajęlę
> *O yi ṣe nan pe ji l'ojọkọ rẹ* [bis]
> You can't have one pregnancy by two persons
> Wife of Ajęlę, to whom does the pregnancy belong?
> You can't have one pregnancy by two persons
>
> *Taní l'ọmọ taní l'oyún rì?*
> *Oyún ṣẹ d'ijà n'ile Ajęlę*
> *Taní l'ọmọ taní l'oyún rì?*
> *Oyún ṣẹ d'ijà n'ile Ajęlę*
> *O yi ṣe nan pe ji l'ojọkọ rẹ* [bis]
> *Àí l'oyún kan f'ènìa meji*
> *Ìyàwó Ajęlę talo p'oloyun ni rì?*
> *Àí l'oyún kan f'ènìa meji*
>
>   [Recorded at Emado Quarter, Aiyetoro, 1971]

In a second song concerned with sexual behavior Ọrọ Ęfę expresses a clear-cut opinion about morality and alludes to several traditional values that have been violated. The first and most serious crime is adultery, referred to in lines 3–4 when Ọrọ Ẹfẹ asks, "Did Ogunṣọla marry his wife for you?" A second transgression compounds the crime, for it is committed by a rich and conceited man against his elder. In the traditional setting, wisdom based on age determined status. But with changes in the economic system, money has begun to play a determining role in prestige and power. In this case, money makes the junior feel superior to his elder, thus upsetting the social and moral laws of the ancestors. Ọrọ Ẹfẹ, as the advocate of order and justice, exposes the foolishness of a man who would "pull on a snake's neck" and voices the Yoruba belief that "sinners will not go unpunished" (cf. Idowu 1962:146):

1 The conceited man with all his money is teasing his elder
2 The conceited man with all his money is teasing his elder
3 Did Ogunṣọla marry his wife for you?
4 Did Ogunṣọla marry his wife for you?
5 Wicked person who pulls on the snake's neck
6 Wicked person who pulls on the snake's neck
7 If the viper bites you should I be concerned?
8 Wicked person who pulls on the snake's neck

1 *Onígbéragá owo wó loní o tówa fi ndùgbo l'ẹgbẹ baba ẹ́*
2 *Onígbéragá owo wó loní o tówa fi ndùgbo l'ẹgbẹ baba ẹ́*
3 *Ogunṣọla fẹ́'yàwo fún ẹ nidán*
4 *Ogunṣọla fẹ́'yàwo fún ẹ nidán*
5 *Olòṣì to nlọ́ fà'rùn ejò*
6 *Olòṣì to nlọ́ fà'rùn ejò*
7 *B'ọka bu ẹ jẹ ọ kan mi a bi o kan mi [ṣe o kan mi?]*
8 *Olòṣì to nlọ́ fà'rùn ejò*

[Collected in Emado Quarter, Aiyetoro, 1971]

Men and women have clearly defined sex roles in a polygamous and patriarchal society. The most senior male of the compound is expected to play the role of arbiter. Although women have economic independence, they have less overt power in their domestic roles as co-wives since they are strangers in their husbands' compounds. In such a situation it would be regarded as ridiculous for a man to "cook," "wash," and "grind pepper" as it would be for the wife "to threaten her husband with a cutlass," an instrument that symbolizes masculinity and physical force. Ọrọ Ẹfẹ, as critic supreme, utilizes striking contradictory imagery to underscore the absurdity of the situation and of the individuals involved. In line 5 he implies the wife is "something else" since she wreaks havoc. The husband is called "Ṣango," a male deity noted for his strength, courage, and hot temper, in order to highlight his lack of these qualities. Biting sarcasm and repetition combine to create an unequivocal statement on improper behavior:

1 For a husband to grind pepper and grate cassava
2 For a husband to grind pepper and grate cassava
3 For a husband to cook cassava meal and wash pots
4 For a husband to cook cassava meal and wash pots
5 The wife you married, Ṣango, is something else!
6 She threatened her husband with a cutlass at the market
7 She threatened her husband with a cutlass at the market
8 I heard him shout to all around, "help me!"
9 She threatened her husband with a cutlass at the market

1 *K'ọkọ ó l'ọta ko tun rin p'aki*
2 *K'ọkọ ó l'ọta ko tun rin p'aki*
3 *K'ọkọ ó t'ẹba ko tun fọ ṣasùn*
4 *K'ọkọ ó t'ẹba ko tun fọ ṣasùn*
5 *Ìyàwó t'efẹ fun Ṣango ma kọ yọyọ*
6 *O y'àda s'ọkọ ni salẹ ọjà*
7 *O y'àda s'ọkọ ni salẹ ọjà*
8 *Mo l'ọkọ nki gbe gbogbo aradugbò "ẹ gba mi!"*
9 *O y'àda s'ọkọ ni salẹ ọjà*

[Recorded in Igan Okoto, 1971]

Politics is another popular topic in Ẹfẹ songs. Ọrọ Ẹfẹ concerns himself with both external and internal affairs. The former include wars or disagreements with neighboring towns or areas, boundary disputes, colonial administration, and, after independence, political parties; while the latter usually involve chieftaincy controversies, headship claims, and land disputes.[15] In these songs, Ọrọ Ẹfẹ utilizes positive and negative reinforcement or merely serves as mediator of the dispute by emphasizing the community's desire for settlement.

A mid-nineteenth-century political Ẹfẹ song seems to have been preserved by Ajiṣafẹ (1964:107), although he does not identify it as such. In 1856 the Aibo people in Ẹgbado challenged the Ẹgba with a song after they had destroyed the Ẹgbado town of Ilogun. The lyric "by your destroying Ilogun—you thrust your hands between the teeth of a poisonous serpent" provoked the Ẹgba to retaliate by destroying Aibo the following year. Ironically, the song may have brought internal unity to the Aibo community, but it also brought destruction by external forces.

In the following song, Ọrọ Ẹfẹ attempts to settle a dispute between Panku and Epo, two towns within the political domain of Ketu. He reminds the protagonists that they are one and should not disagree (lines 3–7). In line 5 he calls for the return of balance with "The right cannot do without the left." Ọrọ Ẹfẹ rebukes the opposing parties in line 8, stating that there is no glory in disorder ("dust") in a household, and in line 11 he asks Aka to reconcile both sides. Ọrọ Ẹfẹ stresses intelligence and reason in order to restore equilibrium and order in the society:

1 Panku must join together with Epo
2 They should not disagree
3 Do not be annoyed child of Ori, we are of the same blood
4 Do not be annoyed child of Ori, we are of the same blood
5 The right [hand] cannot do without the left
6 It is not good in front of Janesi [Jeunesse = youth?]
7 Let us not hear of disunity
8 I have not seen the glory of dust in the house
9 Broken wall must be rebuilt for biting tongue can belittle our town
10 Rebuild for disagreements can belittle the town
11 Unite to convince Aka in this matter
12 That Ketu may rise to success

1 *Panku wọn ko papọ m'Épó*
2 *K'ẹnu kọ bá de*
3 *Ẹ ma ibinu ọmọ orí nitorí irú itíni irú itíni*
4 *Ẹ ma ibinu ọmọ orí nitorí irú itíni irú itíni*
5 *Ọtún kọ ma lọ mọ òsì*
6 *Ko da a l'oju Janesi*
7 *Ẹ ma ijẹ k'agbọ́*
8 *Nko tí rogo a ti rafú nle*
9 *Alapa ẹ nde mo l'ẹnu koko ni sọ'lu ini di kekere*
10 *Ẹ ko nde ẹnu ko papọ ni isọ ini di kekere*
11 *Ẹ gbajọ kẹ ba ni ba m'Aka sọ̀rọ̀ yi*
12 *Ki Kétu me kun run ko yeje*

[Recorded in Ketu, 1971]

A more contemporary commentary refers to the mid-1960s crisis in Nigeria that led to the demise of the government. Ọrọ Ẹfẹ chides those politicians whose carelessness, audacity, and disregard for the people led to their downfall at the hands of the mothers and praises those who have worked for their constituents:

This world is harsh for you politicians
Anyone who wants to live in this world must be very careful [*bis*]
Watch what you say, for the world is heavy
You politicians, the world requires caution
Those who were doing it whom we told were not doing it properly
"The world" cut them away as bananas are cut from the stem
Those who were doing it whom we told were not doing it properly
"The world" blew them away like shafts from wheat
Sardauna died, we saw Balewa no more
"People of the world" killed Bello, Okotiebo packed up and left
Adegbenro with Ọdẹbiyi prepare to avenge
You did not allow a single child to suffer

Those who behave wickedly the "people of the world" will curse
It is a bad death that Akintọla died

Àiyé wọnyi ṣoró ènyin ọmọ òṣelú
Ẹniti oba gbaiyé ko ṣọ ra e [bis]
Ko ṣ'ọnu torí aiyé wuwo
Ènyin òṣelú aiyé di pèlépèlé
Awọn to ti kọ se ti a pe wọn ó ṣére
Aiyé bẹ wọn d'anu bi ògèdè
Awọn to ti kọ ti a pe nwọn ó ṣére
Aiyé fẹ wọn d'ànu bi ìyàngbó
Sardauna ó si, A ó rí Balewa mọ́
Ar'aiyé pa Bello, Okotiebo ko ti è lọ
Adegbenro murá pèlu Ọdẹbiyi ìjà nyin langbe
Ẹ maṣe je'yà ó jẹ́ ọmọ kan
Ẹ ni ba ṣé'kà o l'ar'aiyé o fi ṣ'èpè
Iku oro l'Akintọla ku

[Recorded in Idofoi Quarter, Aiyetoro, 1971]

Ẹfẹ songs also deal with the expected behavior in the performance of religious obligations. The proper execution of fundamental religious rites is necessary for continuity and stability in the community. Ọrọ Ẹfẹ condemns any divergence from the accepted, traditional norm. In the following song, Ọrọ Ẹfẹ cites a funeral at which certain adults showed great irreverence for the deceased. The mourners had carried the coffin to the market, where they slaughtered a goat and shed its blood on the ground. Afterward, as one group was about to take the meat home to prepare and share it, a fight broke out regarding the rightful owner of the goat. Ọrọ Ẹfẹ, in condemning foolish and sacrilegious behavior, explicitly reproves the individuals. Directness and repetition reinforce the harsh judgment of lack of character *(iwa)*, which is equivalent to lack of wisdom, a regrettable situation for elders whose wisdom is expected to surpass that of the general population.

Because of the deceased's goat you began to fight in public
Because of the deceased's goat you began to fight in public
Ọkanlawọn came and claimed to own the goat
Ọkanlawọn came and claimed to own the goat
You elders have no character
You elders have no character
Tell Disu that the goat he is collecting belongs to Ẹgbẹdokun
You elders have no character

Nitori ẹran ori posi lẹ ṣe nko ja loju titi
Nitori ẹran ori posi lẹ ṣe nko ja loju titi
Òkanlàwọn b'òde o si jẹlẹ ran
Òkanlàwọn b'òde o si jẹlẹ ran

A d'àgbalagbà ma mọ ìwa hun
A d'àgbalagbà ma mọ ìwa hun
Ẹ sọ fun Dìsu ẹran Ẹgbẹ́dokun
A d'àgbalagbà ma mọ ìwa hun

[Collected in Imala, 1971]

The last category of social commentary deals with hierarchy based on age. Such ordering reflects various levels of wisdom, for it is age, not wealth, position, or "book knowledge," that brings wisdom. Thus, in a society that is undergoing rapid social change with the resultant loss of traditional social controls, Ọrọ Ẹfẹ often criticizes youths who think they know more than their elders. In the following song obvious exaggeration (line 1) mocks the foolishness of youth, while pointed understatement completes the satire (line 2). In allegorical imagery, the one who was sent simply to collect the soup presumptuously tried to improve it, failing to consider that the specialist is more knowledgeable (lines 3–4). These lines are a reminder to impetuous youth that men, like animals, acquire their own special capabilities through experience, but they may be suitable for one thing and not for another (line 5). This lesson is also embodied in the proverb "If a young man wants to behave like an elderly man, the date of his birth will not let him" (Delano 1966:132):

1 Ah, truly young children are very wise
2 However I say they are not as wise as their elders
3 We called you to get the soup, but you went to add water to it
4 But you are not as wise as the one who cooked it
5 A goat is different from a horse, a white man is different from a
   Hausa
6 You are not as wise as the one who did the cooking

1 *Òtitọ́ l'ọmọde kekere gbọ́n*
2 *Mbimo ni o le gbọ́n t'àgbalagbà*
3 *À ni o wa gb'ọbẹ̀ ó lọ́ ta'mi sí*
4 *Ó lé gbọ́n t'ẹni o mọ se ọbẹ̀*
5 *Ewure ya f'ẹṣin òyìnbó ya fun gàmbàrí*
6 *Ó lé gbọ́n t'ẹni to mọ se ọbẹ̀*

[Collected in Idofoi Quarter, Aiyetoro, 1971]

History

Ẹfẹ songs not only comment on the contemporary scene but also record and preserve the past by means of historical recitations. In the major Yoruba capitals such as Ọyọ, Ketu, and Ile-Ifẹ, there has always been a court lineage responsible for the preservation of oral tradition (cf. Parrinder 1967:23–24; Johnson 1973:3). These accounts include royal

genealogies and prominent historical events or conditions that characterized each reign. Smaller towns and villages, however, often have no
official court historians. The task is left to Ọrọ Ẹfẹ, who, in song, not only
preserves recent occurrences but also recalls past events and personalities
spanning many generations. Such historical Ẹfẹ songs include genealogies and significant political events as well as cult histories. The following historical Ẹfẹ song recalls the names of six kings (ọba) who have ruled
at Aiyetoro, Ẹgbado, since its founding early in this century (c. 1902).
Ọrọ Ẹfẹ does not simply enumerate them; he characterizes their reigns
and embellishes the text with praise names:

> Seriki was the leader who enjoyed life like a king
> The turn of events overcame him [bis lines 1–2]
> Debeọdẹrọ was next to enjoy life
> He fought well and died [bis lines 3–4]
> Pẹluọla spent a short time before his death
> Then came Akinọla, the hero who reigned at an old age [bis lines
>   5–6]
> It came to Aṣamu, the king who stepped with dignity
> Life came to you Omidokun, be tenacious

> *Seriki ni ọgá to kó yayé bi ọba*
> *Bìribìri l'aiyé nyi aiyé yi po*
> *Debeọdẹrọ lo y'aiyé tẹ a e*
> *O bo gún ja o bogín lọ*
> *Pẹ̀lúọla ṣe sá kan ko to ré èbì*
> *Òkán Akínọla óró a fi emi àgbà*
> *O kán Aṣamu ọba ogbẹṣe gb'ola*
> *Aiyé yi kan ẹ Omidokun, ko mura girígirí*
>   [Collected in Idofoi Quarter, Aiyetoro, 1971]

A song collected by Father Thomas Moulero (1970:20–22) in the vicinity
of Ketu credits a man named Ẹdun—a name given to a twin—with the
introduction of Gẹlẹdẹ and its spread throughout thirteen towns in the
Ketu kingdom:

> Ẹdun of Ibadan was going on a trip
> When the evening came, the drumming of the ocean could be heard
> Father, where does one dance at this hour, asked the people?
> It is Ẹdun who brought [imported] Gẹlẹdẹ [bis]
> It is Ẹdun who brought it
> And we are proud of it [bis]
> The [Gẹlẹdẹ] dance arrived at Iranjin, then from there to Igan-Gura
> It is Ẹdun who brought it!
> We are proud of it [bis]
> The people of Ika went with two small goats [as payment] to ask for it
> The dance quietly made its appearance at Ofia

The people of Omu having learned about it came to be initiated
From there Gẹlẹdẹ arrived at Odogbo
The people of Iju quickly went to get permission to do it
The children of Ibepẹrẹ having learned of it came to be initiated
Quietly the dance came to Awayi
In the same way it made its appearance at Idiẹ
Those of Gbogburo ran to receive it
Those of Issaba ran to be initiated
Father, this is the history that was told to me and which I have kept in
   my memory
It is not before me that Gẹlẹdẹ began, it existed a long time ago
Men and women, you must take it seriously
Those of you who are present, inform those who are absent
Men and women, be attentive
That was the work of Ẹdun the originator

Ẹdun Ibadan l'o lọ l'ajò
Igba o di l'alẹ, l'olokun nlu
Baba, l'ibisi wọn njó l'awoyẹ?
Igboyi Gelede ti l'odun bọ [bis]
Ẹdun l'o lọ mu wa le
L'a nfi ṣe ihalẹ [bis]
Ijo wo'Ranjin, o yọ s'Igan-Gura
Ẹdun l'o lọ mu wa le, ko ṣẹ!
L'a nfi ṣe ihalẹ [bis]
Ọmọ Iká wọn l'ẹran meji fi gba a
L'ijó ṣe gbẹrẹ yọ s'Ofia
L'ọmọ Omu wọn gbọ l'a wa gba
Ijo ṣe gbẹrẹ yọ s'Odogbo yi
Ara Iju wọn sare wa gba a
Ọmọ Bekpẹrẹ gbọ a wa gba a
Ijo ṣe gbẹrẹ o wọ'lú Awayi
O ṣe gbẹrẹ ode ẹta Idiẹ
Gboburo wọn sáré a wa gba a
Issàbà wọn sare a wa gba
Baba, itan a kpa mi fi s'ọkàn
Ìgbà ijo ti ṣẹ jinna
K'ẹ kọ lẹ ṣa, ẹ t'akọ t'abo
Oni yi o wa ibi k'orohin f'ọni ko wa
K'ẹ kọ́'lẹ ṣa, ẹ t'akọ t'abo yekun
Okile Ẹdun kọ na

Funeral Commemoration

Funeral commemoration songs are heard at the annual festivals and
at special Gẹlẹdẹ ceremonies in honor of a recently deceased member of
the society or a prominent citizen in the community. On such occasions

Ọrọ Ẹfẹ commemorates the deceased with songs of praise and honor. He recalls the person's stature, character, and role in life and prays that his positive influence may still exert its power for the good of the community. In the following commemoration, Ọrọ Ẹfẹ urges the chorus to sing more to honor the death of a great man (lines 1–2). Lines 3 and 4 seem to be equating the death of a prominent man with that of an elephant and buffalo, two impressive and powerful animals. The meaning of the "pot" in lines 3–4 is obscure. One possible explanation may be related to what Fadipẹ (1970:280) refers to as ọ̀run àpâdì, "the abode of the dead with which potsherd is associated." He states that in a funeral ceremony, the soul of the deceased is summoned to appear before his relatives in order for it to be released from its earthly abode. If it fails to appear by the third calling, it is usually threatened with ọrun apadi, which Abraham (1958:57) translates as "hell." A more obvious explanation is that no matter how powerful an animal may be, it eventually dies and becomes nothing more than meat cooked in a pot.

Ọrọ Ẹfẹ admonishes the chorus to sing well and to continue calling their deceased father home. He then asks other Ọrọ Ẹfẹ—several sing at Ẹfẹ in some Ẹgbado towns—to sing with mournful voice; this probably indicates that the deceased, a society member and singer, died at a relatively young age (lines 7–11). In line 11, the whisk symbolizes what traditionally belongs to a family—something hereditary, as in the Yoruba saying, "the horse dying leaves the tail behind; the children survive the parents" (Beyioku 1946). Thus, although the father has died, his presence continues, a reflection of the Yoruba belief that the lineage is eternal:

1 I am looking at you to see how you do the ceremony
2 You chorus have not sung enough
3 Elephant died in the farm and the pot ate it up
4 Buffalo died in the farm and the pot ate it up
5 You sang well during Bello's performance
6 All Ọrọ Ẹfẹ who are in the market
7 We must all use mournful voice in singing
8 We are calling upon you to come, come, father Adebayo, sleep no
     longer away from home
9 We are calling upon you to come, come, Akewe Bello, sleep no
     longer away from home
10 He could no longer rise up, could no longer sing
11 Father Labode, death caused the whisk to fall from the hand of
     the cult member

1 *Mo nwo nyin loye be ó ti ṣ'awo si ni*
2 *Ẹ̀gbẹ́ Akinjẹlẹ ẹ ò ma ṣ'ere to*
3 *Erin ku l'oko magudu fi jẹ*

4 *Ẹfọn ku l'oko magudu fi jẹ*
5 *Ẹ ṣeré ti Bello ko dara*
6 *Gbogbo èfẹ to wa l'ọjà*
7 *Gbogbo wa ni ka sá ma f'ohun aro ṣ'èfẹ*
8 *A npe ẹ kò dide ko dide Baba Adebayo ko ma sun mọ etíle*
9 *A npe ẹ ko dide ko dide Akewe Bello ko ma sun m'etíle*
10 *Ko tún lé dide ko da'rin mọ*
11 *Baba Labọdé iku gb'ejọ l'ọwọ awo*

[Collected in Idofoi Quarter, Aiyetoro, 1971]

The final song, commemorating a departed mother, wishes her well in her journey home to the afterworld. Ọrọ Ẹfẹ thanks the family of the deceased for its generosity during the funeral rites (line 4) and prays that the mother will watch over her family:

1 Grandmother slept, mother went to the afterworld undisturbed
2 I say the afterworld is home, Grandmother greet them when you reach your abode
3 Mother of Juli went to the afterworld a good person [*bis*]
4 Greetings for spending money, greetings for looking after the house of the deceased
5 Mother will protect your home

1 *Ìyá Àgbà bi sun Ìyá lọ s'ọrun gbẹrẹ*
2 *Mo l'ọrun n'ile o, Ìyá Àgbà ki wọn bi b'ode n'le*
3 *Ìyá Ijúli lọ s'ọrun ẹnire*
4 *Ẹ ku inawo o, è ku aṣehinde*
5 *Ìyá ẹ sọ'le fun nyin*

[Recorded in Ketu, 1971]

Summary

Ọrọ Ẹfẹ directs his songs to spiritual forces, especially to the mothers, either explicitly, as in the *ijuba,* or implicitly, as in the songs of social commentary concerned with antisocial behavior. Sanctioned by the mothers, the Ẹfẹ ceremony becomes the epitome of united communal voicing with choral repetition and audience involvement. The entire community participates—young, old, male, female, Christian, Muslim, devotees of all the Yoruba gods, and the mothers. So do those not of the world, but of *ọrun,* who influence the lives of men either positively or negatively. The power of Ẹfẹ, however, does not reside in the act of voicing alone; indeed its power also derives from the masks and costumes that give Gẹlẹdẹ its reputation as the ultimate spectacle.

4

The Masks and Costumes
of Ẹfẹ Night

In addition to its efficacious words, Ẹfẹ spectacle is a display of enormously diverse masks and costumes. Such diversity suggests a certain antiquity and illustrates the range of creative images designed to appeal to and to entertain the "gods of society" throughout western Yorubaland. At the same time, however, a number of themes persist and recall the mythic origin of Gẹlẹdẹ.

Opening Masquerades

Night masquerades of assorted forms open Ẹfẹ performances, that is, bring them into the world. The program of these masquerades can be quite extensive or very basic. In some communities the opening process begins about a week before the actual ceremonies with the appearance of the herald, Amukoko. Representing a Dahomean warrior with a gash and welts on his face (pl. 14), he wears a pointed cap covered with medicine gourds and rectangular Islamic amulets and smokes a pipe. Another variation of what appears to be a herald mask shows a seated male wearing a pointed cap and smoking a pipe (pl. 15). The allusion to the kingdom of Dahomey is unclear, yet references to Dahomean (Fon) warriors are a popular theme not only in Gẹlẹdẹ but also in Egungun masquerades among the western Yoruba, where they are a satiric comment upon incessant Dahomean attacks throughout much of the nineteenth century (cf. Drewal and Drewal 1978:35, pl. 16 and Schiltz 1978:53, pl. 12). The Dahomeans are typically shown with long gashes on their faces and protective amulets clustered on their caps, which together testify to their ability to survive in the heat of battle. Pipes refer to a popular nineteenth-century pastime among Fon men and women. There also appears to be an oblique reference to Ẹṣu/Ẹlẹgba both in the func-

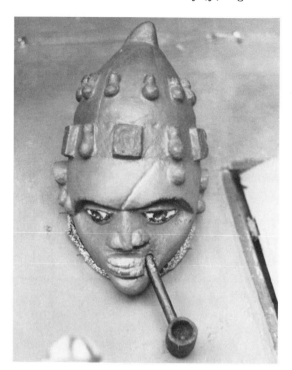

PLATE 14. Amukoko represents a pipe-smoking Dahomean warrior, with welts and a gash on his face, wearing a pointed cap covered with medicine gourds and Islamic amulets. Lagos, 1978.

PLATE 15. A mask, probably a herald or Amukoko, depicts a snake encircling a seated pipe-smoking man with pointed cap. Musée Ethnographique, Porto Novo (55.9.20).

tion of the masker as herald, i.e., messenger, and in the depiction of pipe-smoking, which is common in Ęṣu/Ęlęgba's iconography (cf. Frobenius 1913:228).

In many places Ęfę opening ceremonies include elaborate programs of masquerades. One type is Ogbagba, said to represent Ęṣu/Ęlęgba, the divine mediator whose attire is drawn from the realms of culture and nature—cloth and leaves. In some instances Ogbagba comes in two forms. His initial appearance is as a "young boy in a white cap and raffia skirt," and people sing, "Eshu comes, with light leaves" (Beier 1958:9). Later, Ogbagba appears as a grownup wearing banana leaves and iron anklets. The combination of white woven cap and raffia skirt, the trans-formation from youth to adult, and the leafy costumes destined for the rubbish heaps at the edge of town, all capture the unpredictability and liminality of Ęṣu/Ęlęgba.[1]

Another type of masquerade is Arabi Ajigbalę, "The-One-Who-Sweeps-every-Morning," completely covered in raffia fiber and cloth with iron idiophones around his ankles. In Ketu, Arabi looks like a small haystack, but a Lagos version dons a carved mask (pl. 1). Commonly referred to as Agbalę, "The Sweeper," this mask is painted white with a black dot on the forehead and, like the Ketu examples, tops a long raffia fiber costume. At Ketu, this masquerade evokes Ogun, god of iron. Ogun, the one who clears the bush for the shrines of the other gods, who opens the way for the living, has as his special clothing young raffia palm leaves, known as *mariwo*. Initiates possessed by Ogun's spirit are dressed in these palm fronds in a fashion very similar to the Arabi masquerade. This costume construction and the iron anklets suggest Ogun's symbolic complex. In Lagos, however, Arabi Ajigbalę is said to represent Ęṣu/Ęlęgba. Literally "sweeping" the arena with his broomlike costume of palm leaves, Arabi Ajigbalę "clears the way" *(tún ọ̀nà ṣe)* or opens the festivities, a function that is shared by both Ęṣu/Ęlęgba and Ogun.

In another variation of Ajigbalę from Ęgbado, a masquerader with leggings and a palm leaf skirt, covered with bundles of raffia fiber burn-ing brightly, charges back and forth four times. The way is cleared im-mediately. This masquerader appears to be a combination of two separate performers: Arabi Ajigbalę, with the fiber costume, and Pa Ìná Njáko (literally "Fire starts without Warning"), an uncostumed person carrying a pot of fire on the head. Thus, this Ęgbado Ajigbalę seems to be a condensation of two masqueraders and fulfills both roles at the same time.[2]

These various introductory masqueraders share a number of visual as well as symbolic elements. Their appearances are brief, for they exit as quickly as they enter. Their roles (opening, clearing, sweeping) and im-agery (pipes, palm fronds, fire) allude to two principal Yoruba deities, Ogun and Ęṣu/Ęlęgba—deities who in the context of sacrifices and ceremonies are always invoked first to "clear the way."[3] They are the spiritual links between men and the other deities; they mediate the transition between everyday, ordinary activity—that which exists in the world—and spiritual activity—that which invokes the deities and ancestors resident in the otherworldly realm and brings them into the world. Likewise, introductory masquerades carry the festival into the world. In so doing, they enter the realm of the "owners of the world," the mothers. It is at this point in the process that the materialization of the Great Mother occurs—swiftly, covertly, yet dramatically. Her appearance signals her approval of what has gone before and sanctions the ritual spectacles to follow.

Nocturnal Mother Masquerades

The sacred images that appear immediately following the opening masquerades give expression to the awesome aspects of the mothers.[4] They represent the essence of Gẹlẹdẹ and constitute, as informants explain, the very "foundation" (*ìpilẹ̀sẹ*) of the society. These masks are of two distinct forms yet are conceptually and functionally related. They dramatize the spiritual side of womanhood in two of its aspects—a bearded woman, often called the Great Mother (Iyanla), and Spirit Bird (Ẹyẹ Ọrọ).[5]

Simplicity, boldness of motif, and massive scale distinguish the Great Mother mask (pls. 2, 16–23). It has two parts: the head, and a long flat, boardlike extension below the chin, although in one (pl. 19) the lower face is extended on the board. Together the head and projection (between 15 and 36 inches in length) produce a massive headdress. The head is hemispheric to fit over the upper portion of the performer's head and forehead. The features are strong, massive, and clearly defined. Deep-set, bulging eyes often dominate the face, while heads are shaven or simply indicate a hairline, a variety of hairstyles, or, more dramatic, a prominent tuft of hair (*òṣu*) crowning the center of the head (pl. 20). The only other motifs are a snake encircling the head (pl. 21) or a bird perched on top. Ears, when shown at all, may vary from the standard Yoruba style and position to small pointed ears placed high on the temples (pl. 22).

The lower portion, probably the most distinctive feature of the headdress, is a long, flat or slightly curved projection that emerges from the jawline or chin of the head and generally extends one or two feet. Some have three to seven dark blue or black vertical lines painted on the surface, while others are left unmarked (pls. 21–22). Only one example (pl. 23) exhibits a more elaborate painted design; it consists of three wavering vertical lines interrupted by five horizontal bars. The word *yèyé*,

PLATE 16. A Great Mother mask, its face dominated by large, deep-set eyes and a long beard, creates a dramatic image of covert power. Seattle Art Museum. Photograph by Paul M. Macapia.

PLATE 17. A plaited coiffure, lower lip plug, and a broad beard characterize this Great Mother mask. From Clouzot and Level (1926:pl. 38).

PLATE 18. Having received countless sacrificial offerings that have worn a hole in the beard below the mouth, a mother mask with bulging eyes lies secluded in the Gẹlẹdẹ shrine. Ṣawonjo, 1978.

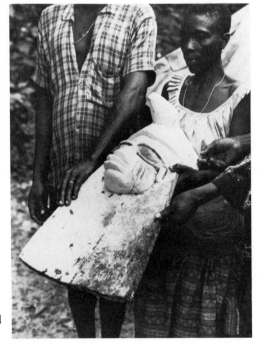

PLATE 19. In this headdress, probably a variant of the Great Mother mask, the nose and mouth are extended onto the boardlike projection of the face. Musée Royal de l'Afrique Centrale, Tervuren (R. G. 75.49.1).

PLATE 20. Held by female and male cult leaders, a Great Mother mask displays a prominent tuft (oṣu) as a symbol of medicines and spiritual power. Ibaiyun, 1975.

PLATE 21. This Great Mother mask has a snake wrapped around the brow and three vertical lines adorning the beard. Benin (R. P. B.), 1975.

PLATE 22. Three Great Mother masks with animal-like ears rest within the Gẹlẹdẹ shrine. A white curtain covers the older ones in the background. Iwoye, 1973.

PLATE 23. Decorating the elongated beard of a Great Mother mask are three wavering lines, five horizontal bars, and the word "Yeye," a term of endearment for mothers. Benin (R. P. B.), 1975.

a term of endearment meaning "mother," is painted across the bottom of the projection. Aside from these few designs, surfaces are plain, somewhat rough, and almost always white.

The boardlike projection from the chin of the Great Mother mask is identified explicitly as a beard (*iruǹgbọ̀n*). A beard defines an elder (*àgbàláàgbà*), with all the connotations of knowledge and wisdom that such status implies. But in the feminine realm the beard takes on additional meanings, for by definition a bearded woman possesses extraordinary spiritual power. Beards depicted in other Yoruba sculpture are much smaller and are sometimes darkened. The exaggeration and elongation of the mother's beard emphasize her extraordinary nature, for the beard on a woman "will not be like a man's own." The length of the beard implies longevity and commanding status. The additional element of whiteness emphasizes these qualities, for the Yoruba say, *ewú logbó, iruǹgbọ̀n làgbà,* meaning "old age [wisdom] is shown by white hair, maturity is shown by a beard" (Abraham 1958:169). The beard also suggests the transformation powers of the mothers. A devotee of one Yoruba deity remarked, "If you see any woman with a bearded chin, she is 'one possessing two bodies' (*abáàra méjì*). You will see her one way during the day, and at midnight she will turn to another thing."

Other icons associated with the bearded mother mask either suggest or depict transformations. In some headdresses (pl. 22), the ears are decidedly nonhuman. One carver (Olupọna 1975) described a more explicit reference to transformation, in which a bird surmounted the head of a bearded mother mask. Birds, it will be recalled, are a common symbol of the mothers in transformed state. A song offered in one community toward the close of bearded mother's appearance invites the mothers to dance:

> Honored elder *apake* come and dance with us
> All birds come dance with us
>
> *Ọlájogún apake ko ba ni jó*
> *Gbogbo ẹyẹ ko ba ni jó*
>
> [Collected in Ibaiyun, 1975]

Another carver (Ogundipẹ 1975) said, "in the midnight, when the drums are playing, the mask can turn to a bird." In some Ketu and Ẹgbado communities, the nocturnal mother mask literally takes such a form—Ẹyẹ Ọrọ or Spirit Bird, which plays upon the mothers' praise name of Bird-of-the-Night, Ẹyẹ Oru (cf. Beier 1958:6)—highlighting explicitly her powers of transformation and her nighttime activities.

The bird mothers, like the bearded mothers, are awesome in their bold simplicity (pls. 3, 24, 25). The whiteness of the cloth and mask dominates. The long, sharply pointed beak thrusts outward from the

PLATE 24. With blood-red beak and women's plaited hair, Spirit Bird exemplifies the mothers' powers of transformation. Ṣawonjo, 1978.

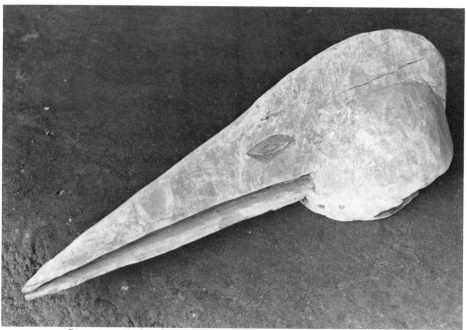

PLATE 25. A simple yet bold Spirit Bird mask displays a long, pointed beak and crested head. Ibeṣe, 1977.

domed or crested head with its small eyes. The beak's lethal quality is heightened by its blood-red tip and recalls "the one who makes noise in the midnight, who eats from the head to the arm . . . the liver to the heart." These sculpted images closely resemble descriptions of the mothers transformed into night birds. A story collected in Ṣala-Orilẹ describes the bird of the mothers as "one with the large beak which was blood-red. Its feathers were white. Someone touched it with a stick and it cried like a witch."[6]

Other features highlight the liminality of the bird mother image in the synthesis of human and animal features. In one (pl. 24) called by its custodian "elderly woman" *(àgbàláàgbà obìnrin)*, plaited hair crowns the head. In the other (pl. 3), Ẹyẹ Ọrọ has human ears. Spirit Bird epitomizes the praise names of the mothers—"the one with two bodies" *(abaara meji)* or "the one with two faces" *(olójú méjì)*. The power of transformation referred to in these praises originates in concepts of the nature of women's life force *(aṣẹ)* and their spiritual head, or *orí inún.*

Yoruba conceive of the individual as having both exterior *(òde)* and interior *(inun)* aspects (cf. Abiọdun 1980b). A person's exterior reveals little or nothing about his true being, character, or intentions; it is simply his outward physical appearance. The inner aspect controls all thoughts and actions. The character, personality, and potential of an individual reside in the spiritual head or *ori inun* (literally "inside head") to distinguish it from the outer or physical head, *ori ode.*

Individuals make a conscious effort to conceal the nature of the inner head as a means of self-protection, for persons reveal this aspect only when thoughts are uttered or acted out. Revealing *ori inun* can bring repercussions. Informants explain that "if someone voices out something which is bad, then people will be thinking bad of the person and the person can be poisoned. . . . What is voiced out comes from inside and that is what we Yoruba call *ori inun.*" A well-known prayer conveying the same concern for concealing and controlling the inner self requests, "May my inner head not spoil the outer one" *(Orí inún mi kò má bà ti òde jẹ́).*

Yoruba perceive a fundamental difference between females and males in their ability to conceal *ori inun.* Male informants stress this distinction in such words as "Women are more secretive than we. . . . But we men usually open our secret to anybody" and "Women have many secrets that they will never tell . . . except [to] their mothers." Secrecy is believed inherent in femaleness. The ability to be self-contained emerges in the concept of *ìrọjú,* a quality possessed by all women. *Iroju* is patience and perseverence (Crowther 1852:157). It connotes the control of self, of *ori inun,* and is matched by another female attribute attested to in the saying *ọwọ́ ẹ̀rọ̀ l'ọwọ́ obìnrin* ("soothing are the hands of a woman") (Odugbesan 1969). The cool female exterior reflects a composed inner self. This personal essence is based on the concept of life force. These notions about women are central to the images representing the mothers.

According to Yoruba belief, the concentration of vital force in women creates extraordinary potential that can manifest itself in both positive and negative ways. Terms such as *oloju meji*, "one with two faces," *abaara meji*, "one with two bodies," *aláàwò méjì*, "one of two colors" aptly express this duality and allude to the alleged powers of transformation attributed to certain women, which allow them to turn themselves into nocturnal creatures such as bats, snakes, rats, and especially birds. The Yoruba word for these special powers and a woman possessing them is *àjẹ́*, which has been translated as "witchcraft" or "witch." Ulli Beier (1958:6), however, argues that the English word "witch" is not a very accurate translation of *aje* since *aje* "represents rather the mystic powers of womanhood in their more dangerous destructive aspect." Any elderly woman, her longevity implying secret knowledge and power, may be regarded as an *aje*, as are all who hold important titles in cults for the gods and ancestors. The feeling is that in order to fulfill her role properly she must possess such power.

These elderly women and priestesses are considered neither antisocial nor the personification of evil. Rather they form an important segment of the population in any town and tend to be shown much respect and affection. Because of their special power, they have greater access to the Yoruba deities. They occupy a position subordinate to those of the supreme deity, Olodumare, and of Ọrunmila, god of the Ifa divination system, and equal or superior to that of the gods.

When angered, the mothers operate surreptitiously to seek out and destroy their victims. Their attacks are believed to result in stillbirth and conditions such as elephantiasis, impotency, infertility, and false pregnancy (which "turns to water") or debilitating diseases—attacks that destroy the victim slowly without outward sign. The inscrutability of the mothers and their mysteries intensify their power in the minds of men. Contrary to images of males that express overt aggression in themes of war and hunting, female images express themes of secrecy and covertness. Disguised as birds, the mothers operate at night in the middle of the town or farm, as one of their praise poems proclaims:

> My Mother Oṣoronga, famous dove that eats in the town
> Famous bird that eats in a cleared farm who kills an animal without
>   sharing with anyone
> One who makes noise in the midnight
> Who eats from the head to the arm, who eats from the liver to the
>   heart
>
> *Ìyámì Òṣòròngà, afínjú àdàbà ti'njẹ láàrín ìlú*

Afínjú ẹyẹ ti'njẹ ni gbangba oko ap'ẹrọn mahagun
Olókìkí oru
A ti orí jẹ apá, a t'ẹ̀dò jẹ ọkòn

[Collected in Ilaro, 1975]

Young girls who are impatient, lack self-control, and exhibit anger are not thought generally to possess this supernatural power, for their temperamental or fickle natures would expose and dissipate a power that must remain a mystery. In other words, "they don't have secret minds, cool minds." Informants say that when slandered, cursed, or slapped, women possessing such power will "just look at you and beg you. Then some time later another thing will happen." Elderly women, those past menopause, are most likely to possess this power, not only because of their cool, covert, secretive characters but also because they retain blood that possesses *aṣẹ*, vital force. A praise name for the aged mothers is "the one with the vagina that turns upside down without pouring blood." Composure and containment are thus essential qualities of the mothers. "If you offend them, they won't be annoyed. They will just be laughing together with the person, but what they will do to the person is inside." Their very restraint communicates complete control of awesome qualities unequaled by the most commanding male. These qualities emerge in these most sacred masquerades of the Gẹlẹdẹ corpus.[7]

The procedures used in sheltering the Great Mother's image between performances reveal very graphically the attitudes of reverence and awe toward this most sacred form. At the Ketu Gẹlẹdẹ house, Isalẹ-Eko, Lagos, while Gẹlẹdẹ masks hang openly on the walls or rest on rafters, the mother mask remains in the shrine, or Aṣẹ Gẹlẹdẹ, a small white house with a locked door. Palm fronds over the doorway serve a protective function, and they warn of an area restricted to initiates because of the presence of spiritual forces. The male cult leader *(babaláṣẹ̀)* murmurs a greeting to the Great Mother and carefully knocks three times before opening the door. In the center of the darkened room, raised on a concrete dais, is Iyanla. A spotless white cloth called *oloya* or *aṣọ funfun* envelops her completely, barely revealing the form. Only the *babalaṣẹ* and his assistant are permitted to approach the mask, and women of childbearing age are prevented from even glancing into the interior of the shrine.

In small Ọhọri, Ketu, and Anago Yoruba communities, the shrine is usually located in a small clearing within a sacred forest linked by a narrow path with the Gẹlẹdẹ performance area. At Ibaiyun, an Ọhọri village east of Pobe, the shrine is a small thatched shelter in the center of a clearing enclosed by a palm frond fence with palm fronds spanning the entrance to the grove. The thatched roof covers the remnants of an earthen mound that probably served as the altar. In the darkness of the eaves, resting on the rafters, is the Iyanla mask. Before Iyanla could be brought out into the open, elaborate arrangements were made to prevent certain people from seeing her countenance, primarily young girls and women of childbearing age, who, informants explained, might "see the face while dreaming," i.e., be visited or attacked by the mothers in night-mares. Several males stretched long bolts of cloth in front of the grove entrance, completely blocking the view of those who might be en-dangered.

In other towns, the mother mask may dwell in slightly different contexts. At Ṣawọnjo (pl. 18), she no longer emerges from the shrine but serves as the centerpiece for the altar. The countless offerings of food to the Great Mother placed on her image below the mouth have worn a hole in the wood. At Igbogila, the Great Mother is linked with Odua and kept in her pot-filled shrine (pl. 26). The cloth completely covering the image can be removed only by cult elders at the time of annual festivals, when a spotless white cloth replaces the soiled one.

A more complex shrine exists at Iwoye, in Ọhọri country. A thatched structure stands in a small clearing some distance from any compound. At the end of the path is a small shrine for Eṣu/Ẹlẹgba, messenger and confidant of the mothers. A bamboo enclosure at one end of the roofed area contains a rectangular earthen mound on which three logs provide a platform for three mother masks (pl. 22). A carefully draped white cloth veils the two older masks. Despite their age and loss of pigment, they have been carefully maintained in the shrine. They are no longer used in performance but remain on the dais as a focus of worship. Only the newest (in the foreground) emerges from the shrine to perform at night and only on certain occasions—annual Gẹlẹdẹ ceremonies, during repa-ration of the shrine, or in times of serious communal distress such as epidemics or drought. In a shrine, then, the mother masks remain par-tially or completely concealed whether located in an inner shrine, locked in a room, wrapped in cloth, or veiled by a curtain.

The iconographic simplicity of these masks and the secrecy attend-ing them in performance and in the shrine are expressions of the practice of endowing the object with vital force. After such masks are carved, the elders apply certain invisible substances, or "medicine." The infusion of substances possessing aṣẹ plus invocations activate the mask and ensure efficacy.[8] The concentration of these substances in an object or at the shrine or face (ojúbọ) of the deity constitutes that deity's power or essence. As explained to us, "She [the mother mask] cannot come out without medicine. That is why they don't like people to be near it." The radiating power of the medicine is believed to cause amenorrhea, infertility, insan-ity, or blindness.[9] These same medicines allow her to serve as guardian of

PLATE 26. A Great Mother mask concealed in cloth lies within the shrine of the goddess Odua. Igbogila, 1978.

the community, warding off destructive forces, for "she is the nightwatch for the town" *(ti a fi ṣọ ìlú)*. The drums accompanying this type of mask invoke some of these essential materials to set them into action:

Chewing stick, come and dance
Rope from the forest, come and dance
Anthill, come and dance
Dust from the road, come and dance
Honored ancestor *apake*, come and dance

Oringbo, wa ka jo
Okun igbo, wa ka jo
Bodipẹtẹ, wa ka jo
Kukubọlẹ, wa ka jo
Ọlajogun apake, wa ka jo

[Collected in Ibaiyun, 1975]

Oringbo, okun igbo, bodipẹtẹ, and *kukubọlẹ* are among the substances that activate the mask, and, like the expression *iyami*, which is used for both mother and a woman with supernatural powers, may have double meanings. The term *kukubọlẹ,* for example, may be translated as "come

down join us," and *bodipẹtẹ* can mean, in addition to an anthill, "turn to
something easy," whereas titled Gẹlẹdẹ members confirm their more
esoteric connotations. *Kukubọlẹ* is dust taken from the road on which
people walk, an ingredient used in the preparation of Iyanla. Reportedly
it is also used by traders in medicinal preparations to draw customers to
their places of business.[10]

Medicines invested in the mother masks are an essential part of the
image and determine, as much as any visible motifs, people's ideas, attitudes, and reactions concerning the form. What is unseen, yet intellec-
tually and emotionally acknowledged by the spectators, must be
considered part of the work of art. In responding to questions about
different aspects of the mother mask, a carver and diviner from Pobe
said (Ogundipẹ 1975), "Yes, there is something else but I don't know
what it is. . . ." Pointing to a closed container, he said, "Do you see this?
Can you tell me what is inside? We can only see the outside of Ososomu
[the Great Mother], but we cannot say anything about what is prepared
inside—except the elders. . . . Ososomu is prepared with medicine." The
mask's relatively uncomplicated iconography and the invisible substances
are as effective in evoking a response as forms with accumulated visible
substances or complex imagery. Without medicine, the mask is simply
wood; with medicine, it becomes a receptacle for the spirit of the Great
Mother. So while one usually thinks of a performance or spectacle as
implying observation by an audience, for the Yoruba, spectacle means
both actual sights and mental images of ethereal entities. In this case the
spectators are purposely given very limited access to the image and may
in fact never see it, forcing them to imagine what the Great Mother really
looks like. One witness to a performance of a mother mask could only
describe "the great rush of people," although he could hear the songs
and drums.

What has the greatest impact upon all present is what is *not* seen. The
obstructed view, created by extinguishing all lights and forming an im-
penetrable circle of society elders around the masquerader, and concealed medicine give the mask a special aura of power. The mother
mask's awesome power resides in its unknowableness. Like women, as
perceived by men in Yoruba culture, the mother mask is secretive, and
like elderly women it is powerful.

A tuft of hair *(òṣù)* on some mother masks evokes the hidden dimension (pl. 20). An initiate who dedicates himself to a deity will have certain
substances rubbed into incisions on the top of his head to allow the deity
to "mount" his inner head or possess him (Verger 1954:394; 1957:71). A
tuft of hair is allowed to grow over the incisions to mark the place where
medicine has been inserted and to signify the bond between devotee and
deity. The tuft announces ritual commitment and endows the bearer with

the spiritual force of his deity. The Great Mother with a tuft of hair on top of her head declares her position as archpriestess possessing spiritual power. The tuft indicates the presence of medicine.

The full significance of the mother mask's tuft emerges in her nocturnal performance. While the community hails her with songs, the drummers offer one of her praise names, Apọ̀kọ̀dọ̀su (A-pa-ọkọ-di-ọsu), meaning "the one who kills her husband in order to receive an *ọsu*," or, in other words, "in order to take a title," the title being symbolized by the tuft *(ọsu)*.

Mother masks are whitewashed.[11] In the realm of the "white deities" *(orìṣa funfun)*, whiteness is synonymous with outer composure *(tutu)* and covert action—two supremely feminine attributes. White may also suggest the state of purity or cleanliness ascribed to elderly women past menopause, for it is said that "Osọsomu is clean. She doesn't like anything that is dirty. . . . When women are passing blood, it is a bad thing." Yoruba males who regard menstrual blood as polluting explain that its purpose is to "wash out all that has been happening between a man and a woman." More important, menses, which by definition contains *aṣẹ*, can bring misfortune to a man (Prince 1961:798) and neutralize any medicinal preparations. By the same token, the strength of the medicines applied to mother masks "dry off" a young woman's menstruation. Keeping young girls and women at a distance from mother masks protects them from her radiating powers.

The use of white cloth adds a further dimension to these themes. In a shrine, cloth heightens the mystery of the mother's face or conceals it completely. At Iwoye, a sheer white curtain partially covers two mother masks, softening the impact of the bold forms (pl. 22). At Ijio, the mother mask is kept behind a curtain in the inner recesses of the shrine (Harper 1970:75). At the Gẹ̀lẹ̀dẹ́ shrine at Isalẹ̀ Eko, Lagos, and at Igbogila, Ẹgbado (pl. 26), the mask is completely wrapped in a white cloth. Only the general outline of rounded head and projecting board can be perceived.

In performance, the costume of the dancer representing the mother is a long white cloth attached to the wood mask. Sometimes more than eight or ten yards in length, it is intended to trail along the ground behind the masquerader, although sometimes it is held by attendants. The length of the trailing garment implies both the generosity of the community and the great age of the eternal mother. A comparable situation exists in Egungun. Among Ẹgbado Yoruba, masqueraders representing the collective ancestors of various lineages, called Baba Parikoko, have enormous trailing cloths, often described as being up to 100 yards long (cf. Drewal and Drewal 1978:pl. 11). Before each yearly appearance of the masqueraders, lineage members contribute money for cloth to lengthen the garment. Lineages compete to display the longest Baba Parikoko because the length attests to the seniority and status of the father and to the status and commitment of the descendants who paid for the cloth.

In contrast to the purchase of the Egungun cloth as an expression of lineage allegiance, the mother's cloth itself represents extralineal or communal unity and cohesion. When the mother mask appears the community sings:

> The cloth of others is sweet to trail on the ground
> Ososomu has none
> The cloth of others is sweet to trail on the ground

> *Aṣọ alaṣọ dùn igbálẹ̀*
> *Ososomu kò ni kọn*
> *Aṣọ alaṣọ dùn igbálẹ̀*

[Collected in Iwoye, 1973]

The song reveals that the community takes care of its mother by providing her with clothes. Each member of the community is expected to make a small contribution toward the purchase of the mother's cloth, and each year the community provides a new one as a gesture of renewed support. It is common practice in Yoruba compounds for children to bathe and clothe elderly women who have grown so old that they have lost the physical strength to care for themselves. By contributing toward the purchase of a new cloth, the community takes care of its ancestral mother fulfilling its social and moral obligation. This communal act is a sacrifice and, in a sense, represents a visual prayer to "the mother of us all" that has the combined force *(aṣẹ)* of individuals to maintain health, wealth, and stability. A similar procedure of providing cloth occurs during afternoon Gęlędę dances.

Scale is another significant feature of the mother mask. The suffix *ńlá* in Iyanla, meaning "big" or "great," implies both physical size and importance (Abraham 1958:444). Size in costuming reinforces notions of social importance (H. J. Drewal 1979). The size of the head suggests spiritual strength. Moulero (1970:47) describes the mother mask as the "enormous mask" and gives the following song and translation:

> Great god [Iyanla] a e! She has come
> With her enormous head
> Ososomu must not be late
> It is pride that makes her do it

> *Orìṣa nla a ẹ! O de o*
> *Ori ẹ Kpẹkẹtẹkpẹkẹtẹ*
> *Ossossom ki jegue*
> *Ara lila l'o de*

Size distinguishes the mother mask from the rest of the Gẹlẹdẹ corpus and suggests the mother's awesome powers. The head man at Igbeme-Ile described the mother masks he had seen at Isele and Pobe as "she is very big" and "enormous." A carver and priest of Ifa, Ogundipẹ (1975), remarked that when the mother mask comes out "the [young] women must not see her because she is too huge *(tóbi ju)*." The scale of the mask stresses the inner head, the source of women's covert power. The prominence of the forehead recalls descriptions of possession in which the head "swells" *(wú)* with the spiritual presence. This emphasis on size is an expression of awe for something that cannot be encompassed, a power that is omnipotent.

Recurrent themes in the corpus of nocturnal mother masquerades reveal the essence of Yoruba beliefs about mystical feminine powers. Hoary age and whiteness pervade both performance and iconography. The masquerades move in a slow, deliberate manner, often bent over. Measured tread connotes pride, stature, patience, and endurance—the attributes of elders. Icons like the beard, which evokes age, reinforce mimed age. Such old age among women implies awesome spiritual powers derived from the termination of menstruation and the consumption of the life blood (i.e., *aṣẹ*) of victims (cf. Prince 1961:798). Hoary age commands both respect and fear. Whiteness, too, connotes postmenopausal women and intensified force inherent in that state. Furthermore, whiteness conveys the coolness that characterizes covert power and action as well as affirms ritual purity, calmness, and patience—soothing feminine qualities.

Concealment is another dominant theme in the performance, shrines, and iconography of bearded and bird mothers. Most striking is that their impact in performance depends on what is *unseen* rather than what is seen. Spirit Bird with fearsome blood-red beak and Bearded Mother make one circuit through the market, surrounded by society members, before disappearing in the dark. These nocturnal apparitions emphasize secrecy and covertness, properties that characterize the life force of women and their spiritual essence, or "inner head," as well as the more destructive potential of the mothers. In the shrine, the wrapped, veiled, or guarded images sustain an aura of mystery. Through the vested interest of the community, each member having contributed to the purchase of their cloths, mother masks remain accessible but visually restricted.

The austere quality of the masks enhances their visual power: outer simplicity highlights inner presence. The extraordinary beard and sharply pointed ears on a human head and the plaited hair style and human ears on a bird head blur male and female, animal and human categories. The depiction of liminal states of being can be threatening, for they defy ordinary worldly/supernatural categories as recognized by the community. These images of the mothers are most appropriate, for they express the reputed powers of transformation and stress the unknowable, undefinable potential of these powerful entities, "the ones of two bodies," who move freely between realms, unlike ordinary mortals. This enigmatic quality of the mothers gives them great importance in Yoruba society, and their nature demands a cautious, calm, and patient approach on the part of supplicants. The brief appearance of the mother masquerade reminds the community of the awesome powers they must assuage, but it also signals the mothers' approval and their sanction of the spectacle to come—the singing masquerades.

Singing Masquerades

The Attendants

Just as preliminary masquerades prepare the way for the appearance of the sacred mothers, masked attendants sing and dance to herald the impending arrival of the principal performer, Ọrọ Ẹfẹ. Important personages in Yoruba society rarely appear in public without their supporters, and Ọrọ Ẹfẹ is no exception, especially since his performance is a dangerous mission that requires proper procedures and propitiations to ensure his safety and the successful completion of his ritual task. In many areas, a companion singing masquerader immediately precedes Ọrọ Ẹfẹ. These maskers, considered to be his subordinates, take different forms.

Among Ketu Yoruba peoples, Ọrọ Ẹfẹ's singing companion is called Tètèdé (literally "The-One-Who-Comes-Before"), a name given to the firstborn of twins if female. As the junior, she comes to test the world for her brother (Moulero 1971). Others explain Tetede as the "wife" of Ọrọ Ẹfẹ, who represents "the most beautiful woman who pleases the witches" (Harper 1970:78). In one town, this masker is referred to as "Cool World" (Aiye Tutu), for her presence soothes, cools, and placates the various powers present in the assembled community, thus making it safe for Ọrọ Ẹfẹ to appear. Tetede headdresses—similar to some afternoon Gẹlẹdẹ masks representing females with elaborate head ties—are usually surmounted by a tray, bowl, or other container (pls. 4, 27–29). Their white or yellow painted faces distinguish them as night masqueraders. The theme of the sacrificial offerings is suggested by the shape and decoration of the receptacles balanced on the head; in plates 4, 27, and 28, gin bottles—the contents of which are either sprayed on shrines to "alert" the gods or poured as libations—flank large cylindrical containers. On some masks, the container lids are in the form of birds (pl. 29). One unusual mask, possibly a Tetede because of its swirling head wrap and white visage (pl. 30), is surmounted by an *agbe* plant. A snake devouring prey curls around the bush, while birds peck at the head tie.

PLATE 27. Tetede balances on her head the gin bottles and containers used in ritual. Art Museum, University of Ifẹ.

PLATE 28. Above her swirling head tie, Tetede carries ritual items. Art Museum, University of Ifẹ.

PLATE 29. Birds cover the containers on Tetede's head. Igbogila, 1978.

PLATE 30. At the top of an *agbe* tree, crowning the head of Tetede, a snake devours its prey while birds peck at a swirling head tie. Musée Ethnographique, Porto Novo (55.3.36).

Tetede-type masqueraders found in Ketu and contiguous areas wear costumes that contain elements found in most Ẹfẹ and Gẹlẹdẹ costumes—leggings, arm wraps, iron leg rattles, and whisks—but other elements provide decidedly feminine attributes. Several head wraps tied tightly around the performer's torso give the impression of a narrow bodice, a typical feature of Ketu style female Gẹlẹdẹ (pl. 4). A wooden construction of sticks or a cylindrical spool is tied at the waist and covered by a long wrapper *(ìró)* to simulate substantial hips and buttocks. Often a carved breastplate, tied above the narrow bodice and draped with head wraps or a cloth panel, thrusts forward. A transcendent image is produced by a form that exaggerates female features, the rich profusion of cloth, and the elaborately carved headdresses, whose white or pastel features float dramatically in the darkness.

In the Ẹgbado town of Ilaro, Ọrọ Ẹfẹ is preceded by a singing male masquerader named Ajákuena. He wears a broad tray mask with a face in the center (pl. 31). A long sheer cloth covers his upper body and face, and strands of beads, palm nuts, cowrie shells, and/or mirrors dangle from the rim of the tray. The costume also includes leggings, leg rattles, and a long-sleeved man's gown of handwoven, narrow-band fabric tied at the waist with a woman's head tie.

These singing attendants may vary in their form and identity but not in their role. As the name of one such masquerader suggests, Aiye Tutu ("Cool World")—whether seen as wife or sister, brother or companion—their purpose is to prepare the way and make safe or "cool" a world in which Ọrọ Ẹfẹ must perform his courageous and dangerous task in the midst of potentially destructive forces.

Male Ọrọ Ẹfẹ Masquerades

Singing male masquerades are central to the Ẹfẹ ceremony, not only because their songs are featured and carry force but also because they are visually enhanced by rich masks and costumes and by the elaborate program of masquerades, described above, that introduce them. These singing masquerades, known variously as Ọrọ Ẹfẹ, Elẹfẹ, or Apaṣa in different areas, convey masculine images of physical and spiritual power, status, and sacred leadership. Through their headdresses, costumes, and movements they also reflect the historical and cultural influence of Islam. Less obvious yet ever present are oblique references to the omnipotent mothers.

Singing masquerades among Ketu people are among the most ornate of all Ẹfẹ with their huge, elaborate costumes and intricately carved masks. Ọrọ Ẹfẹ's headdress is often composed of three parts (frontispiece, color plates 2, 3, and pls. 5, 32–35): the suspended cloth or veil, the main head or face, and the superstructure. The veil, made of cloth or

PLATE 31. Donning a circular platform headdress with a male
head in the center and cowries, mirrors, and palm nuts
suspended from its perimeter, the singing masquerader,
Ajakuena, prepares the way for Ọrọ Ẹfẹ. Ilaro, 1978.

PLATE 32. The side view of an Ọrọ Ẹfẹ headdress illustrates woodpeckers, turban wraps, a leopard, and a snake flanked by long cutlasses in leather sheaths. A crescent moon crowns the white brow. Ketu, 1971.

PLATE 33. A Ketu Ọrọ Ẹfẹ headdress displays typical motifs arranged in a different fashion from those in plate 32, e.g., the arched snake substitutes for the crescent moon. Bernisches Historisches Museum (CO.68.325.2).

PLATE 34. A mongoose and birds seize a snake above Ọrọ Ẹfẹ's head. Musée Ethnographique, Porto Novo (55.9.2).

PLATE 35. Rectangular amulets and a mongoose crown Ọrọ Ẹfẹ's head. Nigerian Museum, Lagos (59.33.106).

other materials, obscures the face while allowing the wearer to see. The main head portrays a human face rendered in stark, cool white. Clear, sculpted facial features, especially the pierced eyes and the mouth, are given further definition by the use of dark colors set off against the white face. The superstructure, in contrast to the simplicity of the main head, is a complex composition of curving, spiraling masses and spaces in several layers. The curving, circulating forms of pythons, crescent moon, and turban wraps *(láwàní)* are juxtaposed with sharply defined vertical cutlass sheaths, which hang at the sides (frontispiece, color plates 2, 3, pls. 32–33). At the back is a sculpted rendering of a leather panel with an interlace motif (color plate 3). In front, a white crescent moon often crowns the brow of the face. Animal motifs—lion, leopard, snake, mongoose—occasionally command the summit of the superstructure, but more frequently birds perch on top. Blue, yellow, green, and especially red highlight surface patterning and offer a contrast to the whiteness of the main head (frontispiece, color plate 2).

This profusion of imagery proclaims both physical and spiritual attributes pointing to a number of themes—masculine strength and courage; royalty; the supernatural powers of the Yoruba god of iron and war, Ogun; the presence of Islam; and the omnipresence of the mothers. The cutlass sheaths suspended from the superstructure suggest masculine prerogatives, especially those of hunters and warriors. These images also connote a spiritual dimension. One of the three major deities worshipped at Ketu Gẹlẹdẹ ceremonies is Ogun, the tutelary deity of hunters and the god of iron and war, whose primary symbols are implements of iron, especially cutlasses. Hunters play a central role in many Gẹlẹdẹ societies. They serve as guardians and supporters for the masqueraders and as crowd controllers during the performance. There are many references to Ogun in the opening masquerades of Ẹfẹ night and in Ọrọ Ẹfẹ's opening incantations.[12]

The crescent moon *(òṣùpá)* may also refer to supernatural powers. One Ketu Ọrọ Ẹfẹ (Ogundipẹ 1971) explained that the moon and the turban wraps in his own headdress identify him as a Muslim (pl. 32)[13] The same probably applies in another mask in which the crescent moon becomes a row of Muslim amulets (pl. 35).[14] According to another Ọrọ Ẹfẹ performer, the moon "allows everyone to see clearly and enjoy." This comment recalls the Yoruba saying that "the moon over Ọyọ helps the Alaafin [king] to know what is going on in the provinces" (Crowther 1852:225). The monarch, his all-seeing powers symbolized by the moon, knows and exposes all sorts of plots, scandals, or disorders within his realm, just as Ọrọ Ẹfẹ does in the course of his performance. The moon is also a reference to the time of the ceremony and the tradition of a vigil, which sets the spectacle apart from everyday activities. It is a time most appropriate for appealing to the elderly women and other spirits, who are most attentive during the hours of darkness. But whether the crescent moon or a row of Muslim amulets crowns Ọrọ Ẹfẹ's brow, it communicates the powers he possesses to perform his task successfully.

Perched at the top of many Ẹfẹ masks is the supreme symbol of spiritual power, the bird of the mothers. On one the bird's long white beak grasps a scorpion. Our inquiries evoked a rhetorical question, "Can a bird take a scorpion in its mouth?" implying the answer "No." Only a bird of supernatural power, the bird of the mothers, can perform such a feat. In other Ketu Ọrọ Ẹfẹ masks (pl. 32), the birds are identified as grey woodpeckers (akoko), which are associated with the mothers, as in the following verse sung by a night masquerader (Beier 1958:10):

> All powerful mother, mother of the night bird. . . .
> My mother kills quickly without a cry
> To prick our memory suddenly
> Quickly as woodpecker pecks the tree on the farm
> The woodpecker who hammers the tree while words rush forth from
>   his mouth. . . .

The woodpecker on top of Ẹfẹ masks alludes to Ọrọ Ẹfẹ's role as spokesman for the mothers and for society, when "words rush forth from his mouth."

The birds at the top, together with the masker's cloth veil and carved face, recall major iconic elements of Yoruba crowns (cf. Thompson 1970:10) and may be references to the royalty and sacred leadership of Ọrọ Ẹfẹ. In one performance he calls himself the "masquerade of the king" (egun ọba), and in another he asserts, "I have become the King of Ẹfẹ; all youths prostrate yourselves before me." To these royal references can be added the whisks (ìrùkẹ̀rẹ̀) held in his hands, which are the accoutrements of elders, chiefs, and kings (frontispiece, color plate 2, pl. 5). Finally, by putting on Ọrọ Ẹfẹ's headdress, iyalaṣẹ mirrors the crowning of a new king by an elderly female official in the palace (cf. H. J. Drewal 1977b:12). These parallels in iconography and ritual procedure reinforce the themes of royalty and sacred leadership in relationship to the mothers.

Another headdress (pls. 34, 35) portrays a mongoose and birds seizing a snake or snakes. The mongoose, renowned for its quickness and cunning in capturing snakes, is an appropriate metaphor for the courage and cleverness of Ọrọ Ẹfẹ, who "catches" and exposes wrongdoers during his nocturnal performance. The encircling bands with decorated rectangular projections appear to be references to belts or turban wraps with Islamic amulets, which are protective devices for the courageous Ọrọ Ẹfẹ.

Among Ọhọri Ketu people, Ọrọ Ẹfẹ imagery is slightly different. Multiple knives and two felines (leopards?) devouring another animal surmount a bearded face (pl. 36). In another, snakes with birds in their mouths loop at the sides (pl. 37). Strands of beads and coins dangle from a horizontal bar over the main face in imitation of beaded veils worn by kings and important priests in this area. Two other features are more striking: the face is bearded, and the hovering form at the apex of the headdress, usually a bird, assumes another flying form, a four-engine airplane! In a further development (pl. 38) the beard fans outward and two bladelike ears rise dramatically above the head. The crescent moon of the Ketu Ọrọ Ẹfẹ reappears but in reversed position, and airplanes, instead of snakes and birds, flank the face. Despite the substitution of motifs, certain themes persist: aggressive action (devouring motifs), male-associated implements and references to the god of iron and war (cutlasses, guns), sacred leadership (leopard, beaded veil), the mothers in transformed state (birds/airplanes), and Islamic references (moon, belt, leather sheaths, and amulets).

Many of the themes evident in Ketu area Ọrọ Ẹfẹ headdresses are amplified in the costume. The expansion of the chest and torso by means of bamboo hoops or layers of cloth amplifies the grandeur, importance, and stature of the wearer as it intensifies his physical presence (frontispiece, color plates 2, 3, pl. 5). Elaborate embroidered and appliqued panels *(gberi, apá)* display a profusion of motifs. Although the most extensive use of such panels occurs in Ọrọ Ẹfẹ's ensemble, they also can form part of the costuming of daytime male and occasionally female Gẹlẹdẹ (cf. color plate 5). Decorative motifs include crosses, stars, chevrons, lozenges, diamonds, circles, and squares consisting of triangular segments of contrasting colors, opposed spiraling motifs interspersed with diamonds and triangles, interlace patterns, vertical stripes set within a rectangle, and mirrors—circular and rectangular—set into the fabric, all of which are surrounded by a straight or, more often, a sawtooth border fringe (frontispiece, color plates 2, 3, pl. 5). In addition to these geometric patterns, a number of representational images appear: crocodiles, tortoises, and human faces. For example, the Ọrọ Ẹfẹ in the frontispiece has a reptile embroidered on his vest. While colors are variegated, red seems to dominate the background as well as the fringes and some of the figures.

The source of such finely worked panels is uncertain, but an analysis of technique, composition, and iconography suggests some intriguing possibilities. Many of the appliquéd patterns, especially the representational ones, have close parallels with appliqué work in the contiguous areas of the Fon to the west of Ketu. In both, light colored silhouetted figures float against a dark background (cf. Harper 1970:49–52). Even

PLATE 36. In this headdress, multiple knives flank Ọrọ Ẹfẹ's face, and two felines attack a third animal. Ajilete, 1978.

PLATE 37. Strands of beads and coins veil the face, snakes hold birds, and a four-engine airplane flies overhead in this Ọrọ Ẹfẹ headdress. Obele, 1975.

PLATE 38. An Ọrọ Ẹfẹ̀ headdress with bladelike ears, beard, and pipe also displays a crescent moon and two airplanes at the sides. Igbeme-Ile, 1975.

more striking are the visual similarities between some curvilinear motifs and Adinkra cloth symbols from Ghana (cf. Quarcoo 1972:32, 46). It seems likely that such similarities may be traced to a common source, Islamic decorative arts. Quarcoo (1972:6) states that "some of the [Adinkra] symbols are stylized forms of talismans believed to have Moslem associations." This is certainly possible since there was a strong Muslim presence in Kumasi by the eighteenth century or earlier (Wilkes 1961:14). Muslim influence is evident in some important Asante regalia, including one worn by the Asantehene during enstoolment and others worn by Asante warriors, as illustrated by Dupuis in 1820 (cf. Lamb 1975:144–146).

Islamic artistic influence is also evident in Yorubaland. The style of Yoruba garments and of much of the embroidery is based on Muslim, more specifically Hausa, Nupe, and Bariba, modes (cf. Johnson 1973 [1921]:110–113; Adamu 1978:124–125). The curvilinear or diamond-shaped interlace pattern, chevrons (color plates 2, 3), "the Muslim knot," double spirals (color plate 3 and pl. 5), and circles are primary motifs in these masquerade panels, but some of the closest parallels come in Hausa calligraphy, embroidered clothing, and appliquéd and embroidered horse trappings (Heathcote 1976:pls. 9, 13, 14, 81, 87). Calligraphy drawn on gowns, primarily excerpts from Koranic prayers, serves as both decoration and protection on "charm" garments, one of which was seen in Yoruba country in 1825 by Clapperton. Writing before 1820, John McLeod (1820:93–95) reported that Muslim artisans at Abomey were well received: "They carried with them scraps or sentences of the Koran, which they distributed to the natives, who generally fastened them to the ends of sticks near their doors as charms against witchcraft." Transformed Arabic symbols as charms against "witchcraft" appliquéd or embroidered on costumes is entirely plausible, particularly for Gẹlẹdẹ. The same motifs may be observed in horse trappings, which had a long history in Hausa as well as in Yoruba country (cf. Clapperton 1829:2). Another striking feature of horse trappings found in both areas is the sawtooth border (Heathcote 1976:pl. 9), which is present in masquerade costumes throughout western Yorubaland, not only in Gẹlẹdẹ but in Egungun (cf. Drewal and Drewal 1978:pls. 1, 2, 3).

Northern, Islamic-inspired decorative motifs that filtered into Yoruba country via Hausa, Nupe, and Bariba are an important part of Ẹfẹ costuming and to a lesser extent of Gẹlẹdẹ, especially in the Ketu area. Muslims have been recorded in the city of Ketu from about 1750. By 1790 they had swelled Masafe Quarter and were important in the defense of the town (Parrinder 1967:41), and they were documented as far south as Whydah and Abomey in the early eighteenth century (cf. Labat 1730; Snelgrave 1734:80; Adamu 1978:113–114). In addition to being traders, many Muslims would have been the craftsmen supplying woven, embroidered and appliquéd material. Muslim references abound in the Ketu Ọrọ Ẹfẹ headdress as well as in Gẹlẹdẹ masks generally: the crescent moon, turban wraps, representations of leather sheaths and panels, and interlace patterns. It seems likely that as the northern peoples became more entrenched in Ketu and neighboring areas and as Yoruba converted to Islam, these elements were incorporated into Gẹlẹdẹ, especially since conversion to Islam did not prevent participation in the society's activities. In fact, given the role of Muslim militia in the defense of Ketu and the involvement of hunters/warriors (the followers of Ogun) in the Gẹlẹdẹ cult, the synthesis of Ogun and Muslim motifs in the Ọrọ Ẹfẹ masquerade seems quite logical. The predominance of the color red also supports this inference. Red is one of the colors associated with warriors and Ogun, and at Ketu a padded red jerkin used by hunters is worn under the appliquéd panels donned by Ọrọ Ẹfẹ. The leg rattles worn by all singing male masquerades also refer to Ogun. They are said to protect Ọrọ Ẹfẹ by providing sounds that scatter negative forces, just as his voice effects blessings and curses.[15] Rattles made of iron effectively invoke Ogun, for it is said that Ogun himself is iron.

In performance, Ọrọ Ẹfẹ paces back and forth at a slow and dignified tempo, terminating each line with a turn that causes his panels to flutter outward. The image of "flying" panels seems most appropriate, for the panels are known as "wings" *(apa),* and the padded jerkin with open sides is known as *àgbe àkàlàngbà,* a name derived from two species of birds with brilliant "puffed-up plumage" (Abraham 1958:27, 56; Harper 1970:78, 93). Such bird attributes are additional references to Ọrọ Ẹfẹ's role as the representative of the spiritually powerful women, "the owners of birds."

Serving the same function as Ọrọ Ẹfẹ among the Ketu Yoruba, but different in both mask and costume style, are the Ọhọri Yoruba singing masquerades known as *apaṣa* (pls. 39–43). The *apaṣa* performers' masks have broad, often striped, carved beards, which fan outward along the jawline, and long, earlike forms or blades projecting upward at the sides, usually painted with horizontal stripes or chevrons. These vertical projections are called either ears *(etí)* or cutlasses *(àdá),* which they more often resemble. Playing upon persistent hunter/Ogun references, some *apaṣa* have guns attached to the blade/ears (pl. 42), and others have knives on an amulet-clad belt (pl. 43). In the latter example, reptiles surmount doubled ears, and the bearded face becomes two. Another shows a hunter and worshipper of Ogun with a knife in one hand and a gun in the other (pl. 166). Note the tall blade/ear forms called cutlasses and the broad but short beard. So while the form of the Ọhọri night masks is dramatically different from the Ketu type, some of the same themes persist, namely masculinity, hunters, warriors, and Ogun.

Ọhọri costuming is completely different from Ketu styles. Almost all Ọhọri Ẹfẹ costumes consist of palm fiber attached to the rim of the headdress to cover the head and upper torso of the masquerader, in contrast to the cloth panels of Ketu. Palm fronds are the "clothes" of Ogun, and their presence reinforces the Ogun references in the headdress. Thus attired, the performers sing Ẹfẹ songs throughout the night.

Certain Ẹgbado and Awori Ọrọ Ẹfẹ headdresses and costumes exhibit quite another style (pl. 44 and cf. Thompson 1978). In fact, the style duplicates that of the singing attendant who introduces them (pl. 31). Like their companion, they wear a headdress in the form of a large circular tray known as *atẹ* Ẹfẹ, which is perforated or painted in triangu-

PLATE 39. A broad, striped beard and long ears characterize the Ọhọri *apaṣa* mask. William and Robert Arnett Collection. Photograph by Gerald Jones.

PLATE 40. The *apaṣa's* broad beard fans out, and bladelike ears tower above the head. Hammer Collection. Photograph by Jeffrey Hammer.

PLATE 41. Bladelike ears and a beard dominate the small head in this *apaṣa* headdress. Photograph by Howard Wildman, Isagba, 1971.

PLATE 42. The bladelike ears and the beard (broken) serve to support the guns, which cross over the *apaṣa's* white face. Iwoye, 1971.

PLATE 43. A double-faced *apaṣa* is
surmounted by a belt decorated
with amulets and knives. It
encircles the blade-shaped ears
topped by reptiles. Iwoye, 1971.

lar segments and has at the center a man's head with peaked cap
(*lábàṅkádà*) carved in high relief. Strands of beads, palm nuts, cowrie
shells, and mirrors dangle from the perimeter of the tray. Cloth also is
attached around the circumference, and a thin lace or gauzelike fabric in
front covers the face but allows the performer to see. The costume consists of leggings, leg rattles, and a long-sleeved man's gown made of
narrow strips of fabric tied at the waist by a single woman's head tie. He
wears white gloves as he clutches large horsetail whisks.

Paralleling this type, yet in many ways different, is the Ẹfẹ at Isalẹ
Eko, Lagos (pl. 45). The head, painted a brilliant white, is offset by the
eyebrows, eyes, scarification marks, and especially the gaping mouth, all
painted black. The head is covered with an unusual cap painted in a black
and white checkerboard pattern with shiny metal disks in the white
squares. Over the head is a circular form called *àkàtà*, painted white on
the bottom and with a black-and-white pinwheel design on the top that
may represent an umbrella. Medicinal camwood blades and shiny metal
disks, like those attached to the cap, dangle around its edge, and two
metal braces, vaguely reminiscent of birds, intersect at its center. In per-

PLATE 44. An Ẹgbado Ọrọ Ẹfẹ̀ wears a traylike headdress from which cowrie shells, palm nuts, mirrors, and beads dangle. Ilaro, 1978.

PLATE 45. Shiny metal disks and camwood blades hang from a moving circular platform that surmounts the white-faced headdress of Ọrọ Ẹfẹ. Lagos, 1981.

formance, the *akata* spins and produces a dramatic optical effect not unlike the "constantly whirling umbrella" *(akata, gbiri, gbiri, gbiri)* of a king in procession (Abiọdun 1982).

The Lagos Ẹfẹ costume combines elements seen elsewhere. As in Ọhọri country, raffia fiber tied around the rim of the mask covers the performer's face. His upper torso is clothed in a large, loose-fitting garment of woven strip cloth. The rest of the costume consists of a rich and voluminous wrapper. Two large flywhisks and multiple leg rattles complete the ensemble.

The circular headpieces of the Ẹgbado, Awori, and Lagos people are somewhat related in form to Ẹfẹ in Abẹokuta and other northern Ẹgbado communities just to the west. At Abẹokuta, the Ẹfẹ headdress called *akata* depicts a man wearing a wide-brimmed hat (pl. 46). The entire headdress is white, and, like its counterpart in Awori and Lagos, it has a raffia fringe on the rim. A long white gown covers the body of the performer. He and his companions sit atop a roof to sing, like the birds of the mothers.

In some northern Ẹgbado towns contiguous with Abẹokuta, the carved headdress of Ẹfẹ disappears, yet the shape of the head covering and costuming persists, as does his position on a roof. An actual wide-brimmed woven hat *(akẹtẹ̀)* painted white replaces the mask, and the face of the singer is visible. He wears a full white gown, and his only other regalia is a large square, woven fan used to baffle his voice as he sings from the rooftop.

Despite the variations in the form and iconography of these singing male masquerades, certain themes recur in almost all of them. One of the most dominant is masculinity, expressed in overtly aggressive action, physical strength, and courage projected in the persistent images of hunters, warriors, and references to Ogun: beards, guns, knives, cutlasses, amulets, palm fronds, and iron leg rattles. The color red, principally in Ketu-area Ọrọ Ẹfẹ, connotes heat and masculine aggressiveness and reinforces warrior/Ogun themes. Added to these are references to the sacred leadership of kings, chiefs, and priests: interlace patterns, leopards, veils of beads, shells, medicines, umbrellas, and whisks. These hallmarks of authority unite with the largeness of his costume, his dignified movements, and the songs referring to his elevated status to proclaim Ọrọ Ẹfẹ monarch of the night.

But as with all Yoruba monarchs, Ọrọ Ẹfẹ commands only with the consent of the mothers, whose omnipresence is acknowledged visually in a number of ways. One is the use of the color white, not only for its dramatic visual effect in a nocturnal rite but also for its symbolic connotations. In a myth describing the origin of Ẹfẹ (Moulero 1970), kaolin (chalk) was used to make the mask visible in the darkness. White contrasts with and sets off the eyes, face marks, and especially the mouth of the

PLATE 46. Ọrọ Ẹfẹ (right) and his singing partner are seated on the roof of a stall in the market. Ọrọ Ẹfẹ's white wooden headdress depicts a head with a wide-brimmed hat; his partner's has a cap. Abẹokuta, 1978.

singer, providing visual focus for the source of the "voiced power" of Ẹfẹ. When extended to the costuming as well, whiteness gives shape and distinctness to the performer as it separates him from both the obscurity of night and the assembled crowd. But even more, white symbolically relates the performer to the "white" deities *(orisa funfun),* who are covert and cool in their demeanor. They are primarily the goddesses, their priestesses, and the spiritually powerful women, "the gods of society," for whom Ọrọ Ẹfẹ acts as spokesman. These singing male masqueraders thus balance the red hot heat and overt action of warriors and Ogun with the cool, covert, patient approach of the mothers. The singers call upon them for support and guidance as they bravely praise and condemn the actions of the "children" of the mothers.

The mirrors in some Ọrọ Ẹfẹ ensembles may have connotations akin to those of the color white. As Ọrọ Ẹfẹ moves about in darkness, the mirrors reflect light of candles and lanterns to produce a momentary brightness, as does the white of the headdress. The mirrors may have another function, for in a sense Ọrọ Ẹfẹ holds up a mirror to society as he reveals the foibles of the gathered citizenry.

A most direct reference to the powerful mothers occurs in the images of birds or other flying creatures, such as airplanes, as well as in other nocturnal creatures. More indirect references are Ọrọ Ẹfẹ's "wings" or "puffed-up plumage," i.e., his flapping panels. The appearance of the mother masquerade and her male missive, Ọrọ Ẹfẹ, symbolizes the contrasts in female and male power. The mothers sanction Ọrọ Ẹfẹ to comment on society; his words take effect. This relationship between female and male power parallels concepts about spiritually powerful women and men in Yoruba society, known as *ajẹ* and *oṣo* respectively. Yoruba say that the mothers *(ajẹ)* conceive a plan and their male counterparts *(oṣo)* carry it out. This concept of power, i.e., women as the covert initiators of a scheme and men as the actors, applies not only to Ẹfẹ performance but also to Gẹlẹdẹ, where the males are the masqueraders but the elderly women are the source of their power.

Closing Masquerades

Just as introductory masqueraders bring the festival into the world, other masqueraders mark the conclusion of Ẹfẹ night and the transition from the nighttime to the afternoon segment of the performance. The conclusion of Ẹfẹ night in Ketu, Anago, and northern Ẹgbado areas is marked by the appearance of a distinct kind of masquerader, a towering stilt dancer dressed in cloth, voluminous raffia, and a carved headdress in the form of a hyena, termed *koriko, ikoko,* or *ayoko* (Beier 1958:14; Huet 1978:pl. 85; Bernolles 1973:23). He holds long wooden staffs in both hands, using them for balance and for menacing gestures that complement his gaping, teeth-filled jaws. A hyena mask, carved by the master Omigbaro of Kesan-Orilẹ about 1944 (pl. 6), admirably expresses the humorous ferocity that is the hallmark of hyena's performance. The chief of Kesan playfully remarked, "It used to kill people; don't you see his teeth?" (Oguntade 1971).

Elsewhere, hyena may be joined or replaced by another mask similar in concept to some introductory masquerades, those representing Ẹṣu/Ẹlẹgba. In the Ketu vicinity, a mask representing Ẹṣu/Ẹlẹgba arrives to conclude Ẹfẹ night; his headdress is covered with magical gourds (Moulero 1970:61). The Ẹṣu masquerader who closes Ẹfẹ night in Ilaro, Ẹgbado, is known as Ẹṣu Gbangbade. The mask depicts a head with tufts of hair *(oṣu)* and magical gourds *(àdó),* similar to the Ketu headdress described by Thomas Moulero. Ẹṣu Gbangbade is said to "chase Ọrọ Ẹfẹ from the market," thus marking the end of the ceremony.

Whether animal or god of the crossroads, Ẹṣu/Ẹlẹgba, these closing masquerades communicate a transition: from the concerns of society expressed by Ọrọ Ẹfẹ to the reassertion of forest beings and supernatural creatures as representatives of the realms beyond human society. Just as the introductory performers brought the spectacle into the world, these closing masquerades mark the conclusion of Ẹfẹ and the transition from night to day, from verbal to nonverbal commentary, for, like the words of Ẹfẹ, the dances and masquerades of Gẹlẹdẹ—which commence late on the following afternoon—evaluate society in their own way.

5
The Dance:
Texturing Time and Space

In contrast to "doing" Ẹfẹ (*a nṣẹ* Ẹfẹ), people say, "we dance Gẹlẹdẹ" (*a jó* Gẹ̀lẹ̀dẹ́). Thus dance is an essential medium of the afternoon spectacle. Gẹlẹdẹ dance is stylistically distinct from other Yoruba dances, and it demands, like many others, specialized knowledge and many years of training and experience. With great energy, and embellished by masks and costumes that amplify and define social roles and physical attributes, the masked male dancers of Gẹlẹdẹ project transcendent images of males and females, attesting to their distinct characters and behaviors. But if voicing words evokes or, more accurately, invokes vital force, bringing it into actual existence, then what are the implications for dance, or what Suzanne Langer (1953:175, 187) calls the illusion of "virtual power"? Dance makes vital force visible. Carried further—into the Yoruba context—dance *is* virtual power and is no less instrumental than the spoken word; it brings dynamic qualities into actual existence. Thus Gẹlẹdẹ also has effect, the power of *aṣẹ*.

The Dancer

Children in Gẹlẹdẹ families inherit the authority to perform, but the ultimate decision to become a Gẹlẹdẹ dancer depends on personal interest and talent. Those who do not inherit the right to perform Gẹlẹdẹ may participate as a result of the prescriptions of a diviner, who determines that in order for the individual to lead an unproblematic, productive life he should honor "the mothers" by dancing Gẹlẹdẹ. As a dancer told Ulli Beier (1958:5), "Gẹlẹdẹ is 'the secret of women.' We the men are merely their slaves. We dance to appease 'our mothers.'" Ordinarily outsiders would not begin to dance in Gẹlẹdẹ performances until their teens or twenties, but if a diviner prescribed Gẹlẹdẹ to cure impotency or infertility, a firstborn child might be obliged to become a Gẹlẹdẹ dancer at a younger age.

But no matter why a man becomes a Gẹlẹdẹ dancer—as a result of inheritance, divination, or special talent—the learning process is the same. It involves emulating the masters rather than receiving verbal instruction. With regular, sustained exposure to performances, a young child can assimilate Gẹlẹdẹ dance technique, structure, and drum phrases and, by learning to mark simple drum patterns with his feet, can begin to perform Gẹlẹdẹ by the age of three (pl. 48). With experience, the child becomes more adept. In some areas, such as Pobe, Lagos, and Ketu, intensive dance sessions are conducted to discipline the dancers and to develop and refine their technique and knowledge of rhythmic patterns. According to a resident of the town of Pobe, who belongs to a group of six Gẹlẹdẹ dancers, the dance master conducts training sessions and decides what steps are to be learned and, thus, what drum rhythms are to be played. Every other night from about 8 to 9:30, for several months before the Gẹlẹdẹ festival, rehearsals are held in the privacy of an enclosed compound. The dancers line up, two-by-two, in three lines, the least experienced dancers in front and the most advanced in the rear. When the group learns new steps, the master demonstrates in front; then, he goes to the back and "taps the rhythm vocally. Everyone learns it [the rhythm]. Everyone must know the drum in his mind (ọkàn)" (Aibiro 1973).[1] When the group is prepared to dance, the master calls in another elder in the society to watch a rehearsal. "If it [the dancing] is not good, he will tell us . . . to do a certain gesture in this part of the dance; then, it will succeed."

Most dance instruction, however, is less structured. Students pick up the stepping style and rhythms by observing and imitating their elders informally. As the drums play during interludes in the performance, parents dance with their children, or children on their own dance along to the music. Often young children from Gẹlẹdẹ families will be taken to the performance in costume to masquerade as a masquerader (pls. 47, 48). Whether their costuming is complete or not, the children are encouraged to dance and are rewarded with small change and cheers by spectators.

Older, more accomplished child dancers wear more complete costumes (pls. 49, 50). Usually they are followed closely by an adult male from their lineage who sees to it that they follow the rhythm of the drums and accent the proper beats. In addition, he informs the drummers what rhythmic sequences to play. With preteens, the coach is not so visible, and the audience becomes less tolerant and more likely to scoff at an obvious error. The coach watches from the side but does not hesitate to rush forward to correct a mistake or scold his dancers, putting them back on

PLATE 47. A neophyte Gẹlẹdẹ dancer, wearing only an old, incomplete mask and a long cloth that reaches below his knees, masquerades as a masquerader. Ilaro, 1978.

PLATE 48. A young Gẹlẹdẹ dancer performs wearing bottle caps
in place of ankle rattles to mark the drum rhythms. Ilaro, 1977.

PLATE 49. Carrying the iron anklets in his hands, a Gẹlẹdẹ performer moves toward the drums under the supervision of his coach. Ilaro, 1978.

PLATE 50. Using a metaphor from the world of animals, this headdress of a plump porcupine eating corn relates thematically to a drummed text in which a porcupine is criticized for selfishness and gluttony. Ṣawonjo, 1978.

the right track. Thus, spectacle itself also functions as a training session for novices in Yoruba society. Regardless of the approach to instruction, whether structured or informal, in almost all cases dance sequences are prearranged with the drummers.

The Music

Among the Yoruba, dancing is inseparable from drumming. In fact, the most frequently mentioned criterion for a good dancer is that he understand the musical structure and phrasing of the drums and match his stepping to the staccato rhythms. As a particularly articulate Gẹlẹdẹ patron explained to Robert F. Thompson (1974a:254),

> Drums tell the dancer what to do; if he dances with the drummer exactly, he is called *aiyejo,* the finest dancer. An *alaiye mojo* [is] someone who does not know how to obey the drums. The ankle rattles of iron the dancers wear *must* make the same sound as the drum. If he makes a mistake it will be audible. . . . The dancer has to end the phrase *exactly* when the senior drum ends it. They must balance *(dogba).* A thousand dresses, it does not matter, if you compromise the drum speech you are not a good dancer!

The dancer may perform relatively simple rhythms as long as he is working up to his capacity, but however difficult or complicated the rhythmical patterns he selects, he must perform them correctly. In this way, Gẹlẹdẹ dance, like the entire spectacle, is synonymous with sacrifice. In making a sacrifice, one is expected to give whatever is within one's capacity at that time, but the sacrifice, however small, must be performed correctly.

A Gẹlẹdẹ drum ensemble is composed of two large cylindrical drums approximately three to four feet high and one to three smaller cylindrical drums about two feet high (pl. 51). The three smaller drums, the *omele akọ* or male *omele,* initiate the drumming and provide a constant, underlying rhythmical structure. A young trainee in the drummers' lineage often plays one of the smaller drums, using sticks. The lead drum, the *iyalu* or mother drum, and the second large drum, the *omele abo* or female *omele,* work together to weave irregular rhythms over the underlying patterns.

By placing tar on the drumheads, the drummers can control their pitch. The *iyalu* and *omele abo* can thus approximate the pitch patterns of spoken Yoruba, which is itself tonal, and the drumming can reproduce aphorisms and praise phrases both tonally and rhythmically. Woven on top of the baseline beat, these phrases constitute a drum language, which in the context of Gẹlẹdẹ is known as *ẹka,* a free, linguistically based rhythm that floats over the basic structure and dictates the rhythm of the

PLATE 51. The Gɛlɛdɛ drum ensemble is composed of two lead drums supported by one to three small drums. Ilaro, 1977.

dance steps. Similar structuring can be observed in certain handwoven Yoruba textiles in which free-floating designs are superimposed on the basic weave. The Yoruba term for these floating phrases, *ɛka*, means literally "enumeration" (CMS 1937:75), but in the Gɛlɛdɛ context it is, more specifically, a drummed aphorism or poem to which the dancers must respond rhythmically. Dancers speak of "counting *ɛka*" *(nka ɛka),* but they do not mean that they enumerate beats in any literal sense. Rather, when dancing, they are in synchrony with the drum rhythms. For each beat of the *ɛka,* there is a simultaneous step.

Since *ɛka* derive from Yoruba aphorisms and praise poems, they possess characteristics of poetry—rhythm, phonetic form, repetition, and intonation:

1   We asked him to go to the farm, he didn't go to the farm
2   We asked him to go to the river, he didn't go to the river
3   We asked him to become a fish, he didn't become a fish
4   We asked him to become a crab, he didn't become a crab
5   Words will never make you into a crab [if] you are a fish
6   Words will never make you into a crab [if] you are a fish
7   Porcupine who [does nothing else but] eats palm leaves in great quantities

8 Porcupine who [does nothing but] eat palm leaves in great
   quantities
9 Huge porcupine who eats palm leaves chomp, chomp, chomp
10 Porcupine who [does nothing but] eat palm leaves in great
   quantities
11 Huge porcupine who eats palm leaves chomp, chomp, chomp

1 *A ni ko r'oko, ko r'oko*
2 *A ni ko r'odò, ko r'odò*
3 *A ni ko ṣ'ẹja, ko ṣ'ẹja*
4 *A ni ko ṣ'akàn, ko ṣ'akàn*
5 *Òrọ ti ko ṣe akàn, ẹja ni oṣe*
6 *Òrọ ti ko ṣe akàn, ẹja ni oṣe*
7 *Êrẹkenṣe a bi jẹ'ko fálafàla*
8 *Êrẹkenṣe a bi jẹ'ko fálafàla*
9 *Êrẹagbọn a bi jẹ'ko bite bite bite*
10 *Êrẹkenṣe a bi jẹ'ko fálafàla*
11 *Êrẹagbọn a bi jẹ'ko bite bite bite*

[Collected in Igbogila, 1978]

The first four lines make use of rhythmic repetition, while the final words
of each line shift meanings. They comment on a lazy person who will not
do anything he is asked to do. Line 6 repeats line 5 to reaffirm that
talking about doing something does not mean that it will be accomplished. Shifting focus, the final five lines suggest that a lazy person, like
the porcupine, is self-serving; he does nothing in life but fulfill his own
basic needs, i.e., eating. The last six syllables of lines 9 and 11, *bite, bite,
bite,* are onomatopoeic and refer to the munching sound of a porcupine
indulging in palm leaves. A similar idea may be conveyed in motifs on
masks, for example, by depicting a porcupine eating corn (pl. 50).

Ẹka are not always so lengthy. Often they are brief one-liners con-
densed from longer texts, which can be repeated a number of times. Or
they may be succinct verbal images that evoke a larger context. As a
Yoruba proverb explains, "It is necessary only to give half of a speech to
the well bred person; inside him it becomes whole" (Owomoyela 1979:8);
that is, a fragment suffices to recall an entire text or context. The *ẹka*
below is a fragment that alludes to a popular song:

La la la dance e, moon dance e

La la la jó e, òṣùpá jó e

[Collected in Pobẹ, 1973]

With great brevity it evokes a song about an eclipse, likening it to a fight
between the sun and the moon in which the moon loses. A line from the
song asserts, "The moon cannot fight" *(O le l'oṣupa ko le ja)*. Commanding

the moon to go ahead and dance, the performers of this *ęka* challenge other dancers by implying that they can never outshine them.

Another succinct *ęka*, by alluding to the possession trance dance of the priests of Ṣango, god of thunder and lightning, evokes a broader ritual context:

Thundergod flying outward yęyęyę, Abidogun

Ṣàngó ntú yęyęyę, Abídógun

[Collected in Aibo Quarter, Aiyetoro, 1971]

Abidogun is the name of the dancer performing the *ęka*. It is added to elaborate the rhythm but it could just as easily be omitted or replaced by another name. Freely translated, the *ęka* instructs Abidogun to "make your skirts fly outward as they would do if you were performing the dance of the Thundergod Ṣango." The expression *yęyęyę* is onomatopoeic, imitating the sound of the priests' paneled ceremonial skirts whirling through the air as the dancer turns (color plate 4). The use of idiophonic language, or what S. A. Babalǫla (1966:67–68) calls "word-pictures," is common in drummed texts—as it is in Yoruba poetry generally—and is notable in a number of other examples discussed later in this chapter.

Ęka comment on many aspects of behavior: competition, social matters, dance, and life in general. Equally important is the rhythmic play of *ęka:* the more accomplished the dancer the more difficult and complex the rhythms he will dance.

Competitiveness provokes the drummers to assert their abilities; they warn the dancers that if they try to outdo the drummers in performing *ęka*, they will just exhaust themselves. By alluding to the behavior of a moth, this *ęka* in the form of a proverb makes its point indirectly:

Moth
The one who tries to put out the lamp
It's himself he kills

Àfòòpinǫn
To ló wǫn wo pa fìtílà
Arááre ni o pa

[Collected in Igbogila, 1978]

Another *ęka* cautions that whoever offends a wicked person should anticipate revenge:

[Rhythmical lead into *ęka*]
The Divine Mediator does not hassle the snake
Anyone who treads on a snake
Is one who will be making a sacrifice [to appease the snake]

Ti bete ke, ti bete ke, ti bete ke, ti bete ke
Eṣu ko ṣ'ejò
Eni ba t'ejò mọlẹ̀
Oluwa rẹ lẹ bọ mbo

[Collected in Igbogila, 1978]

Not even Eṣu, who is a troublemaker himself by nature, would threaten a snake; anyone foolish enough to offend a dangerous creature must be prepared to pay the consequences.

Many *ẹka* focus on dance movement, either directing it or simply commenting on it. The following *ẹka* speaks from the point of view of the dancer, who asserts that he is going to activate his body parts sequentially. It attests to a feature of West African dance often observed by analysts, the segmented use of body parts:

I can use my arms to dance, use my arms to dance
I can use my legs to dance, use my legs to dance
I can use my whole body to dance simultaneously

Mo le f'apá jó, f'apá jó
Mo le f'ẹsẹ̀ jo, f'ẹsẹ̀ jo
Mo le fi gbogbo ara jo muke muke

[Collected in Aibo Quarter, Aiyetoro, 1971]

A more complex variation of this *ẹka*, stated from the observer's point of view, goes:

If I were you
I would use my arms to dance, use my arms to dance, use my arms to
   dance
If I were you
I would use my legs to dance, use my legs to dance, use my legs to
   dance
If I were you
I would use my entire body sin sin sin sin sin sin

To ba ṣe pe mi ni wọ ni ni wọ ni
Mba f'apá jo, f'apá jo, f'apá jo
To ba ṣe pe mi ni wọ ni ni wọ ni
Mba f'ẹsẹ̀ jo, f'ẹsẹ̀ jo, f'ẹsẹ̀ jo
To ba ṣe pe mi ni wọ ni ni wọ ni
Mba fi gbogbo ara sin sin sin sin sin sin

[Collected in Igbogila, 1978]

Sin sin sin sin sin sin imitates the sound of the ankle rattles and also serves as a bridge of regular beats so that the dancer may "catch" the next rhythmic pattern.

Ẹka are not always so explicit. They often refer to dance movements metaphorically, as the next one does, evoking the image of a hunter pulling on tree branches so that the disconcerted squirrels chatter and scamper about:

Pulling on a branch of a tree, kuru kuru kuru cried the squirrel

Nfà lo fà'gi yà, kurú kurú kurú odogbo
[Collected in Ketu Quarter, Aiyetoro, 1971]

The dancer incorporates pulling gestures in the arms and shoulders into his dance, as he matches his steps to the beats of the phrase.

Ẹka actually form only a small portion of the entire dance. They are usually embedded in longer rhythmic sequences that introduce and conclude them. The introductory material prepares the dancer, as one dancer put it, to "catch" the ẹka in order to synchronize his steps with the drumbeats, and the concluding material bridges the ẹka with the next verbally oriented material. In Igbanko Quarter, Pobe, a group of six masqueraders dances to only one ẹka during its performance. The ẹka is embedded in a longer rhythmic sequence called *iworo*. Before and after *iworo* come two other drum patterns called *alujo*, a general Yoruba term meaning "dance to the drum." The *alujo* of Igbanko Quarter have been adapted from the Fon and Bariba peoples, neighbors of the Yoruba to the west and north respectively.

The initial *alujo*, imitating a Fon style, is the entrance sequence, which carries the dancers across the performing area toward the drums with a simple, quick, step-close-step, first to one side and then to the other. With their arms extended out diagonally above their heads, the dancers twirl the horsetail whisks at their wrists. The drummers, approximating the tones of spoken Yoruba, beat:

The domesticated pigeon will always be prosperous
The dove will always find tranquility

Íyẹ n'íyẹ ẹyẹlé
Írọ n'írọ àdàbà l'ọ̀rùn

This rhythmic text is sometimes used in prayer and concludes, "So let me be prosperous; let everything be well with me" (Awolalu 1973:87). The pigeon, a domesticated bird used in sacrifices to bring honor, prosperity, and longevity (Abimbọla 1976:206), is noted for "its serenity in flight, its neatness of appearance and its smartness in movement" (Awolalu 1973). The West African red-eyed turtle dove (*adaba*) is considered the sister of the domesticated pigeon and shares the same attributes. The pigeon and the dove are appropriate images for the dancers, who attempt to achieve neatness, grace, and agility. The rhythm functions as a prayer, in effect beseeching the mothers to grant prosperity and peace to the dancers, who are metaphorically doves. This is another sense in which dance is sacrifice.

Collectively, the dancers adhere to the rhythm, but they need not maintain spatial uniformity throughout the *alujo*. Then, as the drummers launch into *iworo*, the dancers prepare "to attack" the *ęka* embedded in it. Assembling themselves in two parallel lines, they step uniformly, matching the beats as the drummers play:

> We have arrived
> We have arrived
> We have gone outside
> We come dancing

> *Àwá lọ dé*
> *Àwá lọ dé*
> *Àwá dé sí ta* [or: *àwá lọ dé ta*]
> *Àwá lí njó*

The dancers perform tiny jumps in time to the rhythm, which is played thrice. Once they have completed the *ęka*, they may break out of line, angling their bodies and veering off to one side or the other to perform the second *alujo*, the delicate *kete* of the Bariba, a moderately paced, gentle dance of small amplitude. The drummers beat:

> Pleasure has come, pleasure has come, pleasure has come, that's what
>   we are engaged in
> We are creating pleasure
> Pleasure is ours
> It's pleasure that we are creating all around
> Pleasure is being created, pleasure is being created, pleasure is being
>   created, pleasure is being created

> *Fàjì dé, fàjì dé, fàjì dé a nṣe*
> *Àwá nṣe fàjì*
> *Nó fàjì làwá*
> *Ìgbàk'ìgbà fàjì l'àwá nṣe*
> *Fàjì l'á nṣe, fàjì l'á nṣe, fàjì l'á nṣe, fàjì l'á nṣe*

The dancers use this sequence to exit, asserting their abilities kinetically, while the drummers support and reaffirm them rhythmically in a pattern that exudes pride and self-confidence.

The structure of individual dances may vary significantly from place to place. The Pobe form is most similar to that of Ketu and vicinity, and it resembles the forms used by the Ketu Gęlędę societies in Ṣawọnjo, Igbogila, and Isalę Eko, Lagos. But throughout northern Ęgbado and in Abęokuta and Ilaro, performances are ordered differently. Gęlędę families collect and dress in their compounds and, when they are ready,

PLATE 52. A family of devotees of the iron deity, Ogun, dances
to the marketplace along with its masqueraders, who represent
hunters, motorcyclists, and marketwomen. Ilaro, 1978.

dance in groups to the marketplace (pl. 52.) As each group arrives it tells
the drummers which *ęka* to play, and all the masqueraders and others
from that compound who wish to dance join in. Meanwhile, other compounds may rush into the arena, too, until the performance space becomes so packed that the dancers' movement is limited (pl. 53). As more
participants crowd the dancing space, observers see less and less of individual masqueraders. Although uniform in their rhythm, the dancers are
individualistic in their use of space, entering and exiting spontaneously,
not at all like the more organized dance-group approach in Pobe, where
the introduction and conclusion are pre-choreographed.

Wherever Gęlędę is performed, its rhythmic sequences tend to be
strung together in serial fashion. Aside from the fact that these various
patterns occur in the same context, they otherwise have no inherent
relationship either rhythmically or textually. They can be reordered or
changed since they are discrete, self-contained units. This type of
framework allows for great variety, flexibility, and spontaneity in performance.

PLATE 53. In Ẹgbado, a congested dance space limits the
performer's freedom of movement. Ilaro, 1978.

In addition, there is no formal thematic relationship between the masks and the dances or between the masks and the drummed texts. And although in some instances drummers may comment spontaneously on particular masks or dancers, on the whole there is no inherent thematic link between the drummed texts and the dance steps or mask motifs. Likewise, the masks themselves have no thematic relationship to each other, and the program has no predetermined sequence other than that children tend to dance first. The program on any given occasion is the result of the convergence of masks, which have been commissioned at different times by various participants. What holds the whole together and moves it along is the rhythm.

The art forms that make up Yoruba spectacle operate collectively and yet autonomously, each carrying its own information, which is not necessarily related to that of others. The convergence of art forms conceived and created independently results in a multifocal spectacle. Its artistic elements compete for attention, and in its midst, the spectators too are inspired to join the competition.

In the great interplay among participants, spectators become performers and performers become spectators. Spectators may sit down to drum and drummers may break to rest and observe. Dancers or family members can tell drummers what to play or drummers can initiate music, and spectators are free to join in the dancing. Thus individuals mold and shape the performances spontaneously, making each one fluid and unique.

The Costumes

The cloth of Gẹlẹdẹ costumes, like that of Ẹfẹ, is an important means of defining self. Cloth is one way of expressing status, and the Yoruba proverb "Children are the clothes of men" *(Ọmọ l'aṣọ eda)* equates it with the people's most valuable possession, children. Clothes, like children, are what a person shows to the world, and society judges accordingly (cf. H. Drewal 1979:189–190).

Gẹlẹdẹ dance costumes differ from those of Ẹfẹ night in a number of respects. First, ensembles made of grasses or palm fibers, used by several night masquerades, are rare to nonexistent in the daylight masquerades. Second, while embroidered and appliquéd panels may occur in some towns, notably Ketu, Idahin, and Meko (color plate 5), the vast majority of Gẹlẹdẹ costumes consist only of a multitude of women's head ties *(òjá)*, baby wrappers, and skirts *(ìró)* tied in various ways (color plates 2, 4, pls. 52, 54). Third, in contrast to the tailored and elaborately decorated outfits commissioned by some Ketu Ọrọ Ẹfẹ, Gẹlẹdẹ performers borrow cloths from women and assemble their costumes anew just before each performance. This form of assemblage is important to our comprehension of the significance of Gẹlẹdẹ.

Membership in a Gẹlẹdẹ society, it will be recalled, is open to all. Usually certain lineages play a major role in the society's activities and may claim hereditary rights to certain titles, but anyone, especially those "troubled" by the mothers—those who are experiencing such difficulties as sickness, impotence, or barrenness—can join the society. Thus, in its membership, Gẹlẹdẹ stresses communality as well as lineage identity. In this respect, Gẹlẹdẹ contrasts with the Egungun society, whose masquerades honoring the spirits of ancestors give emphasis to kinship and lineage identity. As one Gẹlẹdẹ elder put it (Adepegba 1971):

> You will never hear an individual say "my Gẹlẹdẹ will dance today." Gẹlẹdẹ belongs to the town. If you have money, you can buy cloth, as many kinds as your money can buy to make an Egungun, but you will never see a person owning Gẹlẹdẹ.

Gẹlẹdẹ "belongs to the town" and that is why special performances, in addition to festivals, are arranged to deal with communal disasters such as epidemics, droughts, or famines. The fact that no individual or lineage really "owns" Gẹlẹdẹ, that it belongs to the entire community—the children of the mothers—is reflected in the way Gẹlẹdẹ costumes are put together.

Cloths borrowed from women constitute the essential part of Gẹlẹdẹ costuming (pl. 54). There are no tailored costumes, no selection of particular fabrics. Donations from women in the dancer's compound or in neighboring households are collected before the afternoon performance. Head ties are the major source of cloth, but wrappers and other pieces of women's clothing are incorporated. The assembled cloths are referred to as *aṣọ ẹgbẹ́*, "cloth from the society" (Ogundipẹ 1971); Gẹlẹdẹ is "the one that goes about collecting cloth. It is a day-collector-of-cloths" *(enit-o-y'aṣọ-l'ọ̀sán)* (Akinwọlẹ 1971).

Gẹlẹdẹ costumes seek to define, embellish, and amplify certain physical attributes of the sexes in order to create extraordinary images epitomizing maleness and femaleness (*akọgi* and *abogi*). Male Gẹlẹdẹ costumes in Ketu areas are constructed in essentially the same manner as Ketu Ọrọ Ẹfẹ, but the fabrics may differ (color plate 5). Instead of the embroidered and appliquéd panels, multiple layers of head wraps are usually tied onto a bamboo hoop, expanding the girth and impressiveness of the chest and torso to exaggerate the male physique (color plate 7). This massive cylinder of fabric conveys solidity and substance, prestige and stature. Such costuming transcends reality and proclaims the patronage of the community's women. Although it does not attempt

PLATE 54. At Ibara, Abẹokuta, the dancers wear a costume
made of borrowed cloths that hang down to the ankles and
another cloth that covers the face and torso. 1978.

to imitate male fashions, it produces a similar effect—that of enlarging and enhancing the stature of the wearer through an ostentatious display of cloth.

Male Gẹlẹdẹ in Ẹgbado and Awori generally follow the Ketu styles. Long-sleeved jackets, usually red, are overlaid with an encircling mass of knotted head wraps that descend to the dancer's knees (color plate 8). Bamboo hoops are absent, so the girth is not as great as in Ketu. Only rarely do male Gẹlẹdẹ vary their costuming. When they do, it takes the form of women's cloth head wraps covered by a long man's gown of men's weave *(aṣọ oke)* tied at the waist by a single head wrap (pl. 55), as in Ẹfẹ costumes in Ilaro (pls. 31, 44).

Female Gẹlẹdẹ costumes feature a wooden spool, woven fish trap, or stick construction tied around the waist to exaggerate the hips and buttocks (pl. 56). It is called *bèbè*, a reference to women's body beads worn around the hips. The *bebe* is then covered with a woman's wrapper to

PLATE 55. At Ilaro, a male Gẹlẹdẹ wears a man's long woven gown tied around the waist with a woman's head tie. Underneath the gown are other head ties. 1978.

PLATE 56. In female Gẹlẹdẹ costuming, a fish basket tied at the waist and covered by a large wrapper serves to exaggerate the hips and buttocks. Lagos, 1978.

create the illusion of large, protruding buttocks hung with strands of waist beads, which are supposed to make women alluring. Another distinctive female costume item, a wooden breastplate *(ǫmú),* is tied on with a cloth or rope harness and then secured with other head wraps above the bodice (pl. 57). Most breastplates are carved very simply and painted brightly (pl. 50), but some take the form of statuettes or twin figures (pl. 58) or are elaborately carved to include figures such as monkeys and lizards (pl. 59). In all cases the breasts themselves are firm and assertive. In the Ketu area, a cloth such as a head tie or an embroidered and appliquéd panel is draped over these wooden breasts, and the ends are often held by the performer and manipulated during the dance (pl. 10). To cover the face of the dancer, a cloth known as *aṣǫ* Gẹlẹdẹ is attached to the lower rim of the headpiece by means of wooden pegs or nails. The mask angles slightly forward over the forehead and is tied under the dancer's chin and at the back of the head with cords *(ìgbagbǫ̀n).* Cloth covers the arms and legs, and ankle wraps *(agbèkù)* support the numerous leg rattles *(ìkù).* Sometimes a female wears a blouse or short jacket over which several bands of cloth head ties are wound tightly around the torso from waist to chest and tied at the back, creating a narrow bodice (pl. 60). Horsetail whisks, one for each hand, complete the ensemble.

The girth of the male image contrasts vividly with the narrowness of the Ketu female Gẹlẹdẹ costume, whose sexual attributes are portrayed in the protruding buttocks and hips and the thrusting breasts. These contrasts are reversed in the costuming of Ẹgbado and Awori areas, where female costuming produces a massive girth of layered cloth (pls. 54, 56), and the males are slenderer (color plate 8, pl. 55). At Ilaro and Ajilete, for example, the bottom layer of female Gẹlẹdẹ costuming consists of leggings, rattles, stockings, hip/buttocks construction, arm wraps, blouse, breastplate, and wrapper—elements common to all areas. From this point, however, costuming styles diverge, for after the wrapper has been tied, once around the waist and once just under the breastplate, a long band of cloth with a whole series of head wraps tied onto it is wrapped around the upper chest and over the breastplate so that the variegated cloth hangs down to about the knees of the dancer, forming a cylinder (pl. 61). After this a long sheer or lace *aṣǫ* Gẹlẹdẹ is attached to the rim of the mask, and the headdress is placed on the performer's head. Thus, Ẹgbado and Awori female Gẹlẹdẹ can be as broad as male Gẹlẹdẹ. A somewhat different costume mode exists at Ṣawǫnjo, an Ẹgbado town that has been influenced strongly by Ketu (color plate 11, pl. 62). The style is midway between Ketu and Ẹgbado fashions. Here, the knotted head wraps tied over the breastplate bulge outward over a finely embroidered wrapper (color plate 6), but another cloth strip under the

PLATE 57. A wooden breastplate, held in place by a harness, is
draped with a cloth. Ketu, 1971.

PLATE 58. A masquerader with drums on his headdress substitutes twin statuettes for breasts. Jọga/Imaṣai, 1965.

PLATE 59. Lizards and monkeys adorn the breasts of this masquerader. Imaṣai, 1971.

PLATE 60. Characteristic of Ketu-style female Gẹlẹdẹ costumes is the narrow torso tightly wrapped with women's head ties. Ketu, 1971.

PLATE 61. Tying numerous head ties loosely around the upper
chest and breasts produces a bulky image in the female Gẹlẹdẹ
of Ẹgbado. This headdress depicts snakes wrapped around
medicine vials. Ilaro, 1978.

PLATE 62. At Ṣawonjo, headwraps tied both above and below the breast plate and an elaborately designed wrapper over the hip and buttocks construction create a sense of compactness in a basically bulky form. 1978.

breasts pulls them in to create a degree of compactness in a basically bulky upper torso.

Female Gẹlẹdẹ at Lagos, despite cultural links with Ketu and Ẹg-bado, have a unique and distinctive mode of dressing. All the basic re-galia are the same, although a large cylindrical, woven fish trap is used to create enormous buttocks. The knotted head ties, rather than completely surrounding the masquerader, dangle in front between the wooden breasts and are secured around the waist. Then, over this massive torso fits a special square cape (ẹ̀wù), frequently with a scalloped fringe and a hole for the performer's head (pl. 63). In front is an apronlike garment with three rectangular bordered panels said to represent the three tute-lary deities of Gẹlẹdẹ in Lagos—Ẹṣu, Ogun, and Iyanla. A photograph taken circa 1945 shows a female Gẹlẹdẹ in Lagos whose costume com-bines traditional handwoven and imported fabrics of the day (pl. 64). A reversal of imagery thus occurs; males in Ketu have massive torsos more akin to female Gẹlẹdẹ in Awori and Ẹgbado, while females in Ketu are slender, like Awori and Ẹgbado males. At Lagos, where Ẹfẹ is said to be "male" and Gẹlẹdẹ "female," we did not witness any male Gẹlẹdẹ mas-querades. In a number of instances, primarily in Ketu areas, parts of old and discarded paneled costumes were being incorporated into newer ensembles. Some of these panels were backed with animal skins or cloth that simulated such skins (color plate 8).[2]

Young children wear costumes that reflect their status as neophytes (pls. 7, 47). Their masks are frequently old, cracked, or poorly carved or are simply painted calabashes. Knee-length cloth is sometimes attached to the rims to cover their faces, but often it is eliminated so that the children can see where they are going. Most of the youngest performers wear a smock or their regular clothing rather than the women's cloth or head ties of the typical Gẹlẹdẹ costumes. Rattles are omitted, or simulated with strings of bottle caps around the ankles, or are actual iku, which are carried in the hands (for protection) rather than worn (pls. 48, 49). As young masqueraders become more serious about their dancing, their ensembles become more complete and proper. Those depicting females are given blouses and skirts, while male Gẹlẹdẹ use knotted head ties wrapped around their chest. Some are also given leggings, leg rattles, arm wraps, and either whisks or leafy branches to hold in their hands (pl. 48). The addition of the buttocks construction and wooden breastplates to the female or bamboo hoop and head wraps to the male usually signals postadolescence and maturity as performers.

For adults, costuming must be complete to be acceptable as tribute to the mothers and, therefore, efficacious. The mythic essentials of the en-semble—image, head wraps, and leg rattles—must be present. Beyond that, they can be enhanced, extended, embellished, and magnified to create convincingly transcendent images of females and males. Serrated

PLATE 63. A female Gẹlẹdẹ in typical Lagos fashion sports a
square cape *(ewu)*, which covers the breasts, and an apronlike
garment with three rectangular panels said to symbolize Eṣu,
Ogun, and Iyanla, the divinities of Gẹlẹdẹ at Lagos. Lagos, 1978.

PLATE 64. A portrait taken circa 1945 shows a Lagos female Gẹlẹdẹ with *ewu*, apron, and a combination of traditional handwoven and imported cloth. Nigerian Museum archives.

edges and the male Gẹlẹdẹ embroidered panels sewn over animal skins (color plate 8) are consistent with some Egungun costuming and suggest that the attire performs a protective or medicinal function. The same may be true for a Gẹlẹdẹ wearing parts of an old costume underneath a newer ensemble. Remnants of a forefather's costume, like the skins of animals, are efficacious and honor one's predecessors, adding an element of power and protection to the ensemble.

Dance Structure and Style

Typical of both *akọgi* and *abogi* (male and female) Gẹlẹdẹ is the doubling of dancers in identical masks and costumes (pls. 10, 65). One Gẹlẹdẹ dancer explained why masqueraders dance two-by-two in identical masks (Aibiro 1973): "It is because women give birth to twins as children. That is why there are two masks. It is that we are born by the same mother." Indeed, Yoruba women have one of the highest rates of twin births in the world, but the dancer's explanation is not merely a statement on fertility. It implies that the mothers can control life itself by being able to bring two identical human beings into the world.

The marketplace is important to twins in that their mother is often

PLATE 65. Ketu-style female Gẹlẹdẹ, reversing their forward-inclined torsos, cause their breasts to bob provocatively. Then, with great force, they stamp toward the drums, raising their feet and presenting them forward across the midline of their bodies. Idahin, 1971.

required to dance there and beg for alms. As a worldly realm where spirits intermingle with humans, it is an appropriate environment for spirit children and an appropriate place to synchronize worldly assertions with spiritual efficacy. The concept of matching the drum speech during the ẹka is dramatized by pairing identical masqueraders. Thompson (1974a:204) notes the virtue of comradeship in the pairing of Gẹlẹdẹ masqueraders. Data collected in Pobe and Isagba suggest a strong spiritual dimension in certain types of friendship. When two partners make a pact and adopt a common secret name, they often choose to dress alike and may be mistaken for twins. By virtue of their pact, the friends mutually guard and protect each other, and it is implied that the two can communicate by mental telepathy. Similarly, during the nighttime Ɛfẹ ceremony that precedes Gẹlẹdẹ in Ketu, the singer portraying Ọrọ Ɛfẹ is protected by a medicinally prepared, reduced replica of himself, which accompanies him throughout the performance. Thus doubling seems to imply increased spiritual force and transcendency. Some informants believe that twins share one soul or that one twin is the spirit double of the other (Houlberg 1973:23). Perhaps this concept of a double operates as a spiritual backup to Gẹlẹdẹ's worldly assertions. In this context, twinning may be a visualization of the individual in his worldly and otherworldly manifestation, the two aspects appearing simultaneously in the marketplace during spectacle.[3]

In any case, Gẹlẹdẹ dance can be distinguished further on the basis of style. A sampling of opinions by Gẹlẹdẹ dancers scattered throughout western Yorubaland reveals that they generally agree, in theory at least, on the stylistic distinctions between male and female masquerade dances. A northern Ɛgbado dance master explains (Adepegba 1971):

> When women are created they are created to do things easily [ẹ̀rọ̀] and beautifully [ẹ̀yẹ]. . . . When a male dances, his dance is strong [le], for men are to do things that require power [agbára]. . . . When a female Gẹlẹdẹ is dancing she would be allowed just enough space to dance for everybody to see her dancing and to enjoy and appreciate her dancing, unlike a male dancer who will be jumping here and there.

Rene Aibiro (1973), an Anago Yoruba dancer from Pobe, states that female Gẹlẹdẹ

> don't disturb themselves very much. . . . The dance of the female we say is a dance which is for pleasure [fàjì]. It is not a strong [le] dance. . . . The female must dance gently, carefully [pẹ̀lẹ́pẹ̀lẹ́].

In support of this Anago perspective, an ẹka collected in Ɛgbado area instructs the female masquerader:

Begin diligently
Begin carefully

Mâ sí lèsòlèsò
Mâ sí pèlépèlé

[Collected in Igbogila, 1978]

Pèlèpèlè implies both carefully and gently. A form of this word appears in the Ifa verse introducing chapter 2, which advises how one should deal with the mothers in order to survive (Beyioku 1946). The verse begins:

Prudence was the ancient wisdom among the Ęgba
Prudence was the ancient wisdom among the Ijęsa

Pèlè ni ns'awo wọn lode Ęgba
Pèlè ni ns'awo wọn lode Ijęsa

The verse then instructs Ọrunmila, deity of divination, that to avoid death he should put on a mask and costume to enter the town of the mothers. The text advises that carefulness or prudence is the proper demeanor for approaching the mothers or, more specifically, for dancing Gęlędę. Continuing his comparison of males and females, Aibiro adds that when the male appears,

> He is always courageous. . . . He dances and he does something very difficult, because men are hot. They are always hot. That means to do something very rapidly. . . . *Akọ* must dance hard [*le*]. *Ijo yoya.* He must not dance gently. He must dance *haṣa, haṣa, haṣa!*

An Aiyetoro man (Akinfęnwa 1978) says, "Anything that requires energy [*agbara*] will be referred to as *akọ igi* [male mask]." Yoruba scholar A. Ọlabimtan (1970:193), originally from Ilaro, states,

> The male must always behave in a really masculine manner whilst the female, though actually a man, must not for a moment behave like a man. Whilst the males are fast in their dancing steps, the females tend to be slow and sluggish.

And, finally, an Ajilete informant in southern Ęgbado describes males as "hot" and "hard" and females as "cool," dancing "in a highlife mood" (Thompson 1974a:203). An *ęka* from Pobe, concluding with the male whirling around so fast that he often falls, asserts that masculine physical power is so strong as to overwhelm the female mask:

> Don't accidentally kill the female mask
> The male mask comes very quickly
> It's the male coming very quickly
> Quickly approaches the female

Ko sí ma p'abo
Akọ dé wéré wéré
Si li s'akọ wéré wéré li s'akọ
Wéré wa wa li s'abo

Following the *ẹka*, the drums play "*igberete*" to instruct the male mask to turn *(ìgba)* forcefully.

In spite of the clear emphasis of informants upon the greater strength of the male masqueraders and the gentleness of the females, the female-type dance is more energetic, on the whole, than most other Yoruba dances. Actually, both male and female-type masked dancers maintain extremely high energy levels, and the distinction between the two is to be seen in the way they use dynamics to develop the dance in conjunction with time and space.[4] What informants perceive as a lack of energy on the part of the female is simply a slightly lower level of physical force in comparison to the male, and only in certain segments of the dance. The perception of a lack of energy may stem from the female Gẹlẹdẹ's greatly restricted use of space and, at times, a somewhat slower tempo.

One of the most striking traits of Gẹlẹdẹ is the static quality of the mask, which sits on what appears to be an extended neck. This balance and calm contrasts with the larger energetic gestures of the body from the shoulders down (color plate 4). It is not merely the balancing of a weighty object that dictates this relative stability of the head and mask, but a conscious aesthetic choice. Most masks without superstructures and carved in light wood are easily secured to the dancer's head and allow considerable action. The formal face of the mask, with its symmetry and simplicity of line, enhances the sense of stability.

As with much West African dance, the line of the back appears fairly rigid, straight, and inclined forward from the hips. Slightly flexed knees accommodate the inclined torso (pls. 10, 50, 56, 65, 66). This posture provides a solid base and allows the dancer to maintain close contact with the earth, while freeing his body from the waist down for speed, force, and agility in the transferral of weight. The male Gẹlẹdẹ tends to maintain a very wide stance (pl. 66). His body position and, in Ketu area, the bamboo hoop around his chest accentuate this width. The female in Ketu area, in contrast, tends to step from a relatively narrow stance, which is echoed in her tightly wrapped torso (pls. 10, 50, 57, 60, 65). Both male and female utilize movements of a very wide amplitude, carving out space with big, fully realized gestures. They extend the full arm parallel to the ground. Horsetail whisks *(ìrùkẹ̀)* held by many dancers emphasize the reach of the arm. The horsetail whisks symbolize heredity, for the Yoruba say, "The horse dying leaves the tail behind; the children survive the parents" *(B'ẹsin ba ku a f'iru de'le, ọmọ eni ni ns'ẹhin de ni)* (Beyioku

PLATE 66. Stamping erratically from a wide stance, the male
Gẹlẹdẹ communicates physical power and impetuousity. Idọfa,
1971.

PLATE 67. A male Gẹlẹdẹ with appliquéd panels grips the
bamboo hoop under his costume and moves it rhythmically
during his dance. Idahin, 1971.

1946). Ketu males vary their arm carriage by tucking their arms into their
sides and gripping the bamboo hoop around the chest in certain movement sequences (pl. 67).

Differences in the use of ground space sharply delineate males from
females. Whereas the female pursues a fairly straight path toward the
drums, the male darts here and there, covering the area impetuously (fig.
2). Recall the words of an Ẹgbado dance master, "a female Gẹlẹdẹ . . .
would be allowed just enough space to dance . . . unlike a male dancer
who will be jumping here and there." He is explosive and erratic, while
the female appears outwardly controlled, restraining her energy for release in the ẹka section of the dance. Her stamps are strong yet confined
in space.

In the Ketu area, female masks usually perform in pairs. When they
are ready to dance, they position themselves at the entrance to the arena
with their backs to the audience. Marking time to the drums with deliberate steps, they move alternate feet diagonally forward on the first beat of
each measure; the arms and torso incline toward the forward foot. The
drummers finally launch into the alujo, the entrance pattern, as the
dancers whirl around and majestically stamp into the arena. With great
force, their feet are distinctly raised and presented forward before being

emphatically placed on the ground. The crossing of the feet over the midline of the body emphasizes the narrowness of the tightly wrapped torsos and characteristically narrow stances. Most often the torsos are inclined forward, and the arms create large sweeps, working in natural opposition to the incisive legs, which are either carried only inches above the ground or raised chest high. On one occasion, radically reversing their forward-inclined torsos, a pair of female Gẹlẹdẹ thrust out their stomachs and breasts and, with sharply undulating torsos, swung their breastplates upward so that they bobbed provocatively in the aftermath of each emphatic stamp (pl. 65). Their forearms, which flanked their torsos horizontally, circled backward with each undulation. This stamping pattern, and its variant above, may incorporate single pivot turns as the free leg is carried high. The overall impression of the entrance sequence is supreme composure and controlled power as the paired females pursue a direct line toward the drums. The drummers repeat the sequence until the dancers have reached them, then they give notice for the second rhythmic pattern.

The *ẹka* is embedded in the second drum pattern. The movements that accompany it throughout Gẹlẹdẹ areas are a series of small, extremely rapid, rhythmically complex jumps (pl. 68). The dancers initiate these jumps subtly from a central impulse in the pelvis, which raises them onto the balls of their feet, their toes barely losing contact with the earth. The *ẹka* can also be translated into slight shifts of weight from one foot to the other. The costume construction, which builds up the buttocks, bounces and swings, exaggerating the hips and emphasizing the subtlety of the movements. The intent of the dance is clear in an *ẹka* that accompanies this dance motif:

> Lying *ẹléwẹlẹ* around the hips, body beads make a woman's buttocks
>   stick out *sesesesese*

> *Ẹléwẹlẹ ìlẹkẹ, m'obìnrin sọ'dí sesesesese*

[Collected in Aibo Quarter, Aiyetoro, 1971]

A variation on this theme is:

> Lying *ẹléwẹlẹ* around the hips strung together one after the other
> Beads become a woman's friend, sticking out
> *Bẹrẹbẹrẹ, bẹrẹbẹrẹ, pa rí* [bridge]

> *Ẹléwẹlẹ ẹléwẹlẹ ẹléwẹlẹ*
> *Ìlẹkẹ, b'obìnrin s'ọrẹ, ẹlérẹbẹ*
> *Bẹrẹbẹrẹ, bẹrẹbẹrẹ, pa rí*

[Collected in Igbogila, 1978]

Both *ẹka* refer to the body beads (*ìlẹkẹ*) worn by women around their hips and covered by a wrapper. *Ẹlẹwẹlẹ* is a word-picture that evokes the way

Male

Idahin

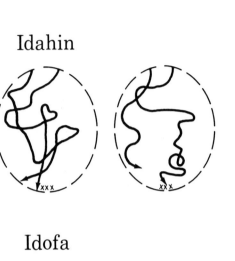

Idofa

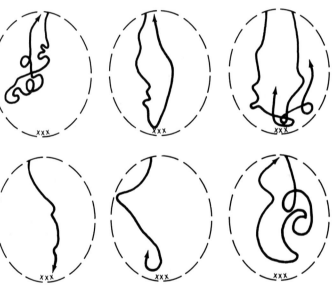

approximate limit of dance space — — —
drum ensemble   xxx

Fig. 2. Performers' use of ground space, Ketu region.

Female

Idahin

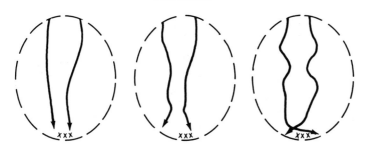

Idofa

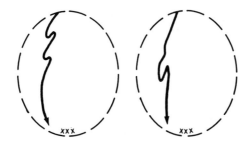

Ketu

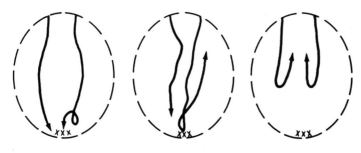

PLATE 68. A female Gẹlẹdẹ executes *ẹka* with a series of small, extremely rapid and rhythmically complex jumps. Ilaro, 1977.

strands of beads fall naturally in response to the contour of a woman's hips. Small girls sometimes wear them before they are old enough to dress fully. Body beads are considered beautiful because they build up the hips, as the two *ẹka* assert. The second *ẹka* alludes further to the bouncing action of the buttocks created by the tiny, powerful jumps performed from an inclined body position. A wooden spool tied around the dancer's hips simulates and, at the same time exaggerates, a woman's buttocks bearing body beads.

Another *ẹka* refers to these jumps, characteristic of female Gẹlẹdẹ, by alluding metaphorically to a frog. To the rhythm of the *ẹka*, the dancers coordinate raising and dropping their shoulders with their jumping feet:

Frog jump into the river, jump into the river, jump into the river,
  jump into the river *sere, sere, sere*

Kònkò bẹ́ s'odò, bẹ́ s'odò, bẹ́ s'odò, bẹ́ s'odò, ṣẹrẹ, ṣẹrẹ, ṣẹrẹ
[Collected in Aibo Quarter, Aiyetoro, 1971]

Ṣẹrẹ is a word-picture that conjures up a frog slithering into the water.

The female jumping motif, with buttocks bouncing and swaying, is small in amplitude but powerful. Dust flies, and sometimes the ground is literally torn up. Informants who describe female Gẹlẹdẹ as gentle are speaking in relative terms. The emphasis of this jumping pattern is down into the earth; each sequence is terminated with an emphatic stress to balance *(dogba)* the drum phrase (Thompson 1974a:203). The body is maintained predominantly at one level with only slight variation. The head remains posed and calm, and the stance is narrow. In contrast to the forward progression of the entrance sequence, the female generally executes the *ẹka* in place, moving only slightly backward or forward. The great rhythmic sensitivity, speed, and virtuosity of this pattern excite the audience, as the good Gẹlẹdẹ dancers match the beating of their feet to the beating of the drums.

In one brilliant performance, two female Gẹlẹdẹ from the town of Ketu initiated their dance with an extremely rapid and rhythmically complex *ẹka*, digging into the earth with great power and agility. After a long, involved pattern, they emphatically hit a last beat, suddenly whirled around, and majestically stepped into the arena. They swept their arms up and down in opposition, and every now and then they punctuated their steps with pivot turns. The audience threw up its arms, yelled, and cheered. Not only had the dancers performed a difficult and challenging pattern brilliantly but they had dared to attack it in the beginning, in an improvisational reversal of the usual sequence. They were confident enough to ignore the advice presented in the *ẹka* "begin diligently; begin carefully." With the *ẹka* concluded, the dancers may break out of their uniformity to exit in a more moderately paced sequence, like the *kete* of Pobe, that allows them to bask in the glory of a task done well.

The male Gẹlẹdẹ, on the other hand, stresses physical prowess, daring, and freedom. He must stamp so powerfully as to stir up clouds of dust, as an *ẹka* for the male Gẹlẹdẹ suggests:

Clouds of dust appear from above the market, clouds of dust *yẹyẹye*

Érukú lá tá'ke ọ́ja, érukú yẹyẹyẹ
[Collected in Aibo Quarter, Aiyetoro, 1978]

The sharp *k* sounds hint at the male's staccato gestures, and *yẹyẹyẹ* is the sound of the dust flying. Male choreography exhibits great variety in stamping. The male approach toward the drums differs from the restrained and regulated progression of the female Gẹlẹdẹ. Working from a wide stance, which echoes his expanded chest in the Ketu areas, the male Gẹlẹdẹ constantly fluctuates in his movement, making him seem spontaneous and agile (pl. 66). His body levels vary from an upstretched posture, his feet barely skimming the earth, to a low, plunging position. As he traverses the performing area, he continually shifts direction, angling from side to side. He may perform a kind of freeform hopscotch, or energetically track sideways while forcefully raising his knees, or merely stamp in one spot. In an unexpected movement he completes a full turn with vigorous stamps, and, as excitement builds, he whirls around with such impetus that he nearly leaves the ground. His arms are extended to the sides, and the profusion of head ties knotted around his chest fly out on the wind as he turns. As if to exhaust the potential of his dancing space, he rushes at the audience, forcing them to fall back and make room. Or in a charge he may suddenly toss his horsetail whisks into the air and dart off abruptly in another direction. He attacks his space with such great vigor that sometimes his attendants must point him in the right direction. He is quite unlike the female, who takes a relatively straight and narrow path toward the drums.

In Ketu area, where male costuming includes a bamboo hoop suspended around the chest with multiple cloths attached, the dancer manipulates the hoop with his hands. He may rotate it as his body twists, bounce it as his body rocks, or jump it in time with his shoulders, greatly enhancing and extending his range of movement. In northern Ẹgbado the male's playful, erratic sojourn is accompanied by a series of *ẹka* strung together, called *ewulu*, a word-picture that evokes a musical pattern composed of assorted rhythms following each other in rapid succession. As the Pobe dancer says, "When the male [Gẹlẹdẹ] comes he is always courageous. . . . He dances and he does something very difficult because men are hot. They are always hot." Thus, it is the artistry of the male masquerade to be daring, to command the entire space, to dazzle and surprise the audience as he asserts his power, his cunning, and his freedom.

A stylistic analysis of the male and female Gẹlẹdẹ masquerades from Ketu area generally corroborates the statements of dancers and other critics. What is curious is that stylistic analyses of Ẹgbado and Awori areas do not bear out the statements of dancers and critics from those areas. Male and female masquerade dances are not nearly as distinct as these critics indicate. Thus, the statements cited above from an Ẹgbado dance master on the distinctions between *akọgi* and *abogi* apply accurately to Ketu but not to Ẹgbado. It also happens that the ratio of males to females in Ketu area is more balanced than anywhere else. In Ẹgbado there is an overwhelming preponderance of female masks, and in Lagos all the Gẹlẹdẹ masquerades seem to be female. Male masquerades appear, however, in Ẹfẹ night, and there is general agreement among members that Ẹfẹ is male and Gẹlẹdẹ is female. That Gẹlẹdẹ is considered female throughout Ẹgbado, Awori, and Lagos perhaps explains why there are fewer males generally and why the dance styles of *abogi* and *akọgi* in those areas are less distinct.

Compared with Ketu style, Gẹlẹdẹ dance in Ẹgbado and Awori areas is in general less energetic and more moderately paced. As in Ketu, however, a calm countenance reigns over a more active body. Also similar is the dance posture, the straight, inclined torso and flexed knees. Whereas the use of space sharply delineates male and female masquerades in Ketu area, it is not so distinct further south; females seem not to be so restrained spatially, and at the same time males are not nearly so erratic in their approach to space. Added to these differences are certain contrastive features in performance format between Ketu and Ẹgbado/Awori areas: shape of space, orientation to space, order, grouping of dancers, and point of entry into the arena.

In Lagos, identical pairs of female Gẹlẹdẹ form two long parallel lines to begin the afternoon's performance (pl. 69). The entry is processional. Flanked by women shaking sacred rattles, the lines of Gẹlẹdẹ in a simple step-together-step movement parade toward the drums and then circle leftward, returning to their starting point to begin again. They repeat this procession several times, then exit, and each Gẹlẹdẹ pair or single returns to dance separately, first paying homage to the drummers (pl. 70). Female Gẹlẹdẹ in Lagos, in contrast to those of Ketu and Ẹgbado areas, are indeed gentle, and their dance steps are extremely simple and repetitive. Another feature unique to Lagos is the striking way the Gẹlẹdẹ end their dance sequences. Guarded by male attendants, they abruptly throw their torsos forward and go into a rapid spin, like a top (pl. 71). There is a concept in Yoruba dance of spinning like a shell (*jijó bí òkòtó*), but these concluding spins, unlike those in other dances, are performed

PLATE 69. Lagos Gẹlẹdẹ line up in identical pairs in preparation for a processional that opens the afternoon performance. Isalẹ Eko 1978.

PLATE 70. A female Gẹlẹdẹ kneels and pays respect to the drummers before beginning a solo. Lagos, 1978.

to give the impression of loss of control, as though the dancer were being spun by a force outside his body. Lack of control is further suggested by the responses of attendants. They rush forward instantly to break the thrust of the spin, catch the masquerader around the waist, lift him, and hold him off the ground to prevent his falling (pl. 72). These concluding movements may allude to Gẹlẹdẹ's association with the god of the sea (Olokun), who fights with the "sound of shells" (*Olókùn ajàró òkòtó*). When the Ẹfẹ ceremony opens in Lagos, the singer invokes Olokun with this praise name (Beyioku 1946). On one level it refers to the sound of the leg rattles, which are likened to the sound of the sea. The spinning evokes the dynamic with which shells wash up on the beach. This particular feature of Gẹlẹdẹ is peculiar to Lagos.

Regional variations in the amount of space and the concern for controlling it may account for variations in format and, particularly, in the use of space. Marketplaces vary in size, capacity, and shape, and these factors will necessarily affect the performance. The marketplace in Ilaro, for example, is full of permanent sheds and stalls that significantly limit the dance space. Markets may also be vast open spaces in which women set up temporary stands on market days. In such a setting, crowd controllers regulate the size and shape of the dance space by attempting to manipulate the crowd of spectators. Often they are able to maintain a relatively large space, anywhere from 10 to 30 feet wide and up to 150 feet long.

In Ketu and Ketu-related towns, the open space that the crowd controllers maintain is usually a long, narrow rectangle (pls. 67, 72) with a clear separation between the performers and the audience. The dancers have a long runway for their dramatic entry and can parade across the space before they break into the *ẹka* just in front of the drums. In contrast, the dance space in Ẹgbado area tends to restrict the dancers. Less crowd control allows the space to shrink around the dancer(s), creating a confined circular or ovular shape (color plate 4, pl. 61). Other masqueraders may interrupt spontaneously, and the space may then become so crowded with masqueraders that there is no longer any distinction between audience and performers (pls. 8, 9, 11, 52, 53). Since the dancers adapt to the available space, the space ultimately affects the style of the dance in a particular marketplace. In towns where permanent stalls infringe upon the dance space or where crowd control is of little concern, the dancers' movements are necessarily restricted to a small area just in front of the drums.

What do these differences imply? The fact that Awori and Ẹgbado performances on the whole are less structured and more spontaneous, and the portrayals of males and females are less distinct than informants actually describe them, suggests either that Gẹlẹdẹ in Ẹgbado and Awori areas changed dramatically from its original style and structure or that in

PLATE 71. A female Gęlędę dancer goes into a rapid spin. Lagos, 1978.

PLATE 72. Before the dancer loses his balance from the momentum of his spin, attendants rush forward to grab him and lift him up off the ground. Lagos, 1978.

Ketu it became more structured and more distinct. Three points are relevant in this regard and suggest that the former is the case. First, it is significant that throughout Ẹgbado and Awori areas the origin of Gẹlẹdẹ is attributed to Ketu. Second, dancers and critics from Ẹgbado and Awori areas stress distinctions between male and female masquerades that do not exist in those areas but apply more accurately to Ketu. This suggests that there has been a more dramatic change in form and style in those areas than in Ketu. Whether it occurred during the diffusion of Gẹlẹdẹ from Ketu or after its establishment in Ẹgbado/Awori areas, perhaps because of the upheavals of civil wars, remains to be considered. Third, although it is stressed universally that Gẹlẹdẹ masqueraders perform in pairs, that does not occur in many Ẹgbado towns. Although masks are frequently carved in pairs, they often perform singly, perhaps because performers are not available in certain areas. In a number of Egbado communities today it is difficult to amass enough dancers to put on a Gẹlẹdẹ spectacle. Elsewhere, as in Badagri, Gẹlẹdẹ has completely died out. Gẹlẹdẹ in Ketu thus represents the ideal, according to participants throughout western Yorubaland.

Summary

Men perform Gẹlẹdẹ as a "plaything" for women. The dance reflects men's perceptions of themselves and of women, creating "a play of powers made visible" (Langer 1953:87). Men as choreographers, trainers, and performers create a powerful image of humanity, which characterizes what is ordinarily invisible in the world or, rather, what normally is concealed inside human beings. In a tightly structured play of great energy, embellished with masks and costumes that amplify and define social roles and physical attributes, males externalize and make visible the vital natures of men and women, identifying and defining their life force, *aṣẹ*. The dynamics of movement thus evoke innate, ordinarily invisible vital power. Images of male *aṣẹ* emerge as the man aggressively consumes the space surrounding him, his explosive manner flaunting unrestrained power. Female *aṣẹ*, as expressed by the male masquerader, is made visible in the narrow stance and controlled and channeled movement, which pursues a direct line toward the drums with a strength and speed uncommon in Yoruba women's dancing. The male does not attempt to imitate female dances; rather he expresses something much deeper—the inner power, the vital potential of female *aṣẹ*, which is covert, concentrated, composed, and mysterious. Similar to the act of voicing, the performers by acting out the vital forces of men and women through the dynamics of the dance bring those life forces into the phenomenal world where they can be observed and studied. In this way Gẹlẹdẹ not only affirms life but secures it.

6

The Masks of Gẹlẹdẹ

The energies made visible in Gẹlẹdẹ dance and enhanced by the costuming are matched by the enthralling imagery of Gẹlẹdẹ headdresses. Depicting practically anything that might be seen in the Yoruba universe, Gẹlẹdẹ masks document and comment on the domain of the mothers, that is, the world. Yet despite the enormous diversity of images in Gẹlẹdẹ, the form or morphology of the masks themselves varies little. By contrast, the morphology of the nocturnal Ẹfẹ masquerades, such as Arabi, the nocturnal mothers, or Ọrọ Ẹfẹ, varies significantly from area to area and even within communities.

Form

Gẹlẹdẹ masks consist of a head representing a human or an animal, sometimes with a superstructure. The superstructures either amplify a theme in the lower portion of the headdress or, more often, develop a different subject. Some superstructures are sited directly on the head or coiffure (pls. 48, 53, 58, 61, 62, 73), while others rest on rectangular or circular platforms that project to the sides or are raised above the head (pls. 74, 75). In the Yoruba (and African) tradition, they are carved from a single block of wood. Some portray intricate mass/void compositions of humans, animals, and objects. Often, the bilateral symmetry of the head is mirrored in the superstructure, but there also may be striking asymmetrical compositions that contrast with the relative simplicity of the head. Like the creators of Egungun and Ẹpa headdresses, some Gẹlẹdẹ artists demonstrate their mastery of the medium by developing extremely complex and complicated imagery within the confines of the basic cylindrical mass of wood. For example, an Ẹgbado masterpiece honoring carvers (pl. 102) shows one at work with a knife, his adze over

PLATE 73. The superstructure of this mask is sited directly on the head. Musée Royal de l'Afrique Centrale, Tervuren (R. G. 72.38.72).

PLATE 74. A covered tray of bananas balances on a cylindrical
support in this female-type mask. Ijale Ketu, 1978.

his shoulder, while the face of the mask is itself covered by another
carved face from the same block of wood. Many other carvers take just
the opposite approach. Rather than accept a solely subtractive approach
to their material, they may also add on wood to demonstrate their virtuosity. The result is an array of extensions and attachments—stationary,
interchangeable and moveable (pls. 9, 52, 59, 76, 77). Such superstructures are indicative of the sculptural freedom and innovation in Gẹlẹdẹ
art and distinguish it from the more conservative approaches to much
shrine sculpture and masquerade headdresses for Egungun and Ẹpa.

Extensions and attachments are achieved in various ways. Some
Gẹlẹdẹ headdresses have a cylindrical or conical projection at the top,
which supports the attachment (pls. 47, 78). Gẹlẹdẹ images of marketwomen carrying wares in containers on their heads are often constructed
in this manner since it allows the container's diameter to be much greater
than that of the head (pl. 111). It also allows either the headpiece or the
superstructure to be replaced should one or the other break or rot. To
extend forms into space, far exceeding the dimensions of the original
wood cylinder, the carver expertly carpenters and fits attachments using
a variety of joints (pls. 76–78, 139, 144, 145).

Some ensembles are even more ambitious. At Igan Okoto, Ẹgbado,

PLATE 75. Platforms on the sides of this mask support two standing figures who in turn hold tumblers. Museum für Völkerkunde, Berlin (III C 41149).

PLATE 76. Moveable chains are suspended from joints on both
sides of the head. British Museum, London (1942 Af 7.10).

there appeared a life-sized equestrian masquerader. The horse's head
and tail were carved, and its torso consisted of a lightweight wooden
frame covered in cloth. A hole in the center of this construction accom-
modated the rider, who was a typical Gɛlɛdɛ masker. A similar horse was
documented in Ibara Quarter, Abɛokuta, by T. J. H. Chappel (pl. 79).
This particular innovation may have been inspired by the work of the
master carver Duga of Mɛkɔ. Bascom (1973:78), citing a letter from an
interpreter at Mɛkɔ that described an important Gɛlɛdɛ funeral commemoration in 1953, reported that

> Duga for the ceremony carved a horse of wood and gave it four wheels
> to walk on, and he made it so that four people could be hid in the mat
> which he covered round the horse. Two people pushed it forward and
> two people pushed it backward. He trained the people to push it as if it
> were alive, and he trained the rider to dance with it as if he were riding
> a live horse. It was very wonderful and interesting indeed.

Some artists are not content with simply extending their forms in

PLATE 77. The creator of this headdress demonstrated his virtuosity by assembling a variety of attachments and media, including a mirror and metal disks. Musée Royal de l'Afrique Centrale, Tervuren (R. G. 62.42.1).

PLATE 78. The flowing form of a woman's head tie embellishes a sculptural coiffure. Nigerian Museum, Lagos (289).

PLATE 79. An ingenious Gẹlẹdẹ masquerade of a king on horseback demonstrates the inventiveness of Yoruba artists. Photograph by T. J. H. Chappel in Abẹokuta, 1964. Nigerian Museum archives (neg. no. 46.5.B.5).

PLATE 80. Hinged joints allow the carved representation of cloth to fly outward as the masquerader turns. Ofia, 1971.

space; they want to activate them as well, using hinges and other constructions. In headdresses at the Nigerian Museum, Lagos, and the Santa Barbara Museum of Art, the face swings to the side to reveal another carved face behind it. This display of sculpting virtuosity may also offer a philosophical comment on the entire phenomenon of masking.[1] Otooro Oduṣina of Ketu has created a mask with two sets of wooden hinges that allow the carved representation of cloth to fly outward as the performer turns (pl. 80). In another example, two enormous snakes clutching antelopes in their mouths emerge from the heads of a pair of female Gẹlẹdẹ masks (pl. 81). The long snake forms are hinged near the top so that they can be manipulated by the masqueraders during performance. The head portions of the masks were carved by Fagbite Asamu of Idahin, circa 1930, and the snake attachments were finished in 1971 by his son and student, Falọla Ẹdun, after Fagbite's death. Another superstructure, photographed in Ilaro but carved in Agoṣaṣa (pl. 82), depicts two coffin bearers. It is an assemblage—the coffin is attached to the heads, the arms are nailed to the shoulders, the figures are secured to a long rectangular platform, and the whole construction is attached to a cylindrical pedestal projecting from the head of the mask. A type of headdress that is concen-

PLATE 81. Joints make moveable enormous snakes that emerge
from the headdresses, thus adding another kinetic dimension to
the dance. Photograph by Howard Wildman, Idahin, 1971.

PLATE 82. Depicting coffin bearers, this headdress is assembled
from many separate parts. Ilaro, 1978.

trated among Ketu, Ọhọri, and Anago Yoruba incorporates movement in the superstructure by means of articulated figures whose parts are manipulated with cords. These puppetry masks appear during both Ęfẹ and Gẹlẹdẹ ceremonies and depict all kinds of genre scenes: bawdy, humorous, or horrific (pl. 83). Their kinetic aspect literally "animates" further the transcendent images presented by the masqueraders.

In addition to attachments to and extensions of the headgear, Gẹlẹdẹ sculptors create other costume elements, including breastplates (pls. 50, 58, 59), breast and belly plates (pls. 84, 85) (cf. also Huet 1978:pls. 80, 86; Kerchache 1973:12, 24), trunk masks (pls. 86, 87), back plates with babies (Beier 1958:13), and wooden spools covered by cloth to build up the hips and buttocks. All of these pieces intensify female attributes and stress beauty, fertility, and maternity.

Iconology

While there may be little variation in the format of the Gẹlẹdẹ mask, its imagery knows no bounds. Literally everything under the sun, that is, within the realm of the "owners of the world," inspires the creators of Gẹlẹdẹ masks. The headdresses, whether representing Yoruba or non-Yoruba, men, women, or animals, make visible the "children" of the mothers.

Although the themes are virtually limitless, certain ones recur frequently. We have classified the masks in several subject categories, recognizing that some would fit into more than one category. All of them present some sort of social or spiritual commentary—praise, criticism, or simply a documentation of an aspect of Yoruba life and thought. The themes in Gẹlẹdẹ masks, corresponding generally to those expressed in Ęfẹ songs, are role recognition, ridicule, and cosmological forces. In the first, various groups and individuals are honored. The masks commemorate certain age groups; various social, economic, political, or religious roles; and specific deceased individuals. The second category deals in devastating humorous or satiric imagery ridiculing antisocial elements or opponents. The third conveys concepts about the forces operating in the Yoruba cosmos.

Role Recognition

The Yoruba divide all Gẹlẹdẹ masks into male *(akọgi)* and female *(abogi)* categories, which are sometimes based on the subject matter depicted in the mask. For example, a head with a female coiffure would be called *abogi* (literally "female wood"); one wearing a man's cap would be identified as *akọgi*, (literally "male wood"). Male-related subject matter in the superstructure may indicate an *akọgi*, but not infrequently a head with a women's head tie may have a male-associated motif, e.g., hunting

PLATE 83. Headdresses with puppets manipulated by cords provide additional visual and kinetic interest. William and Robert Arnett Collection. Photograph by Gerald Jones.

PLATE 84. Breast and belly plates, whether plain or elaborately decorated with scarification patterns, emphasize the theme of the knowledge of the source of life. Photograph by Howard Wildman, Isagba, 1972.

PLATE 85. Pendulous breasts, an expanded womb, and enlarged labia make visible the inner power of women. Musée Royal de l'Afrique Centrale, Tervuren (R. G. 75.78.2).

PLATE 86. A female holds a head tie around her shoulders in this trunk mask. Harrison Eiteljorg Collection. Photograph by Robert Wallace.

PLATE 87. As in plate 86, a head tie is draped around a female's shoulders. Museum für Völkerkunde, Basel (III 12719).

(pl. 108); or a female costume may be combined with a male mask. But beyond the mere identification of females and males, coiffures, headgear, figures, and objects in association with the main faces of the masks define much more specific roles within these two broad groups.

Fashions not only enhance a person's physical appearance but also reflect and interpret Yoruba life as they express and maintain social identity—one's station or accomplishment in life in terms of occupation, education, inheritance, religion, or wealth. The adornment of the head is an important means of expressing social identity (cf. Houlberg 1979). It will be remembered, furthermore, that the head *(ori)*, consisting of both the physical, outer aspect *(ori ode)* and the inner, spiritual one *(ori inun)*, is, according to Yoruba belief, the site of one's personal essence, potential, and destiny. The dressing of one's outer head for ritual occasions communicates something of one's inner, spiritual self. Certain priests of the thungergod Ṣango, for example, plait their hair in a bridal coiffure to communicate that their heads have been prepared for a special relationship with the deity. Whether male or female, these priests, often referred to as Ṣango's wives *(iya Ṣango)*, are endowed with the power to soothe and placate the god, just as females are perceived to have a soothing effect on their husbands. Thus, the depictions of head adornments in Gẹlẹdẹ masks can have both social and spiritual connotations. Female coiffures, jewelry, and head ties are suggestive of women's roles, while male hairstyles and headgear suggest those of men.

Women's coiffures may receive great attention from the carver. Finely rendered incised lines convey the texture of braids and plaits to evoke the sculptural qualities of the hair (pls. 88, 89). Frequently the hairstyle is accentuated and embellished with other objects (pl. 90) or by the sweeping, curving forms of head ties that wrap around the head or float in space to "crown" the head (pls. 91, 92). Ear and hair ornaments are the most frequently depicted types of jewelry on the main head (pls. 111, 146, 147), but other types appear in superstructures adorned with figures (pl. 120).

Men's fashions are expressed in somewhat less sculptural yet distinctive hairstyles (pl. 93), and often in various styles of hats, many of them derived from northern or Islamic sources. Tight-fitting cloth *fìlà* and caps with dog ears *(fìlà abetí ajá* or *lábànkádà,* a Hausa word meaning "the jaws of the crocodile") appear often (pls. 94, 95), as do other unusual headgear (pls. 96, 97). An elaborate turban (pls. 98, 99) announces the Muslim, while the priests of Yoruba gods are shown with their own distinctive hairstyles (pl. 100).

A fine Gẹlẹdẹ mask from Ṣawọnjo (pl. 101) illustrates how head adornment specifies cultural role—position, occupation, religion, age. It depicts a female devotee of Nana Bùkú, the goddess associated with earth

PLATE 88. The delicately rendered coiffure of the mask mirrors the detail and neatness of the hairstyle of the masquerader's female companion. Lagos, 1978.

PLATE 89. A carefully rendered coiffure crowns the head of a female mask. Institute of African Studies, University of Ibadan (6498).

PLATE 90. Ropes (broken) secure engraved calabashes to each side of an intricate female hairdo. Art Museum, University of Ifẹ.

PLATE 91. A head tie sweeps upward and around the plaited hair. Musée des Arts Africaines et Océaniennes, Paris (64.14.1).

PLATE 92. A head tie floats around the front and back of the head. Museum für Völkerkunde, Köln.

PLATE 93. A tuft of hair distinguishes a head that has been prepared with efficacious medicines. Musée de l'Homme, Paris (91.22.99).

and disease. The coiffure worn by initiates of this goddess signals devotion and, in particular, a head ritually prepared to receive the gods during possession trance (cf. M. T. Drewal 1977).

    Gẹlẹdẹ subject matter is exceedingly diverse, but central to all Gẹlẹdẹ imagery is its concern with *humanity*, humankind viewed in its relationship to other living creatures in the world, animals and plants, as well as to the supernatural inhabitants who move at will between worldly and otherworldly realms. Within this world view very specific yet varied beliefs and attitudes may be discerned in Gẹlẹdẹ imagery. When Yoruba informants say that "Gẹlẹdẹ is the god of society," they are expressing not only the communal nature of the cult but also its concrete impact on social matters. It is no wonder that Gẹlẹdẹ masks contrast dramatically with those of Egungun. Gẹlẹdẹ stresses the human presence in the constancy of the lower portion, the head of a man or woman. Even when the main head is that of an animal, its significance must be seen in its relevance to humans. Egungun, on the other hand, stresses the otherworld and its nonhuman aspects, by dramatically altering the human form and including images and media that focus on the afterlife and the super-

PLATE 94. Two Gẹlẹdẹ headdresses depict male headgear derived from northern or Islamic sources: a cap with dog ears on the left and a tight-fitting *fila* on the right. Nigerian Museum, Lagos (l: 59.35.61; r: 59.35.47).

PLATE 95. The popular cap with dog ears is shown with flaps folded down in this Gẹlẹdẹ headdress. Nigerian Museum, Lagos (66.2.118).

PLATE 96. Surface treatment and pigment capture the textured quality of a man's fringed and tasselled cap. Nigerian Museum, Lagos (44.1.1).

PLATE 97. A perforated cap adorns the head of this mask. Art Museum, University of Ifẹ.

PLATE 98. The beard and turban that frame the face, together with the container on the head, identify a Muslim trader. Nigerian Museum, Lagos (60.6.10).

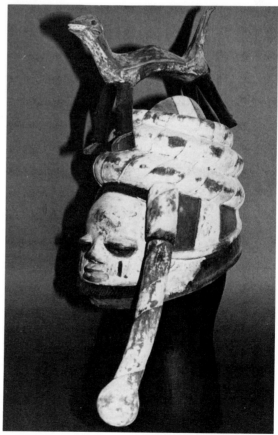

PLATE 99. A turbaned head surmounted by an animal depicts a Muslim. British Museum, London (1942 Af 7.7).

PLATE 100. The carefully shaved head, featuring a central ridge of hair flanked by a circular tuft with a pigtail, identifies a devotee of a Yoruba god. British Museum, London (1959 Af 19.109).

PLATE 101. Coiffures like this one, worn by a devotee of the goddess Nana Buku, mark a head that has been ritually prepared to receive the spirit of the god during possession trance. Institute of African Studies, University of Ibadan (679).

natural rather than life itself. For example, animal imagery in Egungun tends to show parts of the body—horns, skulls, skins, jawbones, and vertebrae—as opposed to the complete and lively animals depicted in Gẹlẹdẹ.

The same focus may be discerned in Ẹpa/Ẹlẹfọn headdresses. While many of the superstructure images depict roles within society—most notably those of mothers and children, kings and courtiers, and herbalists—the lower portion of the headdress, instead of showing a female or male head, presents a highly stylized, almost abstract, and only vaguely humanoid janus form. The supernatural—not the world—is evoked here.

The concern for humanity is expressed in the act of paying homage, an essential ingredient in all Yoruba transactions, whether in felling a tree or appealing to the mothers. Man operates in a world of competing powers, all possessing a life force. He must learn to manipulate the forces at his disposal in order to enhance his own existence and that of people around him. In order to invoke and utilize such forces fully, one must know their proper names, which are often esoteric or secret formulas. A Yoruba proverb explains that "it is not enough to kill an elephant, one must know its praise name." Praise names *(oríkì)* constitute an extremely important part of Yoruba oral literature, in which poetic and often obscure names, places, and images are strung together in serial fashion and fix persons, things, or gods in a larger cosmic system. The voicing of such praises makes up the invocations or homage known as an *ijuba*, like those voiced by Ọrọ Ẹfẹ as a compulsory prelude to his performance. Recognition and honor for the living, for those who have gone before, for those more powerful than oneself, or for those worshipped are essential if any ritual act is to be successful. Just as *oriki* and *ijuba* provide verbal praise, many Gẹlẹdẹ masks, by their appropriateness and completeness according to Yoruba aesthetic concepts (cf. Drewal 1980), pay homage and offer visual praise for persons or groups, living and departed, praise that parallels that cited in an Ẹfẹ song:

> Generation, by generation, by generation, the work of the
>   generations
> The family of Akinoṣo all of them were Maja
> The family of Akinwumi, they were the children Egungun
> The house of Atunde was the house of twins
> He named one child Idowu; he named Akan; he named Aya; he
>   named Ẹdun
> Omilana was the family of hunters and those of Ajobiare were called
>   Ṣango-has-given-me-a-gift
>
> *N'irọn n'irọn n'irọn iṣélẹ ìrọn*

Akinọṣọ́ gbogbo wọ́n lo jẹ́ Maja
Ìrọn Akínwùmỳ ọmọ Egúngún ni wọ́n
Ilé Atunde ni ilé ibẹ́jì
O ṣọ Ìdòwú, o ṣọ Àkàn, o ṣọ Àyá, s'Ẹdun
Omílana n'ìrọn ọdẹ Àjùlé Ajobiare ni nwọ́n ṣọ Ṣàngóbùnmi
[Collected in Idofoi Quarter, Aiyetoro, 1971]

Among those honored in Gẹlẹdẹ masks are artists and craftspersons—carvers, calabash decorators, blacksmiths, tattooers, leatherworkers, potters, weavers, embroiderers, dyers, and beadworkers. Their occupations, like many in Yorubaland, are primarily but not exclusively hereditary. Patience, concentration, foresight, and perseverance are regarded as requisite for success as an artist (cf. H. Drewal 1980:9–10). For art, *ọnà*, involves the design, decoration, or embellishment of an object, and "those-who-create-art" *(onίṣọnà)* are distinguished by their skill in their chosen medium.[2]

The expressive Gẹlẹdẹ mask shown in plate 102 is certainly an unequivocal statement of sculpting virtuosity and self-assertion. It honors its creator, an unknown master carver working among the Ketu Yorubu, who has perfected his technique. The main head is painted white and wears its own mask of blue. Thin vertical bands of wood constitute the outer mask, with the eyes joining the central and lateral portions. Behind this openwork face is another, identical one, separated by less than an inch of space. Perched above and seated on a mat is the carver, with his adze draped casually over his shoulder, shaving a thin sliver of wood from a rectangular board. His trousers and buttoned shirt suggest a certain amount of prosperity, and his hairstyle, with a tuft at the center of a shaven head, may indicate a certain age grade, a special religious status, or Islamic associations, for the rectangular board may be a Muslim writing board.

Less prestigious and more tedious than woodcarving, but nonetheless essential, is the craft of calabash decorating. The mask in plate 103 depicts two boys applying special scrapers to the outer surface of calabash trays, preparing them for incised or pyro-engraved designs. Both their hairstyles and their occupation suggest Hausa or Ọyọ influence, since a great deal of decorated gourd work comes from these areas (cf. Bascom 1969:102; Heathcote 1976:46–48). The mere depiction of two calabash carvers engaged in their trade honors their profession and the families involved in it.

Other male artists are extolled as well. A Gẹlẹdẹ headdress collected at Ilaro in 1964 and called Onίlù (Drummers) (pl. 104) portrays a *dùndúñ* drum ensemble. Up front is the lead drummer with the talking drum, *iyalu* (literally "mother drum"), flanked by players with smaller pressure drums, *gángan, isaju,* or *kerikeri,* and followed by the musician who pro-

PLATE 102. A carver demonstrates his virtuosity by sculpting the main face within an open-work one and by depicting himself at work with his adze over his shoulder. Nigerian Museum, Lagos (67.8.37).

PLATE 103. Using special scrapers, two boys prepare calabashes. Nigerian Museum, Lagos (65.2.81).

PLATE 104. A Gẹlẹdẹ headdress
called Onilu (Drummers) portrays
a *dundun* ensemble with a lead
drummer in front and his
accompanists close behind.
Nigerian Museum, Lagos (66.3.25).

PLATE 105. *Bembe* drums, knives,
sheaths, and tassels suggest
northern cultural influences in this
headdress. Institute of African
Studies, University of Ibadan
(666).

vides a fast fundamental beat with the *gudugudu* drum (Laoye 1959:10–11). The *dundun* is often called the talking drum because its pitch can be changed to reproduce the patterns of spoken Yoruba, for it is these drums that are used to play praise poetry. The subtle contraposto stance of the head drummer captures the playing posture of the musician as he squeezes the tension cords of the drum against his side and hip while sounding the praises of his patrons.

A variant of this theme is depicted on another Gẹlẹdẹ mask (pl. 105), which contains only the drums crowning the head. They are *bẹ̀mbẹ́*, large cylindrical instruments probably introduced into Yorubaland from the north. The knives, sheaths, and tasselled straps reinforce this theme, for these items also come from the northern neighbors of the Yoruba.

Several finely worked masks celebrate hunters, a theme of some importance in Ẹfẹ night headdresses. Hunting figures prominently in both the history and the worship patterns of western Yorubaland. Numerous myths about the origins of towns and villages in this area recall that the founding forefathers were hunters and that Ẹgbado was the hunting ground of both Ketu and Ọyọ peoples. Hunting also has religious significance. Forests are the abode not only of powerful animals but also of spirits. Therefore, hunters arm themselves with both iron weapons, sacred to Ogun, and magical medicines to allow them to outwit animals, disguise themselves, or even make themselves invisible in case of danger. Animals, it is believed, possess their own medicines, which allow them to shed their skins, take on human form, and interact with human society; and there are even legends about hunters married to beautiful women who were, in fact, animals that had removed their outer skins. There is also a belief that a hunter who kills animals indiscriminately will father a child with animal features, who must be thrown into the bush immediately to perish. Images of hunters and their prey must be seen in this complex historical and religious context.

Some headdresses show the hunter's implements, whether a lamp for night hunting or a trap (pl. 106). Another mask (pl. 107) depicts two hunters, their arms and legs entwined, grasping the hind legs of a reptile, possibly a pangolin, as it tries to escape down the face of the mask. Note the long cutlass at the hip and the tailed coiffure of one of the men. The scene conveys a wonderful tension between balance and movement. Another mask sports an elaborate superstructure depicting a lively hunting encounter. On one side (pl. 108), what appears to be a lion with its leg caught in a noose looks away as a hunter in a tree reaches down for his gun (attachments for the branches are missing). On the other side (pl. 109), a hunter armed with gun and medicine packets corners a curious tusked beast. The artist not only captures the adventures and exploits of hunters but also conveys the realm of the forest, where spirits abound

PLATE 106. A trap and containers call attention to the activities of hunters. Museum für Völkerkunde, Hamburg (64.55.595).

PLATE 107. Two hunters work together to hold the hind legs of a pangolin as it tries to escape down the front of the mask. Nigerian Museum, Lagos (68.2.59).

PLATE 108. An elaborate superstructure depicts a hunter in a tree reaching down for his gun, while an animal looks the other way. Nigerian Museum, Lagos (65.9.25).

PLATE 109. On the other side of the mask in plate 108, a second hunter armed with gun and amulets confronts a tusked beast.

and herbal medicines are gathered. All this action rides above a calm head with elaborate head tie and labret.

The principal occupation of Yoruba women is trading. Many Gẹlẹdẹ masks depict marketwomen with wares on their heads—trays or containers of foodstuffs and other commodities, which are an everyday sight in Yorubaland. The women are economically independent of their husbands and have the opportunity and potential to acquire great wealth. It is possible, for example, for a wife to be wealthier than her husband, and he may be a nonentity in the town (Lloyd 1974:38). Husbands help their wives establish trades by giving them some money but, beyond this, husbands and wives borrow money from each other with the expectation of paying it back. In fact, if the wife is a food seller and the husband wants to partake of her wares, he must purchase them from her as he would from anyone else. If the husband is a farmer, he does not necessarily sell produce to his wife even though she may be a marketwoman; rather he sells on the open market. And the wife does not necessarily specialize in selling the crop her husband raises. In one case, the husband raised waterleaf, which he sold to marketwomen for resale, but his wife specialized in bean cakes, a dish that does not take waterleaf. A husband, however, may enlist his wife's assistance in selling because it is generally felt that men can be more easily cheated in the bargaining process than women (Sudarkasa 1973:120).

Since a woman's status derives largely from her reputation in trading, her craftsmanship, and her wealth, rather than from her husband's importance (Lloyd 1963:39), it is understandable why so many Gẹlẹdẹ masks depict females as marketwomen. Images of traders are sometimes generalized. One such mask (pl. 110), carved by an unknown artist working in the vicinity of Likimọn, Ketu, pictures a food seller with a large container flanked by two calabash scoops set upon a calabash tray. Other masks are exquisitely detailed and specific (pls. 111–114). Plate 111 portrays a seller of cooked maize flour, the staple foodstuff in western Yorubaland, which is wrapped in leaves and piled high in a woven basket set upon a decorated calabash. This marvelous superstructure, carved separately from the lower part of the headdress, fits onto a head of a Yoruba woman with traditional stone earrings piercing the ears. Another mask, by Duga of Mẹkọ, depicts a plantain seller with a bird perched on top of a small container in the center of the tray (pl. 112). A very similar and fluid treatment of the head tie appears in a Gẹlẹdẹ pair by the Idahin artist Falọla Ẹdun (pl. 113). Lidded bowls surmounted by a rolled-up mat, all balanced on a metal tray, constitute the marketwoman's loads. Plate 114 shows a female mask with three elegant braids that divide the facial plane and highlight the full eyes. Both the coiffure and the spherical calabash balanced on the head are typical of Fulani women. Contain-

PLATE 110. A trader carries her loads to market on a tray holding a container and scoops. Institute of African Studies, University of Ibadan (6496).

ers of this sort are often used for selling milk, a trade that is virtually monopolized by the Fulani, who are cattle-herding peoples.

Religious activity is another facet of Yoruba life honored in the arts of Gẹlẹdẹ. Devotees of all the principal faiths of Yorubaland are represented: *orisa* worshippers, priests, and priestesses, Muslims and their clerics, and Christians and their clergy. A number of examples illustrate the range and diversity of visual homage to devotees and their beliefs, for it is spiritual knowledge, whether derived from traditional Yoruba sources, Islam, or Christianity, that enables individuals to manipulate forces and improve the quality of life.

In view of the spiritual powers of Yoruba women, it is not surprising that many Gẹlẹdẹ headdresses pay tribute to priestesses and female devotees of various gods. One headdress (pl. 115) from the Ketu region depicts a devotee of the rainbow deity Òṣùmàrè, whose primary symbols, royal pythons, form a double arc over the head—Osumare "who stays in the sky that he covers with his arms" (Verger 1957:237). The opposing directions of the two celestial serpents balance the composition, and the doubling and positioning of the snakes suggest the colored bands of a rainbow.

Long, flowing strands of cowries encircle two female figures in a Gẹlẹdẹ mask (pl. 116) from the Agoṣaṣa area, Anago. While the precise religious reference is uncertain, this mask may extoll the wonders of *orisa*

PLATE 111. A seller of boiled maize flour carries her foodstuff in a woven basket set in a calabash tray. Ṣawonjo, 1978.

PLATE 112. A plantain seller carries her loads to market in a decorated calabash. Nigerian Museum, Lagos (62.21.255).

Oko, the deity associated with the hunt, plants, animal fertility, and the mothers (Ojo 1973:25–26). Devotees of this god signal their ritual commitments by a double lozenge on the forehead, and the cult's principal icon, a large iron staff (*ọpa oriṣa* Oko), is often clad in a garment of cowries or beads (cf. Thompson 1971:ch. 10).

A pair of female Gɛlɛdɛ by the itinerant Ketu carver Atoba evoke a water goddess theme (pl. 117). The specially shaped pots with protuberances are identical to those used to fetch water from sacred sources for rituals involving water divinities such as Olọsa, Yẹmọja, Ọṣun, Iju, and Olomitutu.

PLATE 113. Lidded bowls set in metal trays and rolled up mats constitute the loads of two traders with elaborately looped head ties. Photograph by Howard Wildman, Idahin, 1972.

PLATE 114. The long braids and the spherical calabash with lid suggest a Fulani milk seller, who is often seen in Yoruba markets. Institute of African Studies, University of Ibadan (6497).

PLATE 115. The double arc of royal pythons frames the female figure and pays tribute to the rainbow divinity, Oṣumare, and its priestess. Nigerian Museum, Lagos (60.1.14).

PLATE 116. Strands of cowries encircle two females in a mask that probably honors *oriṣa* Oko. Nigerian Museum, Lagos (66.2.280).

PLATE 117. Special clay vessels
(otun) hold water for use in the
shrines of various water goddesses.
Institute of African Studies,
University of Ibadan (6499,
67102).

PLATE 118. A devotee of Ọrunmila
(the deity of divination) carries on
her head the symbol of the highest
ranking diviners, the *apere igba odu,*
flanked by four bottles for sacred
medicines or libations. Nigerian
Museum, Lagos (59.33.69).

Women play important roles in all cults. In the cult of Ọrunmila, presiding deity of the Ifa divination system, one of the most sacred and secret ritual objects is the *apere igbá odù,* or *apere* Ifa (the "container-for-the-calabash-of-divination-secrets"). Plate 118 shows it being carried by a woman. Only those who have attained the highest rank among diviners, known as *olodù* ("those who have *odu*"), possess such a container. Four smaller containers—traditionally hollow coconut shells, but here bottles—hold sacred medicines prepared with mud, charcoal, chalk, and camwood, ingredients said to represent four principal divination verses (Dennett 1906:253 cited in Bascom 1969:82–83). These containers, kept in household Ifa shrines, are sometimes used as stools by diviners and are carried out in public by certain females during annual Ifa festivals (Ọṣitọla 1982; Bascom 1969:82, 99, and pl. 21A).

Men, like women, are involved in traditional rites and are also honored for maintaining the faith of their ancestors. As case studies of individuals involved in Gẹlẹdẹ among the Ẹgbado show, people are often touched by several divine forces, and that is reflected in their rituals. Thus during Ẹfẹ night, Ọrọ Ẹfẹ honors a masquerader in the Egungun society, a pan-Yoruba society that pays homage to the spirits of male and female ancestors.

Fadapa was king among masqueraders
His tray of images on the head was full of various kinds of beasts
Ẹiyẹfodo was coming
The one who danced to *bata* drums in the wind
Fadapa was king among masqueraders

Fádapa l'ọba ninu égún
Atarí kìkì ẹranko
Ẹiyẹfodo ḿbọ̀
A jó bàtá lo furufù
Fádapa l'ọba ninu egúngún

[Collected at Idofoi Quarter, Aiyetoro, 1971]

Likewise, Gẹlẹdẹ headdresses make reference to Egungun. A mask from the Anago Yoruba displays two types of Egungun masqueraders as they might be seen in performance (pl. 119). The two in front appear to be *alábala,* maskers known for their dancing and the manipulation of their loose-fitting cloth sacks. They often serve as attendants to lineage Egungun. The larger masquerader behind, probably representing a lineage, displays a carved headdress above a tight fitting cloth ensemble.

Two very fine Gẹlẹdẹ headdresses collected in 1887 and now in the British Museum (pl. 120) pay tribute to courageous warriors, devotees of Ogun, and priestesses and their ritual obligations. The male headdress (right) portrays an Awori Yoruba, his head encircled by four warriors

PLATE 119. Honoring those who are active in the ancestral masquerades of Egungun, some Gẹlẹdẹ masks depict different types of masqueraders as they might appear in performance. Indiana University Art Museum, Bloomington (77.104).

holding guns. Standing in the center is another warrior, probably an officer of some rank and a priest of Ogun by his bracelets, carrying a circular tray with several covered containers and a human head in the center. War and ritual sacrifice dominate this mask. In the nineteenth century, much of Yorubaland, including Awori country, was engulfed in internecine warfare in which thousands of Yoruba were captured, sold, or sacrificed (cf. Akinjọgbin 1965; Smith 1969). The last is the case here, for the artist carefully marked the decapitated head of a non-Awori with distinctive Ọyọ Yoruba scarifications and coiffure. This human offering, together with the substances concealed in the covered containers on the tray, probably represents an oblation in honor of Ogun, god of iron and war.

The female Gẹlẹdẹ in plate 120 (left) portrays a kneeling priestess, her distinctive necklaces and bracelets signaling her status. On her head she carries a tray with four receptacles and a human head. Her kneeling position, echoed by the four smaller surrounding females, is a gesture of supplication, humility, and respect appropriate for the presentation of ritual gifts. The act of holding the breasts, depicted in the smaller kneeling female figures, indicates reverence and generosity in soliciting the god's support (cf. Abiọdun 1976:17; Odugbesan 1969:209).

Devotees of other religions—Christians and especially Muslims—are

PLATE 120. Religious devotion and sacrificial offerings are themes in these headdresses. Left, a kneeling priestess and her supporters; right, warriors encircle an Awori priest of Ogun, who carries a tray containing several closed containers and the head of a citizen of Ọyọ. British Museum, London (1887.2-3.2, 1887.2-3.1).

celebrated in Gẹlẹdẹ masks. Since at least the eighteenth century, Islam has had a widespread and significant impact on Yoruba culture (cf. Adamu 1978:123–134). The first to establish a presence, probably Nupe, Bariba, and Hausa, came as traders. They were followed by craftsmen specializing in clothing, embroidery, and leatherwork, and clerics who taught Arabic, divined, and prepared charms and amulets (Adamu 1978:123–134). Their modes of worship must have fascinated the Yoruba, whose response to Islam probably ranged from curiosity or respect to amusement or criticism. The same mixture of attitudes can be seen in Gẹlẹdẹ arts today, for Muslims are among the most commonly depicted subjects. On the one hand, Yoruba admire northern leatherwork and fabric design, as can be seen in the costuming of Ọrọ Ẹfẹ and of Egungun masquerades. They also respect the Muslims' ability to divine and to prepare protective medicines, as evidenced in the frequent portrayals of leather-encased amulets in Yoruba sculpture. Yoruba, recognizing that different peoples, whether Muslims or Christians, manipulate supernatural forces in their own way, adopted and adapted certain ritual practices to suit their own needs. On the other hand, the Muslims were still "strangers" who did eccentric and sometimes amusing things which could evoke a humorous reaction in Ẹfẹ verse and drummed phrases or in the masks themselves. The precise attitude that inspired particular Gẹlẹdẹ headdresses is lost, but the imagery is informative and reflects the keen observations of Yoruba sculptors.

A Muslim cleric straddling the prow of a canoe while the boatman paddles from the stern floats above the main head in a mask by the master Duga of Mẹkọ (pl. 121). The artist realistically captures some of the dress and ritual paraphernalia of the Muslims—the turban with its snake-like wrapping, the tunic, the trousers, the leather sandals, and the prayer beads, as well as the teapots used to wash before praying. Perhaps this mask makes the comment that a devout Muslim, no matter where he finds himself, even in a boat, must be prepared to perform his ritual obligations at the appropriate time. In another mask (pl. 122), the artist elaborates on the serpentine qualities of the turban wraps by building spiraling cylindrical shapes, and by extending them; he thus encloses and almost overpowers the diminutive, bearded face.

While many of the preceding examples probably rendered tribute to living Gẹlẹdẹ society members and other important groups and personages in the community, some may have served to commemorate the dead. In addition to performing at annual and biennial festivals and special rites for communal disaster, Gẹlẹdẹ glorifies the deceased. As the Osunba of the Ẹgbado Gẹlẹdẹ society, Lagos, explained in a letter to Colonial officials (Beyioku 1943):

PLATE 121. A Muslim cleric, his prayer beads in his hands and his teapots for washing at the sides, sits in the bow of a canoe while his assistant paddles at the stern. Nigerian Museum, Lagos (60.1.15).

PLATE 122. A spiralling, serpentine turban completely envelopes the face of a bearded Muslim cleric. Nigerian Museum, Lagos (60.15.8).

The rituals and ceremonies connected with the cult are regarded as sacred religious funeral rites for the repose of the soul of our beloved dead adherents to which every accredited member of the cult is entitled as of rites at death.

Frequently a pair of special Gẹlẹdẹ masks are commissioned for these funeral performances, often with a figure of the deceased shown in a characteristic activity or attitude. The earliest description of a commemorative headdress is by K. C. Murray (1946). He witnessed a Gẹlẹdẹ performance in Lagos at which masqueraders commemorating the late Chief D. C. Taiwo, Olofin of Iṣeri and founder of the Ẹgbado Gẹlẹdẹ society in Lagos, portrayed him "with looking glasses, snake heads, wheels and figures round a central figure." This general composition persists in more recent commemorative masks from Lagos. One (pl. 123)

PLATE 123. A mask commemorates a famous supporter of the Ketu Gẹlẹdẹ society in Lagos, the former Nigerian Supreme Court Justice G. B. A. Coker. Isalẹ Eko, 1978.

pictures the late G. B. A. Coker, a former Nigerian Supreme Court Justice and staunch supporter of the Ketu Gẹlẹdẹ House, Lagos, wearing his robes and wig. With a wonderfully subtle touch, the artist Kilani Ọlaniyan of Ọta, or perhaps a society member, painted the justice's eyes on the slightly curved surface of his spectacles, producing the distortion of eyes as seen through thick lenses. Another (pl. 124) memorializes the former head of the drummers. The trays on the heads of two female Gẹlẹdẹ show him playing the lead drum, flanked by his two supporting drummers—a scene that faithfully reproduces a Lagos drum ensemble (cf. pl. 70). The inscription on the edges of the trays is a prayer for the sweet repose of the departed. These Gẹlẹdẹ masks are thus similar in intent to the Ẹfẹ songs commemorating deceased individuals.

Other Gẹlẹdẹ masks preserve histories or mythic events and the memory of important personages. The elaborate Gẹlẹdẹ mask in plate 125 consists of two heads united by an intricate composition of snakes, crocodiles, monkeys, tortoises, and humans. Two individuals wear the mask, which concludes the Gẹlẹdẹ festival at sunset. The imagery in this mask involves the history of the Gẹlẹdẹ society among Imala and Idofoi people. Imala people say their ancestors went from Ọyọ-Ile to Ketu and from Ketu to their present sites in northern Ẹgbado (Kilomoninṣẹ 1971; Adelẹye 1971). A political dispute at the capital forced the Alaafin's son, Oki, to flee to Ketu. Oki and his followers remained at Ketu for some time before moving first to Idofa, Mẹkọ, and then to a settlement near the Ọyan River, in the vicinity of Imala. The tutelary deity of Gẹlẹdẹ, Onidofoi, was brought from Ketu, and Agbojo, alias Abọdu, and his wife, Apọtun, were the first priest and priestess to worship the deity at their new home. Agbojo and his successor, Ẹlẹmọ, were said to dress like Muslims while performing the Onidofoi rituals. The name Ẹlẹmọ now refers to the male head of the Gẹlẹdẹ society among Imala/Idofoi people.

Muslims at Ketu, it will be recalled, date to the latter half of the eighteenth century, and by about 1790 they occupied the Maṣafe ward of Ketu. Also in the mid-eighteenth century, according to Mercier (cited in Aṣiwaju 1967:13–14), a mixed Bariba group from Boko in Borgu took over Ṣabẹ and instituted a new ruling dynasty. Evidence of Muslim presence in the Ketu vicinity during the second half of the eighteenth century supports Imala/Idofoi oral traditions, which associate their Gẹlẹdẹ origins with Muslims. With these historical traditions in mind, let us consider the imagery contained in the mask for Onidofoi and the details about it provided by the king of Imala, I. O. Adelẹye.

The two heads in plate 125 represent the first priest and priestess of Onidofoi, Agbojo and Apọtun, who brought the ritual practice from Ketu to the Idofoi forest. The snakes, which form the basic structure of

PLATE 124. A masquerade pair offers verbal and visual praise and blessing by memorializing the former head of the Gẹlẹdẹ drummers. Lagos, 1978.

PLATE 125. This special headdress—two heads joined by an intricate composition of tortoises, reptiles, monkeys, and humans—succinctly recapitulates the history of Imala and Idofoi peoples and of the Gẹlẹdẹ and Onidofoi societies. Imala, 1971.

the elaborate composition, represent the supernatural powers of the deity Onidofoi. They symbolize his vital force. The informant states,

> He controls the snakes. . . . The snakes were biting the crocodiles while they carved the image . . . just to show his [the snake's] ability toward other animals.

The bearded figure in the center represents Ẹlẹmọ. Pointing to Ẹlẹmọ, the king said:

> Whenever we wanted to worship Onidofoi, this man was called upon to go and face him. . . . Now the history I am telling you, if you see anything like [a] lie, there you will be confirmed by pictures. . . . This statue of ẹlẹmọ confirms the history.

The female figures

> are the iyalaṣẹ, the women who worship Onidofoi. They sit before Onidofoi. They represent Apọtun [wife of Agbojo, the first to worship Onidofoi]. They worship with kola nuts and are also called "our mothers."

In the back view of the same mask (pl. 126), one can see another figure of a Muslim, holding a cane and the Koran. His identity and significance were explained in this way:

> The carving of a man with a beard was said to be Sule, the founder of Islam in Imala. He was a member of the Onidofoi [Gẹlẹdẹ] cult during

PLATE 126. The back view of the Onidofoi mask in plate 125 shows the figure of Sule, founder of Islam in Imala, holding a cane and the Koran.

his lifetime and helped to carry this mask to the market so, when they carved it, they had to carve him.

Thus the imagery of the Gẹlẹdẹ mask for Onidofoi contains not merely entertaining or fanciful genre scenes, but specific individuals recorded in historical traditions, figures representative of a female ancestor and the living power of the mothers, and animals that recall the mythic power of the cult's tutelary deity. Its images, in effect, recapitulate the entire history of the cult and the community.

Ridicule

Not all Gẹlẹdẹ images extoll the virtues of the living and departed; some satirize and criticize antisocial elements or enemies in devastating images. A popular topic for derision is the prostitute, *aṣewó* (literally "we do it for money"), a character who also appears in Egungun masquerade performances for the amusement of the assembled crowd (cf. Drewal and Drewal 1978:pl. 9). Prostitutes may sometimes be recognized by the indecorous way they wear their head ties and wrappers (cf. Thompson 1971:ch. 14; Harper 1970:82). Graphic scenes of copulating couples (pl. 127) or indecent actions (pl. 128) condemn improper behavior. The masks project an attitude prevalent in the corpus of Ẹfẹ songs:

> You permitted your penis to enter inside completely
> Even before the lights of the truck had been switched off
> He exposed his testicles' amulet [i.e., penis] out in the open
> Yaya was screwing under the truck
> In the s.o.b.'s presence you said Ṣola had no penis
> Yaya was screwing under the truck
>
> *Ẹ jẹ́ kí nfisí k'okó wọlé tán*
> *Iná ẹ̀hìn sinú mótò*
> *Ẹ jẹ́ kí nsí tíra ẹpọ̀n gbangba*
> *Yàyá nfẹ́ wọn n'ìsàlẹ̀ ọkọ̀*
> *Ni s'ojú s.o.b. lè ṣe npé Ṣọlá ò lokó*
> *Yàyá nfẹ́ wọn n'ìsàlẹ̀ ọkọ̀*
>
> [Collected in Idofoi Quarter, Aiyetoro, 1971]

In addition to condemning inappropriate or antisocial deeds, Gẹlẹdẹ imagery may also impugn the character of enemies or rivals—a kind of psychological warfare in art—as evidenced in documentation obtained for a number of masks in the Musée Ethnographique, Porto Novo, Benin. One of these, reportedly carved by the master Kugbenu of Banigbe, Benin (pl. 129), possesses an enormous superstructure of a monkey in a highly uncomplimentary condition. The indisposed monkey with elephantiasis was said to be the totemic symbol of a group trying to rival

PLATE 127. Ridiculing indiscreet sexual behavior, a mask
surmounted by a copulating couple exposes publicly what
should remain a private matter. Nigerian Museum, Lagos
(65.T.11).

PLATE 128. The sight of a woman boldly displaying her private
parts is particularly shocking since they symbolize secrets of
females that should never be exposed. Museum für
Völkerkunde, Berlin (III C 41146).

the Gẹlẹdẹ society. This mask must have occasioned much merriment on the part of society members and audience, and much embarrassment to those associated with the group being depicted.

Gẹlẹdẹ images of foreigners, non-Yoruba peoples, sometimes fall into the category of caricatures, ridiculing those who may have affected traditional Yoruba culture adversely. Colonial officials are a logical target for such playful statements, as seen in a mask from Igbesa, probably the work of Nuru Akapo (pl. 130). The exaggeration of non-African physical traits and the diminution of the pith helmet burlesque the colonial official. The full, rounded forms that generally characterize Gẹlẹdẹ masks are here sharp and angular, especially the pointed nose and jutting jaw, and yellow pigment creates a sallow complexion that sets off black eyebrows, a feature rarely emphasized in Gẹlẹdẹ images of Africans. The result is a thoroughly comic representation of an outsider as seen through Yoruba eyes.

Muslims also may bear the brunt of sculptors' playful images. Despite their contributions in the realms of fashion, trade, divination, and protective charms and amulets, Muslims deprecated the supposed "idolatry" of *oriṣa* worshippers and aligned themselves with the Colonial regime by serving in the British Police Force, the Hausa Regiment (cf. Smith 1969:173). It was probably this force that confiscated one of the earliest known examples of a Gẹlẹdẹ mask during one of its punitive expeditions in an area near Lagos in the 1860s (cf. Willett 1971:87). For these reasons, and perhaps others, commentary on Muslims in Gẹlẹdẹ was probably not always complimentary.

Cosmological Forces

Images of technical as well as cultural innovations brought by outsiders may appear to be primarily humorous, yet they suggest other, more serious themes as well. Some may, in fact, pay tribute to those who have prospered enough to purchase and master instruments such as bicycles and sewing machines, which then, like guns or a priest's regalia, become status symbols. One mask (pl. 131) depicts a Yoruba man in a pith helmet riding a bicycle, and another (pl. 132) shows a motorcyclist and his passenger (pls. 131, 132) (the masquerader is most appropriately accompanied by a man wearing a motorcycle helmet). A third example (pl. 133) portrays a tailor seated behind his status symbol, the sewing machine. The tailoring profession and sewing machines are now widespread in Nigeria. Notice the attention given to the machine and its parts by the size and details—the spool, wheels, gears, and foot pedal. A marvelous headdress at Lagos depicting a biplane (color plate 9) evidences this same kind of emphasis.

In a larger sense, images of new factors introduced into the Yoruba

PLATE 129. The satiric image of a monkey with elephantiasis pokes fun at a rival group. Musée Ethnographique, Porto Novo (55.9.58).

PLATE 130. Playful images of colonial officials burlesque the pointed nose and chin, eyebrows, complexion, and outlandish headgear of Europeans. British Museum, London (1959 Af 19.114).

PLATE 131. An African wearing a pith helmet and riding a bicycle may communicate ambivalent attitudes: a critique of those who try to imitate European ways and, at the same time, a certain admiration for those who have advanced in a system imposed from the outside. Institute of African Studies, University of Ibadan (64.21).

world (whether persons or objects) comment on social, economic, political, or religious change. Gẹlẹdẹ masks, like the songs of Ẹfẹ, continually evaluate the impact of the new in Yoruba life, impugning the antisocial aspects of prostitution as it praises the social benefits provided by marvelous inventions. And it is precisely the magical quality of these inventions that brings us back to the primary impetus of Gẹlẹdẹ—the honoring of "our mothers," who possess supernatural power.

PLATE 132. A mask depicting a motorcyclist and his passenger playfully honors the man standing by in his motorcycle helmet. Ilaro, 1978.

PLATE 133. A tailor sits behind the symbol of his expertise and profession, a sewing machine, which comments on technological changes and their positive contributions to society. Nigerian Museum, Lagos (60.15.16).

To a traditionally minded Yoruba, machines and their non-African creators possess strange and extraordinary qualities. Some Yoruba believe that these inventions are the result of certain spiritual powers, possessed by their creators, which have been channeled in a positive direction. One knowledgeable elder explained that white men used their powers to invent things, whereas the mothers were likely to use their powers for negative actions (Adelẹyẹ 1971). He reasoned:

> The *ajẹ* [destructive mothers] change into birds and fly at night. If they used that knowledge for good, it might result in the manufacture of airplanes or something of the sort. They can go to Lagos and back in very short minutes. They can see the intestines of someone without slaughtering him; they can see a child in the womb. If they used their power for good, they would be good maternity doctors.

Since the mothers are so frequently linked with birds and other flying creatures, depictions of airplanes on Gẹlẹdẹ as well as Ẹfẹ headdresses seem most appropriate. The visualization of innovations perceived to be the result of "positive *aṣẹ*" constitutes a direct and explicit appeal to the mothers to use their powers in constructive rather than destructive ways.

The concept of competing powers—physical, social, or spiritual—operating in the Yoruba universe is communicated in Gęlędę headdresses with two or more human and/or animal images. Yoruba believe that one's existence in the world is shaped by both heredity and destiny. But through divination one can improve one's lot with proper ritual sacrifices. This ontological system is basically open and fluid. In other words, a person born into a Şango-worshipping lineage may carry on familial ritual obligations but, as a result of divination necessitated by circumstances, may also take up the worship of any other deity or supernatural force, recognizing that his/her well-being is determined by multiple forces, some of which may be in competition with each other. Humans, then, must learn how to understand and manipulate these forces in order to enhance their own lives and those around them.

The fluidity that characterizes religious beliefs and practices also characterizes social organization. Much has been written about the supposed rigid, hierarchical structure of Yoruba society; yet relatively little attention has been given to the mechanisms that level and distribute power and authority, more or less equally. Rules regulating the distribution of a man's estate and the practice of polygamy—the wealthier a man was the more wives and children he had to distribute his wealth to—effectively ensured the equality of siblings (Lloyd 1974:190). Furthermore, titles rotated among several families so that sons could not succeed their fathers in office. In the institution of sacred kingship, for another example, the king makers have sufficient power to force the abdication or execution of a ruler convicted of some serious offense (Morton-Williams 1960). And in the organization of Ęgbado Egungun societies, in which titled elders share and distribute authority, the personalities of specific officeholders may determine the precise locus, or loci, of decision-making power (cf. Drewal and Drewal 1978). Thus, Yoruba social organization may be seen as continually in flux—a situation in which individuals compete for power and prestige on the basis of their innate abilities and the appropriate ritual action. As P. C. Lloyd (1974:190) states, traditional Yoruba social structure is "one in which benefits of power and wealth fall more widely upon the entire community, less exclusively upon the children of those in the eminent positions." It is characterized by a great range of upward and downward mobility. Everyone has an equal opportunity to achieve, given his or her personal destiny and the aid of the gods. These basic philosophical and social truths are vividly recorded in Gęlędę masks.

One Gęlędę mask clearly conveys the notion of social ordering and the balance of powers through composition and iconography (pl. 134). The most important personage is centered and elevated on the crown of the main head, while the two flanking figures are relegated to rectangular platforms at the sides. The central figure's cap and fly whisks (the latter

PLATE 134. The scene of a seated chief with a cap and fly whisk (missing) flanked by two attendants communicates balance, stability, and social order. Ilaro, 1978.

PLATE 135. A warthog devours a snake. Musée d'Ethnographie de Genève (38632).

are missing) signal seniority based on age and leadership. At his sides are attendants; on the left, a guard with his club, belted uniform, and cap; on the right, an assistant with his hand covering a container. Together the three figures evoke a segment of leadership patterning in which a head *(olórí)* is assisted by supporters designated by the terms *òtún* ("right") and *òsì* ("left").[3]

Animals, frequently shown in devouring motifs (pls. 135, 136, 137), are another important means of conveying the concept of competing spiritual and/or social forces, both in animal and human realms. One such example (pl. 136) depicts snakes clutching a porcupine.[4] Occasionally such devouring motifs simply record natural occurrences witnessed by the artist (Adegbolu 1971). However, serpents, aside from their didactic connotations, may also be common in Gẹlẹdẹ headdresses for their plastic qualities—their fluid shapes—as well as their visual similarity to ropes, head ties, and turban wraps. Here the sculptor skillfully adapts the serpents to pun upon the manner in which women wrap cloth upon their heads, just as snakes take the place of turban wraps and crescent moons in some Ọrọ Ẹfẹ headdresses (cf. frontispiece, pl. 33). Yet the Yoruba penchant for metaphors, puns, and other devices in both verbal and visual arts suggests that this and other animal images have broader implications.

Animals are metaphors for different kinds of personalities, roles, statuses, actions, and interactions in human society. As such, they occur frequently in proverbs and other aphorisms. A drum rhythm, discussed earlier, uses the allusion of a moth fatally flying into the light, in order to comment on dancers who try to outshine the drummers, only to exhaust themselves. In visual form proverbs about animals appear in Gẹlẹdẹ headdresses. Snakes are among the most frequently depicted animals, and one mask with a serpent coiled on the head cautions vigilance with the saying, "It may be true the snake sleeps but he continues to see" (Drewal 1974b:pl. 10). Snakes seizing and being seized by other animals (cf. pls. 125, 126, 135, 136, 137, 138) explicitly communicate competing powers. They recall the Yoruba proverb "We kill a snake when we find it without its companions" (Abraham 1958:152), which warns people to deal carefully with those who are dangerous or powerful, an allusion already analyzed in an Ẹfẹ song. In this mask, two snakes seize a porcupine. Porcupines, because of their voracious appetites and slow, sluggish movement, are sometimes a metaphor for gluttonous or selfish persons. A headdress depicting a plump porcupine devouring a corn cob conveys something of this creature's greed (cf. pl. 50). Such antisocial behavior eventually leads to trouble, which is just what has happened to this porcupine caught by the two snakes.

Another headdress (pl. 138), probably a wild pig, by its long snout

PLATE 136. Two snakes seize a porcupine, metaphorically acknowledging competing forces operating in the world. British Museum, London (1942 Af 7.6).

PLATE 137. A bird attacks a snake. Museum für Völkerkunde,
Berlin (III C 41133).

PLATE 138. A series of motifs depicting devouring—a pig seizes
a monkey, who in turn seizes corn, while a snake grasps a
tortoise in its mouth—literally conveys a pecking order and
symbolizes the competing forces in the Yoruba cosmos. Institute
of African Studies, University of Ibadan (6628).

and protuberances, provides several devouring themes: pig devours monkey, who devours corn, and, on top, snake devours tortoise. Since all these depictions are unlikely, except for the monkey eating the corn, supernatural forces may be implied.

Animals shown outside the context of devouring compositions communicate a variety of messages. Some are associated with the mothers or with certain divinities. One distinctive masquerade type, a large hollowed-out tree trunk carved in the form of an enormous gorilla, or Ogede, is said to be associated with Odua, the Earth Goddess (Thompson, personal communication, 1974). One version of Ogede (pl. 139) displays awesome power in the bared teeth, gaping mouth, massive torso, pendulous breasts, and outstretched arms and hands—images from the realm of nature that are then synthesized with elements of culture, a white necklace and bracelet, to evoke the theme of transformation seen in the nocturnal mother masks. At Ibara, Abẹokuta, another Ogede carries its immensity to extremes (pl. 140). Enormous arms and hands extend more than ten feet on both sides of a large open-mouthed animal, whose ferocity is heightened by rows of flashing teeth and pointed canines as well as a cluster of bristling spikes on the snout. Both of these masks come out during Gẹlẹdẹ dance performances.

Birds, especially night birds, are among the most pervasive symbols associated with the mothers, since they are the form the mothers are believed to assume on their nocturnal voyages. The *àgbògbò/àgbìgbò*, a large-headed bird who frequently appears in Ifa divination poetry as an agent of supernatural force and a harbinger of disaster, is one of these (pls. 141, 142). According to several Ifa legends, *agbogbo's* distinctive tuft of hair resulted from certain treacherous acts. In one tale he carved a coffin and carried it about on his head, setting it down in front of the house of those he intended to kill. One day he arrived at the house of his father, Ọrunmila. Outside he met Ẹṣu, who found out what sacrifices were necessary to avert death and informed Ọrunmila, who made the proper offerings and survived. Because of his treachery, *agbogbo* was cursed by Ẹṣu. The coffin on his head stuck and became the tuft of hair (Abimbọla 1976:211–213). Thus, *agbogbo*, an infamous character in Ifa literature, reminds us that only proper rituals and sacrifices can ward off bad fortune, just as Gẹlẹdẹ turns the potentially destructive powers of the mothers to the benefit of the community. Another bird (pl. 143) grasps its prey, a mudfish, in its long beak while under its broad wings it shelters its young; it is a powerful metaphor for mothers who must devour in order to protect their children.

Flora is extremely rare in Yoruba art yet is present in a number of Gẹlẹdẹ headdresses. We have already seen one example (cf. pl. 30) in an Ẹfẹ mask showing an *agbe* tree laden with fruit, a snake, and birds—a

PLATE 139. A body mask in the form of Ogede, the Gorilla, combines animal teeth, paws, and human features. Kẹsan Orile, 1971.

PLATE 140. Another Gorilla of surreal proportions flashes his ferocious canine teeth and stretches out his arms and gigantic hands as if he is ready to pounce on a victim. Abẹokuta, 1978.

PLATE 141. The hornbill, an infamous character in Ifa divination literature, serves as a reminder that only proper rituals and sacrifices can ward off bad fortune. British Museum, London (1942 Af 7.11).

PLATE 142. The distinctive features of the hornbill persist despite a different stylistic treatment by the artist. Bernisches Historisches Museum (60).

PLATE 143. A bird grasps a mudfish in her beak and
simultaneously conceals her young under her wings, evoking
two dimensions of the mothers' powers. Musée d'Ethnographie
de Genève (33308).

combination of motifs that points to the probable reason for flora depictions in Gęlędę. Birds, i.e., the mothers transformed, rest in trees, and
spirits of trees, especially *iroko* and *apa,* are companions of the mothers.
References to them recur in the songs of Ęfę night as well as in the
creation of the images of the nocturnal mothers. Other plants (pls. 144,
145) may have other symbolic associations. The plantain tree is associated
with Aráágbó (literally "Being from the Bush"), the tutelary deity of
special spirit children *(àbíkú),* who are born to die, that is, born into the
world only to return shortly thereafter to the spirit realm. The plantain
tree is planted at Araagbo's shrine, and its phallic fruit is favored by
children because it is sweet. In other masks, the depiction of the forest is
used to evoke the realm of operation of hunters (pls. 77, 108, 109).
Whether connoting the meeting places of the bird mothers, the tree
spirits, the shrines for deities, or the realms of hunters and others, flora
invokes a domain beyond human society, one inhabited by the gods,
spirits, and the mothers.

The enormous diversity of Gęlędę visual imagery can be said to

PLATE 144. Although they are infrequently represented in Gẹlẹdẹ masks, plants, such as the plaintain stalk, suggest the realm of spirits, in this case, the shrine of Araagbo, the deity of spirit children. Nigerian Museum, Lagos (58.15.8a).

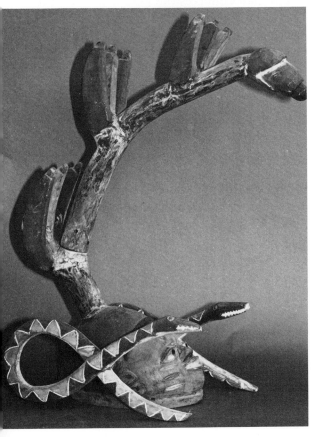

PLATE 145. Another mask with a plaintain stalk projecting from the top also has snakes flanking the face. British Museum, London (1942 Af 7.24).

evaluate everything that exists—women, men, ancestors, gods, animals, plants, and objects—within the purview of the mothers, the "owners of the world," in terms of their influence on the living, who are the "children of the mothers." Roles and personages seen as contributing to the stability and cohesion of Yoruba society are celebrated, while those detrimental to the community are exposed and derided in devastating images. Competing forces operating in the Yoruba cosmos, whether religious or social, are evoked in scenes of multiple human figures or animals in devouring motifs. Similar imagery may also serve didactic functions as visualized proverbs, histories, or myths. Thus, the heritage of the past is preserved and asserted, and at the same time positive innovations are encouraged and incorporated. All these ideas are meant to honor and please the mothers. Having created appropriate images and performed the necessary rites, the living dwell secure in the belief that as long as they continue to act according to accepted norms, they will receive the benefits of the mothers' power channeled to positive ends.

Afternoon Mother Masquerades

The survey and analysis of Gẹlẹdẹ masks above include all masquerade types except one—the one that climaxes the performances, thus signifying the success of these propitiatory spectacles. It synthesizes goddess, ancestress, and priestess, in effect epitomizing the mothers. This closing masquerade possesses many of the same qualities as the nocturnal mother masquerades, yet the mask, costume, dance, music, and song as well as the setting of the afternoon mothers convey different dimensions, other potentials of the spiritual powers of women with regard to their children, the society.

The afternoon mother masquerades, which seem to be most common in northern and central Ẹgbado areas, represent the community's deified ancestress or tutelary deity and simultaneously her representative among the living, her priestess. Throughout this area, she is intimately linked with the origins of the people, their migrations into the area, and the accounts of their settling on the land. Legends collected in Ẹgbado usually mention both progenitors and the gods they brought with them, the two often becoming one in these accounts.[5] The foremother, usually barren, is told by Ifa that she and her husband must search for a new site if she is to bear children. The story traces the journey to their destination, a site often designated by the presence of life-giving water or some other propitious sign. Their arrival at the appointed site heralds the birth of many children. The town prospers, and the founding mother, keeper of the secret of childbirth, becomes, along with her own deity and the land or river itself, the spiritual focus of all women seeking children. The ancestress and goddess become one in the minds of the descendants. It is she who personifies "the mothers" and is honored at the finale of many Gẹlẹdẹ rituals. Just before dusk, surrounded by the community, her masquerade moves to the performance area to signal the end of the Gẹlẹdẹ festival (pl. 13).

The mother masqueraders in a number of Ẹgbado communities present the same themes as do the nocturnal mothers, but some attributes have diminished while others have increased in importance, and still others convey new messages and meanings. At Igan Okoto, tradition claims that a warrior named Ajade led a group of people from Ọyọ to Ẹgbado during the reign of Alaafin Abiọdun (c. 1775–1790), after which they began to perform Gẹlẹdẹ (Oke 1971; Ọlatibosun 1971; Ajibọla 1971; Owolẹyẹ 1971). Ajade's wife, Ọlẹyọ Ejide, progenitor of Igan Okoto people, is identified with a nearby stream. She is also called Iya Olọmọ, "Mother-of-Many-Children," because people "consulted her during her lifetime in order to conceive." Toward the close of the Gẹlẹdẹ dance in late afternoon, Ọlẹyọ emerges from her shrine by the stream where the people first settled. She walks in slow, stately fashion toward the crowded market in the center of the town as children wave branches and sing, "Our Mother, Mother of Many Children is coming" (*Ìyá wá, Ìyá Olọmọ mbọ̀*). The masquerader's ensemble contains a number of important elements that associate Ọlẹyọ Ejide with the most popular water goddess in the vicinity, Yẹmọja. The colors blue, yellow, and especially white predominate, and the blue tips of her breasts recall Yẹmọja's praise, "Mother-of-Moist-Nipples" (Verger 1957:297). Red feathers placed in the head tie are supreme symbols of the mystical powers of the mothers,[6] for they are termed "the cloth of the [female] elders" (*aṣọ agbalagba*) and refer to the power of transformation attributed to these women. These feathers are powerful ingredients that activate medicine and are sold in the market at high prices by elderly women (Akinfẹnwa 1978).

The same red parrot feathers are carved on a pair of masks representing Yẹmọja and her priestess, which conclude Gẹlẹdẹ festivals in the Ẹgbado quarter of Ibara, Abẹokuta (Ọbajia 1978) (pl. 146). White cotton wool depicting hair in these Abẹokuta mother masks, and the whiteness of Ọlẹyọ evoke the cool, covert feminine powers possessed by the eldest and wisest females, i.e., those with white hair. The double iron rattle, or *ààjà*, an essential ritual implement used by female heads in Gẹlẹdẹ and priestesses of Yẹmọja, rings out "so be it" (*aṣẹ, aṣẹ*), as the people sing and pray.

At the neighboring town of Jọga there is a similar mother masquerade (pl. 147). Jọga's ancestor, Ọbalaju, is said to be an Ọyọ prince

PLATE 146. Left, a mask of Iya
Yẹmọja with red parrot feathers
(the "cloth of elderly women")
crowning the head represents the
divinity and her priestess
simultaneously. Right, an Ẹfẹ mask
has a billed cap. Abẹokuta, 1978.

PLATE 147. An afternoon mother
masquerade, Iju Ejide, with white
hair and a ritual pot blends images
of ancestress, priestess, and deity.
Jọga, 1971.

and hunter who migrated to Ẹgbado together with the founders of Iṣaga, Ibeṣe, and Ilaro—three brothers by the same mother. They settled in their various locations and shortly thereafter returned to Ọyọ to defend it against Fulani attacks, which Ajayi and Smith (1964:64) suggest was circa 1825–1840. Ọbalaju and his wife, Iju Ejide, associated with a nearby stream named in her honor, are deities; the mother mask at Jọga represents her (Adeṣina 1971). Her appearance, like that of Ọlẹyọ and Yẹmọja, climaxes the final afternoon of the Gẹlẹdẹ festival. Again certain themes persist: her slow, stately movement, giving the impression of age, an impression made explicit by the white cotton hair attached to the mask, the colors yellow and blue, the large white cloth about her torso, and the double rattle on her lap. Two important iconic features are added in this mother image: the pot on her head and the large cylindrical ear plugs. The pot is a ritual vessel (*ọtùn*) for carrying sacred water from her stream. The ear plugs, a former fashion of Yoruba women, suggest the past, the founding mother, and ancient ritual regalia. This regalia blends ancestress, priestess, and deity into one image.

Not far from Jọga-Orilẹ, in the town of Imaṣai, elaborate Gẹlẹdẹ performances also conclude with the mother's appearance (pl. 13). Imaṣai people say they migrated from Ọyọ through Aro Ketu, stopping at a number of places on the way before settling at their present site. The original forefather, Ojuọla, was a son of Oluaṣo, the eighth Alaafin of Ọyọ, who left Ọyọ on the advice of a diviner because none of his wives could conceive. They followed the Yẹwa River, where they made sacrifices, and the wives began to bear children. Finally, they settled near a dense forest known as Aginju, where they met a woman they supposed was a spirit (*àlìjọnú*). She wore a white wrapper and drew water from the Iju River. The woman called herself Iju, and at every Gẹlẹdẹ festival she would dance last. After her death, whenever there was a Gẹlẹdẹ festival, a masquerader would represent her. Slowly, with great dignity, the mother mask comes from the river. Surrounded by her "children," mother Iju blesses and protects the community. Cool white is her only color, except for small blue dots over her face, headdress, and nipples.[7] Snakes lie coiled on her head as she shakes a double iron bell in benediction.[8]

In a final example at Ilu Ata Quarter, Ilaro, the mother Iya Odua is linked with earth rather than water. Her home is Itolu, a small village west of Ilaro considered to be the oldest settlement in the area and the site of the central Odua shrine. Her performance on the final day of the festival is strikingly similar to that of the other mothers of Ẹgbado. Iya Odua comes at dusk, her white attire shining in the growing darkness (pl. 148). She moves with measured tread toward the main market, shaking the *aaja* rattle at regular intervals. Her priestesses, the Iyalaja and Ọtun

PLATE 148. Iya Odua comes at dusk with her white attire
shining in the waning light. Ilaro, 1978.

Iyalaja, accompany her. Their appearance, identical to that of the ancestral priestess masquerade, visually unites spiritual and earthly realms.[9]

Taken as a group, these afternoon mother masquerades share some traits with the night mothers. But their portrayal of women's powers accentuates the positive, creative elements and minimizes the destructive aspects. As with the nocturnal mothers, slow, stately movement communicates age and thus the wisdom and extraordinary power of elderly women who reign as the "gods of society." Whiteness persists in all mother manifestations as an expression of the covertness and cool demeanor of the inner heads of women and the ritual purity of their post-menopausal state. In addition, white hair conveys unusual longevity, in itself evidence of supernatural capabilities. Yet here the similarities end. In linking the afternoon masquerades with their progenitor, the community stresses its biological link with its mother and invokes the regenerative powers that have produced and sustained the community. The accompanying songs ring with joyous praises of "Mother-of-Many-Children," in sharp contrast to the fearsome nocturnal references to the "One-Who-Killed-Her-Husband-to-Take-a-Title." Missing too are the visual references to awesome power—the extraordinary beard or the blood red beak. Here in the light of day and in full view, the entire community, children and elders, women and men, crowd around the creative, protective mother. She symbolically adds her own impressive life force and blesses her "children" with her sacred rattle, which sounds the critical blessing of *aṣẹ, aṣẹ, aṣẹ* ("so be it, may it come to pass"). The deified ancestral priestess thus basks in the warmth of her children's respect and devotion. Her appearance assures them that the lavish spectacles have successfully "pampered" the mothers and convinced them to use their powers for the benefit of society.

Conclusion

There is little in the Yoruba world that is not visualized in Gẹlẹdẹ masks, for Gẹlẹdẹ honors and serves the "gods of society" by evaluating the state of the world through visual praise, humor, or ridicule. The images in Gẹlẹdẹ headdresses are concerned with the present, the "happenings" involving individuals and groups in the community, as do Ẹfẹ songs. This present, however, is viewed in terms of the past, the accumulated wisdom and precepts of the ancestors, as well as the eternal presence of the supernatural—all realms that the mothers influence. This concern with society, with humanity, is graphically shown (even when alluded to in animal motifs) in the primary form of a person's head, the "inner head." Whether male or female, it is the site of a person's spiritual essence, destiny, and potential. The "outer head" can reveal a person's character or nature as much as it can conceal it. Thus by simply depicting coiffures, fashions, and body arts, or by creating complicated tableaux on these carved heads, the artist comments on the individual's essence, which is then carried into the midst of the assembled community for evaluation. In this way, the visual arts contribute to the shaping of culture as they express the attitudes of the owners of the world. Thus, one finds extremely complex compositions in the mask superstructures; layers upon layers of head wraps, which convincingly document female patronage; multiple iron ankle rattles; and whisks symbolizing heredity. The richness of the resulting ensemble, the layers of meaning, are conceived not merely for dramatic effect but for spiritual efficacy. In the presence of the mothers, the elements of the masquerade ensemble, separately and collectively endowed with force, compel the maintenance of human values. This maintenance is not merely a social function of Gẹlẹdẹ, for from a Yoruba point of view Gẹlẹdẹ has the metaphysical power to make its visual and musical assertions come to pass in the world.

7

A Historical and Thematic Overview

If we are to comprehend the full significance of Gẹlẹdẹ as an artistic phenomenon, we must examine not only the cultural beliefs, concepts, and performances associated with it but also the historical factors that have shaped and continue to shape it. In particular, we will address the following questions: What situations or conditions might have precipitated Gẹlẹdẹ? If the belief in women's mystical powers is pan-Yoruba, as we contend, why is Gẹlẹdẹ found only in western Yorubaland—that is, in the area approximately from Ṣabẹ in the north down to the coast, bordered on the west by the Ọhọri and on the east by the Ẹgbado?[1] And how and why did Gẹlẹdẹ spread to places such as Sierra Leone, Cuba, and Brazil?

It seems fairly certain that the history of the Ọyọ Empire, its political and economic power, and its expansionist policies during the eighteenth century had direct bearing on the spread of the Ṣango and Egungun cults throughout much of Yorubaland (cf. Lawal 1970; Law 1977:43–44, 104, 139–140). Likewise, the nonimperialistic histories of the Igbomina, Ekiti, and Ijẹbu kingdoms explain, at least in part, the limited dispersal of the Ẹpa/Ẹlẹfon and the Magbo/Ekine masquerades in these respective areas. The history of western Yoruba peoples lies somewhere between these two extremes, and, when viewed in relation to Gẹlẹdẹ oral traditions, evidence in the art forms themselves can inform us about the historical development and meaning of this institution. Taken together, these data provide an overview of Gẹlẹdẹ and suggest why it is found principally in western Yorubaland.

Among the dominant themes in Gẹlẹdẹ masks, costumes, and songs, wherever Gẹlẹdẹ is performed in western Yorubaland, are those of marketwomen (pls. 110–114); foreigners, especially Hausas or other Muslims, and Europeans (pls. 98, 99, 114, 121, 122, 125, 126, 130); and foreign trade goods, e.g., sewing machines (pl. 133), bicycles (pl. 131) and motorcycles (pl. 132). These themes have a common link to the marketing network, an economic system well established by the mid-eighteenth century.

Western Yorubaland

Located largely between two major rivers, the Weme and the Ogun, western Yorubaland is a relatively flat territory of low elevation and fertile soil (see map p. xxiv). Its northern portion is savannah grassland with some open forests. An area of thick vegetation, black clay soil known as *lama,* and a generally inaccessible marshland (Kumi) separate the northern and southern sections. Dry open forest extends southward to the coastal plain. Ample water and sufficient drainage are provided by a lagoon network and numerous streams and rivers, especially the Yẹwa, which runs north and south through the center of the area inhabited by the Ẹgbado (literally the "Ẹgba-of-the-Water").

The forests, rivers, and soil of western Yorubaland made it attractive for hunting and farming, activities frequently mentioned in migration stories of Ketu and Ọyọ peoples collected in Ẹgbado area. Its generally open, level terrain permitted easy access and travel in most places, with the important exception of the swamps south of Ketu. Because of its location between the Atlantic Ocean and the interior and its level country, western Yorubaland became an important corridor for trade for both Africans and non-Africans.

Of all the subgroups in western Yorubaland, perhaps the most prominent historically is Ketu. Ketu's antiquity in Yoruba mythology is well established (Johnson 1973 [1921]:7–8), yet its significance as a political and cultural entity has been eclipsed by that of Ọyọ, because of Ọyọ's political and economic expansion in the seventeenth and eighteenth centuries (Akinjogbin 1965; 1966a; 1966b; and Law 1977). Well-documented king lists suggest Ketu origins in the fourteenth century, yet with its territory extending eastward only to the Yẹwa River, the subgroup remained relatively small (cf. Parrinder 1967). Despite the hegemony of Ọyọ, Ketu was almost certainly autonomous until the latter part of the nineteenth century (Atanda 1973:11–12).[2]

Ketu as well as Ọyọ accounts recognize the seniority of Ketu people and their origins at Ile-Ifẹ, for the second child of Oduduwa's eldest son, Okanbi, gave birth to the mother of Alaketu, who was accorded the right to possess crowns (Johnson 1973 [1921]:7–8). Ketu preeminence is also supported by Ẹgba traditions, some of which recognize the Alaketu as "father" or senior to the Ẹgbas' progenitor, the Alake. Other traditions record their joint and ancient migrations from Ile-Ifẹ, and Ketu Yoruba traditions link the title Alake with an important marketplace at Ketu (Ajiṣafe 1964:10; Losi 1924:2 cited in Parrinder 1967:7; Biobaku 1957:3). Even migration legends of the Aja (Popo) of Benin (R.P.B.) and Ewe of Togo mention Ketu as a place along their migration routes (Bertho 1949:121–132). Ketu's preeminence in western Yoruba history is central to the history of Gẹlẹdẹ masquerading.

It is also via Ketu that the Islamic impact on western Yorubaland became evident. Muslims were probably in this area and further south by the late seventeenth century (Adamu 1978:113). At Ketu, Muslims date to the latter half of the eighteenth century, and by 1790 they played an important role in defending the town (Parrinder 1967:41). The introduction of Islam is a key factor in assessing Gẹlẹdẹ history, for there are many references to Muslims in Gẹlẹdẹ oral traditions and in the performance and, what is perhaps more significant, in the style and form of certain costumes.

Another major cultural factor operating in western Yoruba country was the expansion of the Ọyọ Empire (cf. Law 1977). Ọyọ's initial influence in the Ketu Yoruba area resulted from its first trade routes to the coast, which passed west of Ketu territory through Abomey and Aja/Fon country to outlets at Whydah and Allada in the seventeenth century. This corridor to the coast shifted to the eastern edge of the Ketu kingdom during the reign of Alaafin Abiọdun, circa 1774–1789 (Law 1977:89). As a result, during the last quarter of the eighteenth century, Ọyọ immigrant towns were established farther south, along the eastern boundary of Ketu, what is today Ẹgbado and Anago territory, in order to control Ọyọ's trade route to Porto Novo and Badagri on the coast (Morton-Williams 1964a; Law 1977:94–95). Probably one reason for this particular location of the trade route was the natural barrier created by the Kumi swamp running east to west midway between Ketu and the coast, but another was Ketu's ancient territorial claims and its probable alliance with Ọyọ (Atanda 1973:11–12). Although the Ọyọ route was established principally for the slave trade, it seems fairly reasonable that local traders profited from the increased traffic through the area. According to Law (1977:307),

> It seems likely, indeed, that participation in the slave trade acted as a stimulus to local trade and manufacturing. It is sometimes suggested that the Atlantic trade was essentially a state-managed sector which had no direct links with the domestic economy, and it is certainly the case that the slave trade tended to be dominated by a small number of large-scale entrepreneurs, normally the political and military chiefs, with the mass of the population unable to participate directly. Perhaps the only opportunity for ordinary people to benefit directly from the slave trade was in the supply of foodstuffs to trading caravans. . . . But

the Atlantic trade yielded a greater variety of imported goods, and in particular masses of cowry shells for currency. Much of the trade goods and cowries which the chiefs received in return for their slaves was not consumed or hoarded within the chiefly households, but was exchanged for local products, thus spreading the wealth from the Atlantic trade more widely. It is, it may be suggested, not merely a reflection of the point of view of the Ọyọ chiefs that the reign of *Alafin* Abiọdun, the peak of Ọyọ involvement in the Atlantic slave trade, was remembered as a time of great wealth, and more specifically as a time when cowries were abundant.

For a time then, perhaps between 1770 and 1820, western Yorubaland enjoyed prosperity under the stabilizing presence of Ọyọ and Ketu. Agriculture prospered (Aṣiwaju 1976:22), and an extensive trade network leading from the coast far north to Hausaland and Borgu, as well as eastward to Ijẹbu and Benin and westward to Abomey and Asante, traversed the territory (cf. Morton-Williams 1969:83–84; Aṣiwaju 1976:23; and Law 1977:211–228).[3]

This era came to an end, however, for the nineteenth century ushered in a long and painful period of warfare and disruption. The area became a battleground for the armies of the Dahomey from the west; the Ẹgba, Ibadan, and Ijaye from the east; and the Gun from the southeast (Aṣiwaju 1976:26, 31). Unable to forge effective alliances, towns were destroyed; people were forced to flee; and trade was disrupted until the 1880s, when, for economic reasons, the French and British asserted themselves.

The establishment of European rule was first regarded as "an act of liberation" by the peoples of western Yorubaland, since it effectively stopped the depredations of both Dahomey and the Ẹgba (Aṣiwaju 1976:39). Peace and trade were restored to the area. Later, however, certain aspects of Colonial rule, in particular conscription policies instituted by the French during World War I, caused a great deal of unrest. Many Yoruba in Dahomey protested these policies vigorously. They migrated eastward to establish new communities or join older ones in the western Yoruba areas in the British territory of Nigeria (Aṣiwaju 1976:141–143), bringing their cultural institutions with them, including Gẹlẹdẹ.

The enormous political, economic, and social changes that occurred in western Yorubaland, together with the varied origins of its peoples, have produced a complex and often fluid cultural situation. Some of these cultural traits are shared with other Yoruba areas, some are variants, and others appear to be unique to western Yoruba groups. It is our thesis that it was during this relatively brief period of great prosperity, with the movements of people, goods, and new ideas along the trade route, that Gẹlẹdẹ as spectacle spread throughout western Yorubaland. The trade corridor corresponds loosely to Gẹlẹdẹ's boundaries. It produced a large influx of immigrants, especially from Ọyọ, and many new trading settlements. With the trade route also came many foreigners (Hausa, Bariba, Fulani, and others), traders, and palace officials from Ọyọ, as well as slaves, who penetrated the entire area as they had when the trade outlet was at Whydah (Adamu 1978:113–114). At the local level, the people who would have profited most from the increased traffic would have been the marketwomen. In 1826, Clapperton (1829:21) observed wives of the Alaafin of Ọyọ "in every place trading" and "like other women of the common class, carrying large loads on their heads from town to town." The subsequent rapid economic decline of the area and the upheavals of war seem to have limited the spread of Gẹlẹdẹ.

Gẹlẹdẹ Oral Traditions

Oral traditions throughout Ẹgbado suggest that Gẹlẹdẹ originated among the Ketu Yoruba.[4] This may explain why performances are more highly structured in the Ketu area and why observable distinctions between male and female Gẹlẹdẹ are much more clear-cut and consistent with the distinctions described by informants throughout western Yorubaland. One group of Ẹgbado people in particular—those of Imala/Idofoi—not only attribute Gẹlẹdẹ to a Ketu origin but also link it with the introduction of Islam into the area, in the mid- to late eighteenth century.[5] If these accounts are accurate, then, the introduction of Gẹlẹdẹ into Ẹgbado area would appear to be fairly late, i.e., the latter part of the eighteenth century. Given the number of towns that point to Ketu as the source of Gẹlẹdẹ, it is therefore surprising and, we think, significant to find that testimony in the city of Ketu itself and its vicinity identifies the town of Ilobi as the place of origin.

Ilobi traditions, which say the town was founded by a member of one of Ketu's royal houses, traces a long history in the area now called Ẹgbado (Petition 1932; Fọlayan 1967:15–16). One knowledgeable Ketu elder (Ogundipẹ 1971) explained: "Gẹlẹdẹ came from Ilobi . . . Gẹlẹdẹ belongs to Ilobi. . . . Anytime Gẹlẹdẹ is done Abiọdun will be honored because he was the founder [of Gẹlẹdẹ at Ketu]." Another (Taiwo 1971) confirmed this account and sought to explain the prominence of Ketu in Gẹlẹdẹ histories:

> That is so how Gẹlẹdẹ started. . . . The one who had interest in entertainment went to Ilobi to collect it. He went to see the wisdom of Gẹlẹdẹ. . . . When many people say Ketu is the home of Gẹlẹdẹ, our father went to Ilobi to bring it. It is only that the glory belongs to Ketu.

It is just as if a person is an apprentice and, after years of apprentice-ship, he is set free; and sometimes he becomes more popular than his master. It is from Ketu that Gẹlẹdẹ spread to Idọfa, Imẹkọ, and many other places.

Ogundipẹ (1971) added, "Even though Ilobi is a small town, yet it is there that Olọrun [God] ordered Gẹlẹdẹ to start, and they made leg rattles from brass." This tradition is preserved in the following song:

> Children of Ilobi, the ones who own brass o
> They are strikers of brass against brass, Ilobi o
>
> Ọmọ Ilobì l'oniidẹ o
> Ẹ ilùdẹ ludẹ e e Ilobì o

The same verse was cited by the king of Pobe (Odu 1973) and is said to be a song from a divination text linking Ilobi, brass, and Gẹlẹdẹ.

The above evidence was repeated and expanded by Father Thomas Moulero (1970), a native of Ketu and historian of his people.[6] Moulero believed that Gẹlẹdẹ is closely linked with Alaketu Adebiya of the Mefu royal line, who reigned circa 1816–1853, and that its origin was at Ilobi.[7] He provided some elaborate oral traditions to support this assertion. One myth says that "when Alaketu Akibiohu [Akebioru, circa 1780–1795] died fate chose Ẹdun." Moulero identifies Ẹdun, a name given to the second born of twins, as Adebiya. Ẹdun's twin brother, Akan, wishing to rule, plotted to kill him. On the advice of a friend, Adebiya fled to Isalẹ. As Akan prepared to pursue him there, Adebiya was warned and fled to Ilobi. There he prepared the following ruse: He quickly gathered many snail shells and strung them together on two long cords, which he then tied to posts placed on both sides of the path leading to his hiding place. Between these two strings of shells he placed a large trunk on which he had sculpted the face of a man. For clothing he encircled the wood with dry banana leaves. Then he took a piece of calabash, carved it in the form of a mask, painted it white with kaolin, and put it on the head of the figure.[8] When he had finished preparing the trap, he called his followers together and taught them this song:

> Strikers of brass against brass
> People of Ilobi
> It is Ilobi that possesses brass
>
> Afoudè loudè
> Ero Ilobì
> Ilobì ni icholoudè[9]

On the fourth night Akan and his followers came to Ilobi. When Adebiya heard them, he pulled the cords. The noise so frightened the attackers, they fled and vowed never to return. Adebiya returned to Ketu and the throne. Later, people of Isalẹ went to learn how Adebiya had tricked his brother. Adebiya instructed them and said they must use the trick only at night, that it was *ọrọ ẹfẹ*, a "joke," and that its name was *Olóku-ajàró-òkòtó*, which means "man of the sea who fought with the sound of snail shells."[10] Isalẹ thus began to dance at night as instructed by Adebiya. It was much later that people began to dance during the day. This myth and song, therefore, suggest a specific historical period (sometime after the death of Alaketu Akebioru, circa 1795, and before the reign of Alaketu Adebiya, beginning circa 1816), a place of origin (Ilobi), and certain Gẹlẹdẹ ritual elements (nocturnal ruse, costume, white-faced mask, rattles, and song).

Moulero (1970:24–26) also collected an Ẹfẹ song of self-assertion in which the singer claims authenticity by singing that he has come from Ilobi:[11]

> Bringer of the dance, I come from the Ilobi area
> Welcome the dancer
> Tell him your last meeting with him was long ago
> I am a spark of fire
> One cannot put me in a wrapper [cloth]
> Here I am, I the most excellent dancer
> I know very well how to be the Ọrọ-Ẹfẹ
> All of you approach me [come close to me]
> It is from Ilobi that I come. It is truly from
> Ilobi that the Gẹlẹdẹ dancer comes
> I hear your voice Opẹrẹ
> And I come to greet you
> I cannot wait, dancer's escort [or one inside the masquerade]
> Child of Ọjẹ, masquerader of the king
> I could not sing until tomorrow afternoon
> Acclaim loudly
> Sobulu the dancer's escort [or one inside the masquerade]
> I will tell you a wonderful history
> Here I am, I have arrived
> Opẹrẹ has come, the performer, child of Ọjẹ
> Don't my leg rattles sound beautiful?
> I the wonderful joker, the one with reverberating leg rattles, I dance
>   majestically
>
> *Iha Ilobi ni nti mbọ*
> *A ṣeri ijo*
> *Ẹ ṣe awu li barika, ku ijó*
> *Ṣinṣin iná ni mi*

Nko ṣe fu'nu aṣo
Aṣeri ijó de
A mọ ṣe ọrọ-èfè
Ẹ māa sun mọ mi
Iha Ilobi l'awo nti mbọ wa
Ngbọ ariwo iwọ Okpèrè
A ni nya ki yin ni
Ika le duro, atọkun
Ọmọ Ọjè, Egun Ọba
Nka eha mo n d'ọsan ọla
Ẹ māa hó yeye
Sobulu bu Egue
Ngo sọ'tan kan fun yin
K'ẹ yẹ ẹ wo
Okpẹrẹ de, atọkun, ọmọ Ọjẹ
Ki nro wewe
Oliku yeye njo.

Thus Moulero traces the spread of Gẹlẹdẹ from Ilobi.

At a small town only a few miles from Ketu, named Ofia, Moulero
was told that an Ẹdun (not the same as Adebiya) went to Ilobi to learn the
art of Gelede after being granted permission by Alaketu Adebiya. But for
a long time, Ofia was only allowed to "rent" the necessary equipment at
an exorbitant rate. It was not until the French capture of Abomey in 1894
that Ọga Oluguna of Ofia was able to obtain the necessary paraphernalia
at Ika, another small town formerly in the Ketu kingdom, some 30 miles
south (Moulero 1970:27). Information collected at Ofia (Idowu 1971)
supports part of Moulero's account, for it was said that Gẹlẹdẹ was
brought to Ofia from Ilobi by Alareọdẹ Faṣeti at an unspecified time.

At Idahin, also a few miles from Ketu, Moulero was told that one
"Adjalla," originally from Ilobi, went to his hometown with others to ask
permission to start Gẹlẹdẹ at Idahin. After his death, Ajala was buried
where the drums are played during Gẹlẹdẹ festivals. Moulero (1970:29)
was not able to obtain a date for the introduction of Gẹlẹdẹ at Idahin;
however, our own information from Idahin (field notes 1971) essentially
corroborates Moulero and adds a time perspective. We know that the
Dahomean army under Gezo attacked and destroyed Idahin around February 1860.[12] The event is preserved in the oral traditions of Idahin, and
an elder said, "Ajala Aradahin [Ajala of Idahin] brought Gẹlẹdẹ from
Ilobi. We did Gẹlẹdẹ about forty years before the Dahomeans attacked
Idahin." This information suggests that Gẹlẹdẹ existed at Idahin about
1820.

Ilobi itself provides additional yet inconclusive data. An early document (Petition 1932) says that the Ilobi left Ketu because of an accession

dispute and migrated southward through Itolu (near the present site of
Ilaro) to their present location in southern Ẹgbado. At Ilobi, the king
(Ogunbiyi 1973) and his elders could offer no further information on
Gẹlẹdẹ but did produce two sets of leg rattles and three Gẹlẹdẹ masks.
There was clear evidence of a well developed smelting industry in the
town but, contrary to the constant references to brass in the songs, the leg
rattles seen in the field and those presented at Ilobi were all made of iron.
It should be pointed out, however, that present-day Ilobi is not located on
its original site because of the nineteenth-century wars. So the existence
of a brass-casting industry cannot be verified. Since the people had to
pass through the small town of Itolu as they migrated southward (Petition 1932), Ilobi was indeed probably located fairly far south. The only
additional information from Ilobi is contained in a letter from a former
king of Ilobi (Adebowale 1972):

> Gẹlẹdẹ cult worship was *oriṣa olọmọwẹwẹ* [god of ones-with-small-
> children] . . . which the Ilobis of ages instituted. . . . Gẹlẹdẹ dancing
> spread to Ofia . . . and then to Ketu, homestead of the Ilobis. Today,
> wherever an Ẹfẹ/Gẹlẹdẹ has to be made anywhere in Yorubaland,
> Ilobi must be mentioned in splitting the kola-nut.

The first part of the statement confirms Moulero's account of the diffusion of Gẹlẹdẹ. We cannot confirm the second part. While the origins of
Gẹlẹdẹ remain conjectural, the data do seem to focus on the Ketu Yoruba
generally and on Ilobi in particular, a town formerly part of the Ketu
kingdom. The time of these events is still in doubt, yet a number of
independent sources associate Gẹlẹdẹ with the era just before the reign
of Alaketu Adebiya, or circa 1795–1816. These dates fall within the period of Ọyọ's trade route, down through what is now Ẹgbado territory.

The theme of doubling appears in various aspects of Gẹlẹdẹ performance as well as in origin myths. Babatunde Lawal (1978) has suggested links between Gẹlẹdẹ, spirit children, and twins, citing myths and
costuming elements as evidence. Other twin references appear in myths
collected by Moulero (1971), in which the originator of Ẹfẹ was Ẹdun, a
name given to twins. The origin of Ẹfẹ revolved around a dispute between twins as to which one was the rightful heir to the kingdom of Ketu.
A review of our own data reveals additional twinning references. A night
mask from Ọhọri (pl. 43) was said to be "the *apaṣa* of twins," and several
two-faced masks documented in Ẹgbado (pls. 149, 150) as well as the
pairing of Gẹlẹdẹ dancers were also said to represent twins. At Abẹokuta,
a double-faced mask commemorates an ancestress by the name of Eyini
who, according to one account, was the mother of two children (Babalọla
1971). Furthermore, twin memorial figures appear as breasts in one en-

PLATE 149. Double-faced masks represent either twins or the deity Eyini, mother of small children. Ilaro, 1978.

PLATE 150. A double-faced mask representing Eyini carries a
tray of gin bottles for use in rituals. Abẹokuta, 1978.

semble (pl. 58), and both the mothers of twins and Gẹlẹdẹ masqueraders
dance at the market. The history of Gẹlẹdẹ as we have developed it
coincides roughly with the history of twin veneration as put forward by
T. J. H. Chappel (1974). According to Chappel's data, the Yoruba
stopped practicing twin infanticide about the middle of the eighteenth
century, as a result of Ọyọ traders settling among Egun people, who
traditionally accepted twin births. If Chappel is correct, then both the
linkage between the origins of Gẹlẹdẹ and twins who vied for the kingship at Ketu and statements that people with the twin name of Ẹdun
introduced Gẹlẹdẹ into other communities suggest that Gẹlẹdẹ developed after western Yoruba abandoned the practice of twin infanticide.
References to twinning in Gẹlẹdẹ do not indicate a direct or formal link
with the cult of twins, yet they do tend to support our hypothesis of
eighteenth-century Gẹlẹdẹ origins among Ketu peoples.

The Spread of Gẹlẹdẹ

A number of towns in present-day Ẹgbado record a secondary dispersal of Gẹlẹdẹ from Ketu Yoruba towns. At Kesan-Orilẹ, traditions suggest that the original forefather came from Ketu, but that Gẹlẹdẹ was introduced by the forefather's wife, who was from Ijoun, approximately 22 miles southeast of Ketu (Oguntade 1971). In Ketu, Odudua is the tutelary deity presiding over Gẹlẹdẹ but, at Kesan, that position is held by Bọrọmu, whose origin is Ijoun, according to both Ketu and Ẹgbado traditions.[13] Ketu quarter in the town of Aiyetoro claims to have migrated originally from Ọyẹ to Iko and subsequently founded Ijalẹ Ketu with the permission of the Alaketu. Circa 1900 they immigrated to Aiyetoro. Gẹlẹdẹ was performed at Ijale Ketu for the founding forefather, Ata, and continues today at Aiyetoro in a Ketu style (Akinwọlẹ and Ayọdele 1971).

Other towns associated with the former trade route seem to have started performing Gẹlẹdẹ after settling in Ẹgbado. The elders of Jọga contend that their founder and those of Iṣaga, Ibeṣe, and Ilaro settled at the same time and returned to Ọyọ to defend it against Fulani attacks, which Ajayi and Smith (1964:64) date circa 1825–1840. This corroborates claims by Morton-Williams (1964a:40):

> Late in the eighteenth century, Alafin Abiọdun, in whose reign the power of Ọyọ reached its greatest extent, founded a chain of kingdoms in what is now Ẹgbado territory. . . . Trade was now rerouted through these kingdoms, which were permitted less autonomy than the Anago kingdoms had been; and the new trade route, which led to Badagri as well as Porto Novo, was more rigorously controlled by the Alafin.

Abiọdun's reign seems to have been circa 1770–1789 (Akinjogbin 1966b:455; 1965:27); thus, Jọga, Iṣaga, Ibeṣe, and Ilaro would have had close ties with Ọyọ at the time of the Fulani invasions, and their founders would have been contemporaries of Atiba, son of Abiọdun and founder of New Ọyọ, 1836, who had also fought against the Fulani (Smith 1969:146). Jọga local records list eight leaders before 1921 and give an approximate date of 1817 for the first.[14]

Gẹlẹdẹ in Jọga is not linked historically with Ketu, and performance format confirms this. Stylistically consistent with other northern Ẹgbado communities, Jọga's Ẹfẹ performer is unmasked and mounts the roof to sing. Since the founding date of Jọga seems late (c. 1790), Gẹlẹdẹ in that town must also be fairly recent.

Three other Gẹlẹdẹ towns, Igan-Okoto, Emado, and Aibo, also seem to be associated with the trade route to Badagri. Both Igan-Okoto and Aibo say they migrated from Ọyọ to Ẹgbado during the reign of Alaafin

Abiọdun. Indeed, the village listed by Clapperton as "Liabo" is probably Aibo, on the basis of name and location correspondences with Clapperton's data and oral tradition.[15] Likewise, Igan-Okoto and Emado were on the route taken by Clapperton in 1825–26 (Morton-Williams 1964a:36).[16] At Igan-Okoto, Gẹlẹdẹ is said to have begun "the second time they came back from war with Ẹgba," which is fairly securely dated circa 1834 (Oke 1971).[17] Another account from an elder with a war title (Owolẹyẹ 1971) suggests a tradition spanning only three to four generations, or dating from circa 1850. No dates are available for the origin of Gẹlẹdẹ in Emado, but an Ẹfẹ song suggests that performances began there after the towns of Jọga (or Jiga) and Ibara had already instituted it, probably some time after 1825:[18]

> He [Ẹfẹ singer] asks, where did Gẹlẹdẹ originate?
> He asks, whoever witnessed the origin come and say
> E e! Jiga is the origin
> Olubara is next to them
> Whoever does not understand it
> Can come and ask Apena

> *O ní bí Gẹlẹdẹ wọnyí ti ṣe*
> *O l'ẹni ba s'oju e ko wa wi*
> *E e Jiga ni ṣelẹ*
> *Olubara lo kun wọn*
> *B'ẹni ti o ba ye si o*
> *Ẹ wa b'Apena*

Both Igan-Okoto and Aibo perform Gẹlẹdẹ in a style consistent with other northern Ẹgbado towns such as Jọga.

More significant for the history of Gẹlẹdẹ in western Yorubaland is the establishment of Ilaro, the major town on the Ọyọ trade route, and its adoption of Gẹlẹdẹ from the ancient Ketu town of Itolu, only a few miles away. It will be remembered that Itolu is the town cited in Ilobi traditions as a stopping point in their migrations from Ketu southward during the reign of the second Alaketu. Ilaro people recognize the antiquity of Itolu, acknowledging that it existed long before their forefather founded Ilaro. Circa 1770–1789, a son of Alaafin Abiọdun established Ilaro to oversee Ọyọ's new trade route through Ẹgbado territory to Badagri (Morton-Williams 1964a; Law 1977:113–115).[19] Evidence of the historical introduction of a new ruling authority from Ọyọ is suggested by the Ilaro tradition that the Osata of Ilu Ata, the earlier authority, should never come face to face with the Olu of Ilaro, the authority superimposed from Ọyọ. A similar tradition existed, for similar reasons, that the Olu should not come face to face with the Onisàrẹ of Ijanna (cf. Johnson 1921: 227). According to sources in Jọga, the forefather of Ilaro, Oronna, left Ọyọ together with the founder of Jǫga, Isaga, and Ibeṣe, all of them children of Alaafin Abiǫdun by the same mother.[20] Oronna is said to have traveled far south—until his sacrifice sank into the water—through Ado Odo, Ilobi, and Awǫri country and then returned to settle on the present site of Ilaro. This journey seems to correspond loosely with the trade route.

Odua, tutelary deity of Gęlędę in Ketu, is also the deity of Gęlędę in Itolu and Ilaro. During the annual Gęlędę festival, masqueraders used to come out at Itolu before they appeared in Ilaro (Murray 1946), and in the past Gęlędę masqueraders reportedly came out from the central Odua shrine located in Itolu every eight days (Philip Allison 1950). In addition to the major Odua shrine, those of many other Ketu Yoruba gods and the graves of their priestesses line a road through the forest, Borǫmu, Eṣu Panada, Babaluaiye (Ṣopǫnnǫn), and so on. The quarters of Ilaro responsible for Gęlędę are not the same as those that perform the Ǫyǫ-related Egungun. Three quarters—Modeolu, Ilu Ata, and Onǫla—dominate Gęlędę in Ilaro; they maintain close ties with the ancient Ketu town of Itolu, where the central Odua shrine is located. Thus, Ilaro seems to have been settled in the latter part of the eighteenth century to secure Ǫyǫ's trade route to the coast, and it seems to have taken up and continued Gęlędę practice as a result of its proximity to the Ketu settlement of Itolu, which houses the central Gęlędę/Odua shrine.

The dispersal of Gęlędę then seems to have been a direct result of Ǫyǫ's trade route established in the latter part of the eighteenth century and the subsequent large influx of people into the area, particularly from Ǫyǫ, together with movements of Ketu people throughout the area in response to trade. Populations shifted and realigned themselves for economic reasons.

Evidence inherent in Gęlędę performance itself seems to support this theory. Gęlędę as spectacle by its very nature is expensive and requires a community's combined resources to produce properly. It seems likely then that it could have spread only during a period of prosperity. Furthermore, performances of Gęlędę require a large number of performers—singers, dancers, and others—all well versed in Gęlędę practice. A single individual may install a shrine to any Yoruba god in his house and worship there regularly, but it would be impossible for him to put on a Gęlędę spectacle alone. Gęlędę's spread was contingent upon large migrations of people, as was the case during the late eighteenth century. The importance of the marketplace as the setting of Gęlędę and the prevalence of images of marketwomen, foreigners, and foreign innovations in the masks indeed suggest this period in western Yoruba history, when the trade route was flourishing. During prosperous times when marketwomen and foreign traders, many of them Muslim, seemed particularly powerful, it would not be surprising that a society of local men—primarily hunters and farmers—would devise a means of working with the mothers for their own well-being.

The trade route and Ilaro figure prominently in Gẹlẹdẹ's further spread into the coastal area. Gẹlẹdẹ in Badagri shows historical links with both Ilaro and Imala/Idofoi peoples. Seriki Abasi, an ex-slave with family ties to Aibo and Idofoi who was adopted by a wealthy, childless merchant in Badagri, is regarded as the founder of Aiyetoro (circa 1900), a town of Imala/Idofoi peoples, among others (cf. Aṣiwaju 1976:98–100). A mask called Onidofoi, collected at Badagri in 1946, is remarkably similar in form to the Imala Onidofoi example (pl. 125). When informants at Aiyet-oro were told of a similar mask at Badagri, they explained that it "was brought [to Badagri] by Seriki Abasi . . . who came from Badagri" (Mur-ray 1950), presumably some time between 1900 and 1919, the date of Abasi's death. The people of Iposuko, Badagri, however, say they brought Gẹlẹdẹ from Ilaro (Murray 1942). Furthermore, Ilado, Aina-Agbo, Ibereko, and Mosafejo in Badagri area refer to their Gẹlẹdẹ societies as "Ilaro Awori," while Mowo calls its own simply "Ẹgbado" (Murray 1942). The Ilaro migration to Badagri is probably a result of Badagri's rise as an important port (circa 1750–1825) about the time of the founding of Ilaro. During the early period of Ilaro history, the Olu controlled the trade route, but by circa 1820, Ilaro's authority over the southern end of the trade route was checked when the Alaafin placed another political agent, the Onisare, in a town only a few miles from Ilaro (Adewale 1949).[21] It may be that the "Ilaro Awori"[22] Gẹlẹdẹ society was carried to Badagri by Ilaro emigrants moving south along the trade route late in the eighteenth century but before 1820, when Ilaro lost its author-ity to the Onisare stationed in Ijanna (Adewale 1949). By 1942, Gẹlẹdẹ was dying out in Badagri.[23]

In Lagos, the Ẹgbado-related Gẹlẹdẹ society was allegedly estab-lished during the first quarter of the nineteenth century, approximately the same time as it seems to have been introduced into Badagri. A de-tailed letter from a titled elder in the Ẹgbado Gẹlẹdẹ society, Lagos (Bey-ioku 1946), states that "Chief D. C. Taiwo, the Olofin of Isheri . . . introduced the Gẹlẹdẹ Cult into Lagos," and a petition from the same society (Beyioku 1943) places this introduction "during the reign of Oba Eshinlokun." The dates of Ẹsinlokun's reign, according to Talbot (1969:86–87) and Law (1968), are 1820–1829.[24]

Further evidence suggests that Gẹlẹdẹ at Iṣeri has Ilaro origins. Bey-ioku notes that members call themselves Ọmọ Oron-nas ("children of Oronna"), a reference to the descendents of the founding father of Ilaro, Oronna.[25] The Petition cited above from the Ẹgbado Gẹlẹdẹ Society, Lagos, states that Gẹlẹdẹ was performed at Onọla Isalẹ Gangan, Lagos, a place name perhaps deriving from Onọla quarter, Ilaro, where Gẹlẹdẹ is also performed. Finally, Murray (1946) records that the head of the Gẹlẹdẹ society at Lagos is called Gbondu, a unique Gẹlẹdẹ title, which occurs, as far as we know, in only one other town, Ilaro.

These details taken together suggest that Ilaro and the trade route were instrumental in the introduction of Gẹlẹdẹ to the coast. Indeed, it is in Ilaro/Itolu down through Awori country and in Lagos that the Ẹfẹ headdress is a traylike form, called atẹ Ẹfẹ (pls. 31, 44, 45).

More recent dispersals of Gẹlẹdẹ occurred in Ibarapa area and also along the western border of Nigeria. The introduction of Gẹlẹdẹ into Ibarapa seems to date to the early twentieth century, particularly in Igbo-Ọra, Lanlate, and Idere. Evidence in Igbo-Ọra claims Gẹlẹdẹ was obtained from the Idofoi/Imala peoples (Murray 1940; 1960). Igbẹrẹkodo and Pako quarters, which perform Gẹlẹdẹ together, claim that it came from Amala (Imala) people. The same account was given independently at Imala (Adelẹyẹ 1971). A third quarter, Olurin, attributes its Gẹlẹdẹ to Aiyetoro and performs for the deity Onidofoi. This would connect it directly with Idofoi and Imala quarters of Aiyetoro, since those are the only two that worship Onidofoi, and would also place its introduction in Olurin as the early twentieth century, since Aiyetoro was established only around 1900. In addition, one of the principal masqueraders is Ogede, the gorilla (Murray 1940), which is an Ẹgbado—more specifically Aiyetoro, Imala, Kesan, and Ibara—phenomenon (pls. 139, 140). In Lanlate, further north in Ibarapa country, three quarters perform Gẹlẹdẹ. One quarter, Oketagbo, cites Mẹko as the source, while Isalẹ-Logun obtained Gẹlẹdẹ from Imala (Murray 1948). The third quarter, Oke-Ọtun, claims to have begun to perform Gẹlẹdẹ only in 1913, but there is no mention of the source (Nigerian Museum Archives 1960). Another Ibarapa town, Idere, say its Gẹlẹdẹ came from Aiyetoro and is performed for Onidofoi (Murray 1948). Since both Olurin quarter in Igbo-Ọra and Idere identify Gẹlẹdẹ with Onidofoi and Aiyetoro, its origins can be more precisely identified with the Idofoi or Imala peoples and can be dated some time after 1900, that is, after the founding of Aiyetoro. Thus these two places in Ibarapa and Oke-Ọtun Quarter, Lanlate, can be securely dated to the early twentieth century.

A number of other towns where Gẹlẹdẹ appears to be fairly recent have been identified by Aṣiwaju (1976) as refugee centers near the Nigerian border, where there was a large influx of Dahomean Yoruba fleeing French conscription policies. These towns include Ijio (cf. Harper 1970), Ẹgua, and Igbobi Ṣabẹ, Lagos. Traditions in Ẹgua say that the town's founder was an Ọyọ prince who migrated via Ketu during the reign of Alaketu Adebiya (circa 1816–1853) (Folayan 1967:20; Parrinder 1967:100). However, Murray (1946) learned in Ẹgua that its Gẹlẹdẹ society originated in Pobe—just a few miles west on the other side of the Benin border. This claim is supported by the fact that Gẹlẹdẹ in Ẹgua honors Pobe's founding forefather, Ondo (cf. M. T. Drewal 1975). It is significant that Ẹgua, having arrived in the area very late (1816–1853) from Ọyọ, required permission from the Alaketu to settle, yet Gẹlẹdẹ seems to have been introduced even more recently by people from Pobe, perhaps fleeing French conscription policies (cf. Aṣiwaju 1976).

Gẹlẹdẹ's early, and rapid, spread thus seems to be a result of Ketu's cultural influence and Ọyọ's relatively brief economic impact on western Yorubaland. The spread of this artistic phenomenon probably continued throughout the nineteenth century, though perhaps more slowly after 1830 because of the disruptions of war.[26] In the twentieth century, Gẹlẹdẹ extended to Ibarapa from northern Ẹgbado areas, primarily from Imala and Idofoi, and probably to western Nigeria from Benin.

The geographical extent of Gẹlẹdẹ, at least through the first half of the nineteenth century, is confined significantly to Ọyọ's former trade corridor. Its boundaries correspond to the limits of the movements and migrations of Ketu, Ẹgbado, and Awori peoples throughout western Yorubaland for purposes of trade and, later on, for protection from the incursions of the Fon from the west and the Ẹgba from the east who were out to capture western Yoruba peoples for the slave trade. Sandwiched between two hostile enemies from the second quarter of the nineteenth century, the peoples who perform Gẹlẹdẹ were essentially restricted to the boundaries of their own territory for protection. This situation effectively confined Gẹlẹdẹ to western Yorubaland.

Gẹlẹdẹ and Related Masquerades in Ijẹbu, Lagos, and among the Fon

Gẹlẹdẹ's history would be incomplete without a consideration of its cultural and artistic relationships to masquerades in other areas. The Ijẹbu Yoruba masquerade cult known as Agbo (Magbo), or Ekine, pays homage to Olokun, goddess of the sea, and a host of water spirits (cf. Okeṣola 1967; de la Burde 1973:30–32). Derived from the Ijọ Ekine masking society of the western Delta, Agbo masks vary from the Ijọ type of highly stylized, horizontally oriented cap headdresses to those with a strongly Yoruba, and more specifically Gẹlẹdẹ, style (pls. 151, 152). The clearest artistic interactions between Agbo and Gẹlẹdẹ occur in western and coastal Ijẹbu communities with close ties to Lagos, where some carving workshops make masks for both societies. See, for example, masks from the same workshop carved for the Agbo society in Ijẹbuland (pl. 151) and the Ketu Gẹlẹdẹ society in Lagos (color plate 9).

A brief comparison of Agbo and Gẹlẹdẹ reveals some interesting parallels. Human fertility is a concern in both Agbo and Gẹlẹdẹ; in Agbo,

PLATE 151. Similar in form to Gẹlẹdẹ masks are those of Agbo,
used in Ijẹbu area and eastward along the coast. Nigerian
Museum, Lagos (57.25.1a and b).

special children known as Mọlokun (Ọmọ Olokun, literally "Children of
the Goddess of the Sea") are thought to have come into the world
through the intercession of the water spirits. Agbo masquerades represent these water spirits. Like Gẹlẹdẹ, annual Agbo festivals in Ijẹbu come
just before the rains, and a herald masquerade, known as Okooro, appears several weeks in advance to announce the festival date (pl. 152).
Although this Agbo herald's mask can be mistaken for Gẹlẹdẹ, the costume is quite distinct. It is made of tightly woven mats. Certain other
Agbo headdresses are also similar to those of Gẹlẹdẹ, and the costumes
that adorn them, like those at Lagos, consist of layers of rich cloth, which
cover a woven fish trap to produce enormous buttocks. Also as in Lagos,
their dance evokes the grace of corpulent women and terminates with a
sudden off-balance spin during which attendants catch the dancers to
prevent them from falling. Whereas Gẹlẹdẹ traditionally dance in pairs,
Agbo perform in threes, carrying whisks and wooden paddlelike blades,
which they strike on leg rattles made from seed pods (pl. 153).

    The themes of Olokun, water spirits, and fertility in both Agbo and
Gẹlẹdẹ and the coastal trading networks linking Lagos with Ijẹbu and the
Delta may account for many of the artistic similarities observable in these
two masking traditions. The precise nature of their convergence must
await further investigation.

PLATE 152. This Okooro masquerader announces the beginning
of the Agbo masquerade festival. His headdress bears a striking
resemblance to many Gẹlẹdẹ masks. Ijẹbuland, Odomola, 1982.

PLATE 153. An Ijẹbu Agbo
masquerader, whose costume
resembles that of Gẹlẹdẹ, performs
at an annual festival. Akio, 1982.

In Ijọra, Lagos, masks used in performances called Ejiwa show striking similarity to Gẹlẹdẹ headdresses. Ejiwa performances, which usually
occur between March and May, or about one month before the Gẹlẹdẹ
festival, honor Ẹlẹgbara. They are performed for the Idéjọ́, or white-
capped chiefs of Lagos, who trace their ancestry to the Ẹgbado town of
Iṣeri and its ruler, the Olofin (Smith 1969:92). The masqueraders, about
six, wear a massive costume of raffia strips (ìko) attached to the masks.
They appear from behind a palm leaf curtain when summoned by a
priest shaking an iron bell. Murray (1940) photographed a mask, "a bird
with a human face, long beak and human hands . . . holding an axe and a
staff with a bird on the top" (pl. 154), which shows striking similarities
with the spirit bird forms in Gẹlẹdẹ.[27]
    A lesser-known aspect of Gẹlẹdẹ history is its dispersal to certain Fon
communities in Benin (Bay 1974). Among the Fon at Cove, the night
masquerade singer, Ọrọ Ẹfẹ, sings in Yoruba and has his words
translated into Fon during the performance. The nocturnal ritual also
includes the most sacred of all Gẹlẹdẹ forms, the mask for the Great

PLATE 154. An Ejiwa mask similar to Gẹlẹdẹ in form and iconography is used in ceremonies honoring Elegbara and is associated with the white cap chiefs of Lagos. Nigerian Museum archives (neg. nos. 7.12.4 and 5).

Mother, Iyanla (pl. 2). Her movement, costuming, and mask type are identical to Great Mother masks found in the contiguous areas of Ketu, Ohọri, and Anago. Another nocturnal masquerade wears a stark white janus headdress that fuses human and bird images into one and recalls the spirit bird masks of Ẹgbado.

Gẹlẹdẹ in Other Yoruba Communities

Historical events in the early part of the nineteenth century in Yorubaland had a profound impact upon the spread of Gẹlẹdẹ in two ways. First, disruptions caused by the decline of the Ọyọ Empire were detrimental to the spread of the society beyond the formerly Ọyọ-controlled trade route through Ẹgbado. Second, this political upheaval was accompanied by extensive slave raiding activities, much of it in western Yorubaland, in which captives were sold to European slavers on the coast. Some captives were freed by the British and landed at Freetown, Sierra Leone, where between 1822 and 1840 they swelled the ranks of liberated slaves in the colony. It was not long before the predominantly Yoruba communities in Freetown, Hastings, and Waterloo established the cults of Egungun, Oro, Ṣango, Agẹmọ, Ogun, and Gẹlẹdẹ (Peterson 1969). As early as 1837, one observer of a Gẹlẹdẹ masquerade recorded that

one of them, who was dancing for the amusement of the company surrounding him, was partly dressed in women's clothes, with a wooden mask of rather ingenious make, representing a human head covered with a helmet, which had for a crest, a snake in the act of killing a bird. . . . [Warburton 1837:423 cited in Nunley 1981:54].

By the second half of the nineteenth century, these Yoruba societies had also spread to the Susu, Mandinka, Temne, and Creole groups. According to a Freetown missionary newspaper (*Methodist Herald*, 1883), Gęlędę originated among the Aku and so-called Popo groups. It was described as "innocent and amusing, it danced about in the likeness of a female with grotesque breasts." The name Popo was ascribed to the liberated slaves who had sailed from the slaving port of Grand Popo in Dahomey. They were almost certainly Yoruba from Ketu and Ęgbado areas sold by the Fon. Thus Gęlędę spread from its original home to a new one on the West African coast.

Information collected from a number of Sierra Leoneans of Yoruba ancestry leaves no doubt about the society's survival in its new home. One informant (Robinson 1972), whose grandmother was the head of Gęlędę in Freetown, described numerous details common to Gęlędę in Nigeria: the use of an iron gong by the female leader, the society's concern with birth and fertility, the control exercised by female elders, and the use of cloth to cover the masquerader to depict a woman. Another informant (Akinsulure 1972), whose grandparents were prominent elders in the Waterloo, or Akutown, Gęlędę society, described an annual festival in which performers using a mask with a cloth tied around its rim, wrappers over the body, enlarged hips, wooden breastplate, and leg rattles, would come out in pairs.

The same historical events that led to the establishment of Gęlędę in Sierra Leone also fostered its emergence in the New World, specifically in Cuba and Brazil. In Cuba the introduction of a substantial number of Yoruba (Lucumi) dates from approximately 1800. Until 1763 there were not many slaves in Cuba, since many of them were resold from the British Islands of Jamaica and Grenada at exorbitant prices and high import duties. Cuba did not have its own outlet on the West African coast until 1778, and it was not until 1792 that slaves came directly to Cuba on a Spanish ship (Aimes 1967 [1907]: 36–56). While the introduction of large numbers of slaves was late, it continued until about 1865 (Verger 1964a:369). When Gęlędę began is uncertain, but most probably it was in the first half of the nineteenth century. Fernando Ortiz (1906:71–72, fig. 18) published a mask with the figure of a bird as superstructure, which he compared to works from Dahomey illustrated in Rutzel (1888) but attributed to the Congo. It is probably Yoruba-derived, most likely a Gęlędę mask, as Thompson (1971:ch. 14/pl. 3) has suggested. Ortiz (1951:347; 1952:III, 412) also described elaborate feasts for Olokun, who is associated with Gęlędę in Cuba along with Yęmoja. These feasts, known as

"Easter of the Blacks," recall Easter Gẹlẹdẹ performances in Sierra Leone and Lagos. The performance format and costuming described by Ortiz show remarkable similarities with Gẹlẹdẹ practice, especially in Ẹgbado and Lagos areas.

A record of Gẹlẹdẹ in Brazil is preserved in both oral traditions and sculpture. Between 1807 and 1825 massive numbers of Yoruba, probably the majority from Ketu and other western Yoruba groups, were brought to the northeastern Brazilian city of Salvador (Turner 1975), where the first Yoruba-derived cult house, Ile Iya Naso, was founded about 1830. The date of the first Gẹlẹdẹ performance is uncertain, but Carneiro (1954:49) tells of one Maria Julia Figueiredo of Ile Iya Naso, who had the title of Iyalode Erelu and who enjoyed great prestige among black Salvadorans because of the festivals of "*gheledes (mascaras)*" (Gẹlẹdẹ masks) that she held on December 8 at Boa Viagem (Salvador). Others have added to this brief but important account and in the process have revealed other dimensions of Gẹlẹdẹ practice in Brazil. According to Didi dos Santos (1967:44–45) and Juana dos Santos (1976:115), Maria Figueiredo, whose Yoruba name was Ọmọnikẹ, was the daughter of Iya Naso and goddaughter of Ọbatosi, Marcelina da Silva, the first head of Ile Iya Naso. They confirm that until the death of Ọmọnikẹ, circa 1940, Gẹlẹdẹ festivals were held on December 8, the day of Our Lady of the Immaculate Conception of the Beach, which "is associated with Ọṣun" (a river goddess)[28] and, more important, that this is also the date when Onile and the "Iya Mi" (the mothers) are worshipped. Thus two accounts corroborate the presence of Gẹlẹdẹ in Salvador and its links with female spiritual powers, whether a river goddess, Ọ̀ṣun (as in some areas of western Yorubaland), the mothers (as in all areas), or Onilé, the guiding presence of Oṣugbo societies.

A number of Gẹlẹdẹ masks add a further dimension to this fascinating history.[29] After Ọmọnikẹ's death, some masks remained at Ile Iya Naso and others went to another Yoruba cult house *(candomblé)*, Aṣẹ Opo Afọnja, where they were worn by the Babalawo Ọjẹlade, Martiliano Eliseu of Bomfin (dos Santos 1967:45).[30] Despite the demise of the cult, several masks still survive. One (pl. 155) is distinguished by its delicacy of line and form, and it and another (pl. 156) show stylistic similarities with nineteenth-century works from the area of Ọta, Awori, north of Lagos (pl. 93). The morphology, shape, and position of the eye and the structure of the elongated head and the thrusting chin are analogous. However, they differ from the Ọta masks in the more simplified ear form and, most dramatically, in the shallowly carved interior. The latter may be explained by the report that the masks were worn in front of the face rather than on top of the head (dos Santos 1967:45). These changes in style and pattern of use suggest that these masks may have been carved in

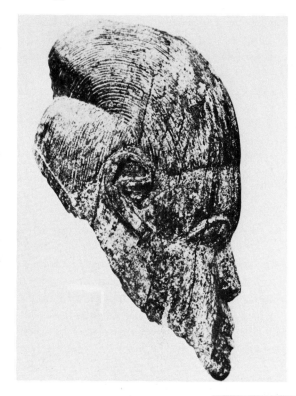

PLATE 155. The style of this Gelede mask in Brazil is remarkably similar to that of Awori. Didi and Juana dos Santos Collection.

PLATE 156. The shallow interiors of a number of Brazilian Gelede masks suggest that they were worn more as face masks than as helmets. Didi and Juana dos Santos Collection.

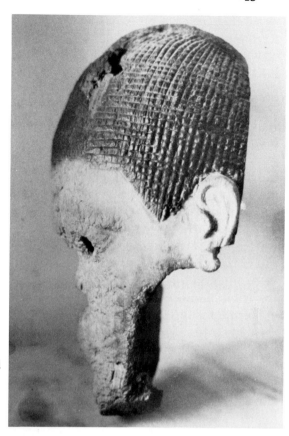

PLATE 157. The naturalistic style of the ear in this Gẹlẹdẹ mask fragment from Brazil closely resembles coastal Ijẹbu work. Didi and Juana dos Santos Collection.

Brazil by an artist of Awori origin.[31] In a final example, only the fineness of the carefully rendered and highly naturalistic ear preserves the former glory of the piece (pl. 157). Such realism suggests a coastal Ijẹbu origin for the Afro-Brazilian creator of this piece (cf. pl. 151). While many Afro-Brazilian ritual forms were used in new ways to serve new needs, the convergence of Onile, *iya mi*, Apaọka, Ọṣun (and Yẹmọja) with festivals of "Ghelede masks" suggests that Gẹlẹdẹ as practiced in Yorubaland survived for a time in Brazil.

Conclusions

The various economic and political factors that had their origins in the Ọyọ Empire and developed in western Yorubaland, beginning circa 1775 with Alaafin Abiọdun's rise to power, appear to have created a social climate that fostered the creation and expansion of Gẹlẹdẹ. The Ketu kingdom, whose cultural and political authority in the area had never been questioned, suddenly was affected by the expansionist policies of Ọyọ, whose economic, political, and military presence rapidly expanded along Ketu's eastern boundary in Ẹgbado, encroaching on Ketu territory. Ketu, unable to respond in any overtly aggressive or military manner against Ọyọ power, possibly asserted its authority through the Gẹlẹdẹ institution. Moulero collected a myth that links the origins of Ẹfẹ with a succession dispute at Ketu, where a ruse or joke solved a political matter. This is not very different from the way in which Ẹfẹ songs curse, ridicule, criticize, and condemn antisocial actions to resolve specific communal problems. Sanctioned by the all powerful mothers, the perspectives on society espoused by Gẹlẹdẹ performances have the authority of law. Therefore, performances of Gẹlẹdẹ might have been the most politically astute means for Ketu peoples to exert authority indirectly in a basically Ọyọ-dominated setting. In a sense, pan-Yoruba concepts about the powers of the mothers, the owners of the world, allowed Ketu peoples, using the institution of Gẹlẹdẹ, to balance to some extent the impact of Ọyọ in the area. Thus, Gẹlẹdẹ spectacle as an otherworldly phenomenon served periodically to reevaluate and shape the world. With the combined economic and spiritual power of women, the Gẹlẹdẹ society of the Ketu people spread rapidly throughout western Yorubaland to the Ọyọ immigrants newly stationed along the trade routes in Ẹgbado, Anago, and Aworị areas. Then, as Ọyọ's power waned in the area and many Yoruba were sold into slavery and carried from their homeland, Gẹlẹdẹ sprang up in new homes in West Africa and the New World, taking with it the ideals of patience and indulgence, which it embodies, as alternative approaches for peacefully managing their new-found situations. In Freetown, Sierra Leone, Gẹlẹdẹ seems to have thrived; however, in Brazil and Cuba, where women maintain positions of power in African derived cults up to the present and where slavery continued late into the nineteenth century, only vestiges of what can be precisely identified as Gẹlẹdẹ spectacle remain.

8
Gẹlẹdẹ and the Individual

Individual participants shape Gẹlẹdẹ practice to reflect their own concerns, situations, or aesthetic preferences. It is our belief that the creative elements within Yoruba spectacle, the contributions of art and of individuals, ultimately change the basic ritual structure itself, making it dynamic rather than static and thus diversifying Gẹlẹdẹ practice throughout western Yorubaland. If one tries to interpret the form and content of Gẹlẹdẹ without knowing the personal lives of its participants, one perceives a static, generalized view of Gẹlẹdẹ spectacle. Likewise, examining individuals and their personal histories without an overview of Gẹlẹdẹ spectacle would be equally unsatisfactory, producing a fragmented view of the Gẹlẹdẹ phenomenon. Viewing both facets will produce a more complete and realistic picture, one that illustrates the dynamics of Yoruba religion and the relationships between art and the individual, between cultural norms and individuality, and between history and diversity.

Yoruba Religion

Yoruba religious practice depends on two factors, descent and divination. In combination they produce a very fluid religious system. Descent provides continuity; divination, in contrast, opens up the system to countless possibilities. In the following case studies of individuals and their Gẹlẹdẹ activities we see the interaction of these two factors, the dynamic context they produce, and the processes that shape Gẹlẹdẹ in particular places and lead to diversity in practice.

It will be recalled that the central Ẹgbado town of Ilaro (see map p. xxiv) is associated historically and culturally with Ketu and Ọyọ, a combination that is reflected in the religious life of the community. The quar-

247

ters that consist largely of lineages that identify with Ọyọ are responsible for the Egungun masquerade (basically an Ọyọ institution); those with ties to the former Ketu kingdom dominate the Gẹlẹdẹ society. Three quarters in Ilaro—Modeolu, Iluata, and Onọla—share responsibility for various aspects of the society, its arts, and its performances. Gẹlẹdẹ titles are distributed more or less equally among the three quarters. Two of them have a masquerader known as Eṣu Gbangbade, who announces the coming of the annual festival as well as closes the Ẹfẹ night portion of that festival. Modeolu Quarter is responsible for the night bird mother masquerade, Ẹyẹ Ọrọ (cf. pl. 3), which sanctions the performance of Ẹfẹ songs; while Iluata Quarter controls the mother mask that "closes" the festival, Iya Odua (pl. 148). During the course of the festival, sacrificial ceremonies *(etutu)* for the masks and participants of the Gẹlẹdẹ lineages in each of the quarters take place on specified days. On these particular occasions it becomes apparent how the histories of individuals, families, and their ritual objects have shaped the society's perception of the meanings and functions of Gẹlẹdẹ.

One Modeolu Quarter lineage, which performs its own sacrificial rite on the third day of the festival, traces its origins to Ketu territory and views its participation in Gẹlẹdẹ as intimately linked with other powerful forces—sacred twins *(ibeji),* the god of iron (Ogun), and the god of thunder (Ṣango). The family's traditional ritual objects are gathered for a purification rite and cooling *(etutu)* by their elderly caretaker, Adeogun (pl. 158). These Gẹlẹdẹ masks and twin figures are intimately related to the history and life of this woman and her lineage, which traces its origins to a forefather, Ojo. According to family traditions, Ojo migrated from the upper Yẹwa River valley town of Oke Odo, in Ketu Yoruba territory, to Ilaro, in the Ẹgbado area, six generations ago, or circa 1795. His title, Olori Agberu, identifies him as head of the Gẹlẹdẹ masqueraders and worshipper of Odua, the goddess associated with Gẹlẹdẹ in Ilaro. It is not recalled whether Ojo worshipped other deities in addition to Odua, but other deities appear in the next generation, perhaps as the result of divination or perhaps through Ojo's wives' lineages. Ogun Akọgbọna, son of Ojo, worshipped Odua and Gẹlẹdẹ, Ogun, and Ṣango. An old Gẹlẹdẹ mask carefully preserved within the family compound was his (pl. 159). It is called Oluwaiye (literally "Owner of the World"), a praise name for Gẹlẹdẹ and the mothers. The mask is simple yet dramatic in its iconography.

The headdress depicts a male with a distinctive hairstyle, the head shaven except for an oval tuft on the crown. In Yoruba belief and ritual practice, the tuft marks the place where incisions are made and "medicines" are inserted to prepare an individual's head, more precisely his "inner," or spiritual, head to receive supernatural forces (cf. M. T.

PLATE 158. Gẹlẹdẹ masks and twin figures gathered together
for a rite of purification by their elderly caretaker document the
interaction of various lineage traditions. Ilaro, 1978.

Drewal 1977). The descendants of Ogun Akọgbọna explain that the tuft
depicted in this mask is unique to Gẹlẹdẹ or Odua worshippers. It may
look like tufts worn by the devotees of Yoruba deities and others, but
each is "prepared" differently, that is, with different spiritual ingredients. The male represented by this Gẹlẹdẹ mask has a tuft prepared for
Odua, like the person who used it during his lifetime, Ogun Akọgbọna.

The correlation between the imagery of the mask and the life of its
owner has become even stronger since the death of Akọgbọna. With the
passage of time, the mask's roles have changed. It has come to represent
the spiritual presence of the forefather. When it broke many years ago, it
changed from a masquerade headdress to an altarpiece for the lineage
and the town. At annual celebrations, the mask serves as a focus for
worship. It receives offerings, elaborate praises, and prayers as part of a
sacrifice *(etutu ilu),* literally "cooling the town," to ensure prosperity and
peace in the lineage and the community.

The Oluaiye mask also ensures the active participation of Ogun
Akọgbọna's descendants in their inherited ritual obligations. The mask,

PLATE 159. A retired mask represents the forefather and serves
as the centerpiece for the household shrine. Ilaro, 1978.

i.e., Akọgbọna, surrounded by images for departed twins, or his "children," is carried by female lineage members to Gẹlẹdẹ performances,
where they dance with the masqueraders from their compound (pl. 160).
From the elders' point of view, the public appearance and participation
of Oluaiye and the twin figures compel all lineage members—living and
departed—to attend the ceremonies. As one explained, "Family members
will come from here and there to help their father during the festival, so
peace (etutu) will come to the town."

Ogun Akọgbọna gave birth to several children, among them twins.
Sacrifices prescribed by Ifa were prepared and offered to the spirit of
twins to allow the twins to remain in the world, but the firstborn, Ẹbọ,
died soon after birth (pl. 158). A memorial figure was carved for her and
cared for over the years. To decorate and beautify the form, the head has
been washed, oiled, and rubbed, the hair dyed, and the body enhanced
with various strands of beads about the waist (one strand carved) and
neck. Her white beads and lead bracelet (ojé) signify Odua, the tutelary
deity of Gẹlẹdẹ and an important lineage divinity.

The second twin was called Orişadi because of special circumstances
surrounding his birth. The name indicates that he was born in the

PLATE 160. A woman dances with a masquerader from her compound while balancing an enamel basin containing a Gẹlẹdẹ mask and twin figures representing departed lineage members. Ilaro, 1978.

placenta *(òkẹ́)*. Lineage members recall this event by saying, "The sack tied by the gods cannot be untied by anyone" *(Òkẹ́ ti òrìṣà di ọmọ ar'aiyé ò le tú)*, to explain that it is a sign from the gods that needs interpretation. A child born with a caul usually has affinities with masquerading; the event is most auspicious, given the importance of Gẹlẹdẹ to Oriṣadi's grand-father and father.

The twin figure representing Oriṣadi is quite different in both style and age from its mate. Oriṣadi lived long and fathered several children. When he died, Ẹbọ was consulted by a diviner to learn whether she (i.e., her image) should be buried with her brother. Ẹbọ said no, that instead another image for Oriṣadi should be commissioned to keep *her* company. Since Oriṣadi lived to old age, the date of creation is probably circa 1895, or 60 years after the death of Ẹbọ, when her own memorial figure was carved. These two figures, together with most of the others, represent the generations of twins born into the lineage of Ogun Akọgbọna. Oriṣadi in particular is important to Gẹlẹdẹ, not only because he was born in a caul but also because he was a Gẹlẹdẹ participant, the forefather who passed the tradition and the authority to perform Gẹlẹdẹ on to his children and his children's children.

The caretaker of the twins and the old Gẹlẹdẹ mask, Adeogun, is the granddaughter of Oriṣadi and the great granddaughter of Ogun Akọgbọna. She is one of the few in her family still willing to maintain her religious traditions. She holds a position in the Ogboni society, inherited from a daughter of her grandfather's brother. She also holds the senior female title in the Gẹlẹdẹ society—Iyalaja, "Mother-of-the-Sacred-Rattle" (the rattle being the symbol of her authority). Because of her age and positions, other priests of Yoruba gods seek out her attendance at their festivals.

Various strands in this lineage history come together during the annual Gẹlẹdẹ celebration for family and community gods. Rites for twins, Ṣango, Ogun, and especially Gẹlẹdẹ (Odua) are performed and ritual objects are renewed to demonstrate commitment to the ancestors. Newly carved Gẹlẹdẹ masks shine with bright enamel paints. The circular Ẹfẹ headdress of Ilaro is given new paint, cloth, and mirrors; and the hair of lineage twins and the head and lineage marks of Ogun Akọgbọna's ancient mask are darkened with rich indigo dye. The elderly caretaker's symbol of authority, the *aaja* or sacred double rattle, lies in her lap. The shrines for Ogun and Ṣango are close by in the corner of the room. Memorial figures for departed twin lineage members stand together with Gẹlẹdẹ images of the past and present, demonstrating the interactions of sacred arts as expressions of lineage dynamics. As lineage members explain, "The *orisa* of Gẹlẹdẹ and twins is the same." Annual rites for the spirit of twins in this lineage occur as part of the Gẹlẹdẹ festival.

In the adjoining quarter of Iluata, another lineage important in the Gẹlẹdẹ society possesses different divinities and ritual objects and, as a result, different worship patterns. This family, Ile Ọmọṣeun Babayinde, is responsible for the preparation and performance of Iya Odua, the goddess/priestess masquerader who closes the annual Gẹlẹdẹ festival (pl. 148). The Ọmọṣeun lineage also honors the spirit of twins and Eṣu/Ẹlẹgba, yet the perceived relationship of these divinities is different from that of the descendants of Ojo. Three generations of twins are represented in the house. Their births and deaths are linked directly with the intercession of Eṣu/Elẹgba and only indirectly with Gẹlẹdẹ. A great grandmother, Ilọ, gave birth to many children who died young. It was learned through divination that she had to take up the worship of Elẹgba if her children were to remain in the world, and this she did. Eṣu's direct involvement with the birth and death of twins in this family is recorded in the juxtaposition of a carved wristlet with cowrie shells for Eṣu/Elẹgba and memorial figures of the departed twins of the lineage in the same calabash. Elaborate prayers and offerings attend Gẹlẹdẹ rites in this household. As representations of lineage members, the twin memorial figures are carried along with the symbol of their deity, Eṣu/Elẹgba, to the marketplace to attend Gẹlẹdẹ performances. This was particularly important at one Efẹ funeral commemoration, for it was essential that the departed twins, as members of the lineage, be present when one of their mates was honored.

Other individuals and their sacred images tell different stories. Members of the Bamboṣe family of Iluata Quarter, Ilaro, are active in two spheres—those of Ogun (god of hunting, iron, and war) and of Gẹlẹdẹ. Therefore they commemorate Ogun in the superstructures of their Gẹlẹdẹ masks (pl. 52). Massive images of equestrian warriors and hunters evoke their past accomplishments, while those of motorcyclists demonstrate their continued involvement with iron and Ogun, for professional drivers and those who use the roads are frequently Ogun worshippers (cf. Barnes 1980). In addition to being Gẹlẹdẹ dancers, Bamboṣe lineage members hold the title of Elẹfẹ Apọnle (literally "flatterers of Efẹ"), for they traditionally escort the Ọrọ Efẹ singers to the market, firing their guns in salute, praise, and protection for the performers. The loud report of their weapons punctuate Ọrọ Efẹ's verbal texts, lending dramatic emphasis to his voiced power.

Similar circumstances occur in the compound of the Olori Agberu, the Head of the Costumers for the Gẹlẹdẹ society. Ogun and Gẹlẹdẹ come together in his lineage shrine (pl. 161). Olori Agberu is also Olori Olọdẹ, that is, Head of the Hunters. During annual festivals for Ogun, the deity becomes manifest in the world by means of possession trance, mounting the head of Olori Olọdẹ, and on the final day of the Ogun festival, an Egungun of the Hunters (Eegun Olọdẹ), emerges from his shrine wearing a platform mask displaying a number of spirits and animals. During Gẹlẹdẹ festivals Olori Olọdẹ places all his Gẹlẹdẹ masks on the Ogun shrine in his compound. The scene is the "cooling" rite (*etutu*) for the ritual forms in his compound. His Gẹlẹdẹ society title is clearly written on the forehead of one of the masks, while in the corner of the room is the shrine for his ancestors and Ogun.

PLATE 161. A Gelede society member, who is also head of the
hunters, has placed his masks on the shrine to the god of
hunters, Ogun. Ilaro, 1978.

Others proclaim their contribution to society with representations of
themselves. A priestess of the goddess Are, with ritual fan, iron rattle,
bracelets of beads, and white blouse, mirrors the representation of an
Are priestess in the superstructure of the mask (pl. 162). The water pot
on the head of the carved figure refers to the water from the sacred
stream of the goddess, used during propitiations or cooling rites. The
priestess and the masquerade honoring her, together with a crowd of
friends and supporters, parade to the market, where the masquerader
performs.

Another Gelede mask depicts an Egungun masquerader with attendant (pl. 163). Its owner, Andele, is active in both the Gelede and the
Egungun masking societies, serving as Alaagba, the spiritual head of the
latter. In addition he is a practicing Muslim. His various religious obligations merge in this Gelede headdress. The figures above represent an
Egungun masquerader of the *elebiti*/*alago* type attended by a servant of
the society (*ilari*, literally "the one with marks on the head") holding a
ritually prepared whip or *isan* (cf. Drewal and Drewal 1978). The field of
white dots on the platform, like the white cowrie shells on the face netting
of the Egungun masker, suggest the spirit qualities of the "being from

PLATE 162. A priestess of the deity Are is accompanied by a
masquerader who honors her by depicting her ritual role. Ilaro,
1978.

PLATE 163. The head of the
Egungun masquerade society, who
is also a member of the Gelede
society and a Muslim, is honored
with a mask depicting an Egungun
on top of a turban-wrapped head.
Sawonjo, 1978.

beyond" *(ará òrun).* Below, the main head communicates another religious sphere, that of Allah, in the striped turban wraps and beard of
Muslim fashions.

These examples demonstrate personal concerns expressed in Gelede
masks and show how these concerns diversify Gelede practice and content. Another example illustrates how this diversity extends to form and
style. It involves Lawani Ojo, who returned to the homestead of his
ancestors in order to obtain a mask that reflects his roots and introduce it
into his new home. As a young man, Lawani's father was told through
divination that he should leave Ohori in order to prosper and to father
many children. He resettled in Imasai, took an Egbado wife there, and
reared his children. Lawani thus grew up in Imasai, and when he became
an Efe singer, following in his father's tradition, he returned to his
father's subgroup, Ohori, and commissioned a headdress typical of that
area (pl. 164). His introduction of the Ohori-style Efe mask, known as
apasa, into an Egbado community, was quite acceptable, since he was a
son of the community on his mother's side, but he is also expected to
follow the traditions of his father. In this example, not only is the source
of the carving outside the locale of the participant but also the form and
style of the mask are unique to the area where it is worn.

PLATE 164. An Ọhọri style Ẹfẹ mask used in an Ẹgbado
community illustrates traveling styles and cultural change.
Imaṣai, 1978.

Patron/Artist Interaction

The histories of individuals and families, as we have seen, explain to a large extent how and why certain images and ritual forms merge and how they are perceived and interpreted by those who may have commissioned, inherited, or acquired them. But art users are not the only ones involved in these decisions, for the work is the result of interactions, or even misunderstandings, between patrons and artists as well as decisions made during the creative process itself.

With Gęlędę's emphasis on spectacle, it is not surprising that its society members are important patrons of artists in western Yorubaland. Any member of the society, male or female, may commission work from a sculptor, although generally the older members, lineage heads or title-holders, make commissions. They initiate the agreement by approaching one or more carvers, sometimes far in advance of anticipated performances, but usually several months before annual/biennial festivals. Other commissions, for a particular performance, such as at a funeral commemoration, are given just before the occasion and often involve clearly defined requirements, such as headdresses honoring the departed (pls. 123, 124).

Gęlędę patrons rely on local talent, as well as on carvers from other towns. Clients often travel to towns with reputations as carving centers in order to commission work. In Ilaro, Ęgbado, a number of Gęlędę masks were carved locally, but quite a few were done in distant towns in Anago, Awori, and Ketu areas, thus producing a great mixture of styles and images. Outside talent, especially for Gęlędę, may be preferred over local artists so that patrons may enhance the spectacle with novel or unique images that have not been seen in the area. Or in the case of Lawani, an individual may introduce a new style by obtaining a mask in his forebears' home (pl. 164).

Not infrequently carvers are "called" to come to the community that is requesting the work. In 1975 the Anago carver Saibu Akinyemi of Agoşaşa went to Ilaro, Ęgbado, to prepare masks for a Gęlędę festival. For three months he worked under a blacksmith's roof, producing a series of headdresses for an important lineage in the Gęlędę society. Under such an arrangement the artist receives food and accommodation in addition to his fee.

Another factor contributing to diversity is the migration of carvers, who move to other communities or subgroups on the advice of diviners or as a direct result of their carving practice. Relatives of Alaiye Adeisa Ętuǫbę, a renowned Ketu carver, are dispersed throughout western Yorubaland, and a number of them perpetuate a distinct Ketu carving tradition. Carving relatives and in-laws of Ętuǫbę migrated to Şabę (north of Ketu), Idọfa (just inside Nigeria), Igbogila, and Ajilete. Until 1978, Ẹtuọbẹ's son, Adegbọla Alaiye of Itaọba Quarter, Ketu, farmed and lived part of the year in the northern Ẹgbado town of Igbogila, where he carved for local as well as distant societies in western Yoruba-land. He traveled between Ketu and Igbogila regularly and maintained his traditional Ketu carving style and repertoire of motifs. Adegbọla's son (Ẹtuọbẹ's grandson), who lives in Igbogila, does not carve but performs Ẹfẹ in a costume that is Ketu in style. His mask was carved by his grand-father, Alaiye Ẹtuọbẹ (frontispiece). These circumstances have resulted in a mixture of Ketu and Ẹgbado elements in Gẹlẹdẹ spectacles in Ig-bogila.

Another source of Gẹlẹdẹ carvings are itinerant artists (cf. H. J. Drewal 1977b:8–9). Our own field data and those of K. C. Murray (Nige-rian Museum Archives) document numerous instances of traveling car-vers—many from Ketu—who worked in various Ẹgbado communities in this century. One of the most prolific and mobile carvers was the Ketu master Atọba, whose work has been widely documented in Ẹgbado, Ketu, and Anago areas (pl. 117).

The Commission

Agreements between Yoruba patrons and artists vary greatly. At one extreme, the artist alone makes the decision on iconography with no input from patrons or clients, since almost anything can be depicted in Gẹlẹdẹ masks. One prolific sculptor simply turned out a large number of masks with male and female themes, such as marketwomen, hairstyles, head ties, and animals—images he thought were general enough and popular enough to sell easily. At the other extreme, the most restrictive commission is the replication of another mask. Often patrons will bring old or broken masks to be copied. These replacements faithfully repro-duce the iconography and sometimes even the style of the original. Of-ten, however, patrons will define their requirements in broad terms (i.e., "two Gẹlẹdẹ masks" or "two male masks") and leave the specific imagery to the artist's imagination, especially if the artist, because of his "famos-ity," as Yoruba put it, has a reputation for innovation and originality. This was the case with Duga of Mẹkọ (cf. Bascom 1973). Open-ended commissions seem to be more characteristic of Gẹlẹdẹ than of the cults of the deities, given the encouragement of new, exciting, enthralling, and often shocking imagery in Gẹlẹdẹ spectacles.

Probably the majority of commissions include both specific require-ments as well as a certain amount of freedom for the artist, as happens with the Ẹfẹ singers and the Gẹlẹdẹ dancers. The patron will probably order a female headdress *(abogi)* or a male headdress *(akọgi)* and give some general suggestions for carrying out the theme, such as the sort of coiffure, fashion, or objects and/or figures in the superstructure. For example, in Ilaro, the Iyalaja, "Mother-of-the-Sacred-Ritual-Rattle," commissioned a mask that would commemorate her role in the Gęlędę society. She suggested to the carver that the superstructure show either a female figure holding a rattle or a rattle balanced on a female head, in imitation of the way Iyalaja often carries the rattle to performances. The final design is often determined by financial considerations, for simple motifs are easier to carve and less expensive than complex genre scenes in superstructures.

One interesting commission involved a senior priest in the Ṣango cult. While Ṣango was the principal divinity worshipped by his lineage, he also participated actively in the Gęlędę society and wanted a mask that would recognize his contribution to both groups. He traveled to the Awori capital of Ọta and gave a commission to the well-known Kilani Ọlaniyan (last in a long line of famous Ọta carvers). Obviously there was a misunderstanding, for instead of depicting a Ṣango priest, the artist sculpted a priestess, thus changing the headdress from male to female (pl. 165). Although the patron was not pleased, he agreed to accept the work and pay the fee. Why he did so is not clear, but several factors may have influenced him: Both male and female devotees, when possessed by the spirit of Ṣango, are known as "wives of Ṣango" (iyawo Ṣango) and plait their hair in feminine fashion. Furthermore, the other ritual symbols of Ṣango—the double-bladed dance wand and the dance skirt—are completely correct. In addition, the patron was apparently able to personalize the headdress and make it more appropriate by painting his god's praise name, Olukoso ("The-Ruler-of-Koso"), on the forehead, thus proclaiming his masculinity, royalty, and divinity simultaneously.

Creating Gęlędę Sculpture

Selecting the wood for an Ęfę or Gęlędę mask involves both practical and spiritual considerations. The Cordia Millenii tree (ọmọ̀) and the Ricinodendron Africanum, or oilnut tree (erinmado/apopo), are preferred because their woods are light in weight, easily carved, and close-grained. Their lightness makes them comfortable for dancing; their relative softness means they can be carved quickly, if necessary, before festivals or special funeral commemorations; and the compact grain permits surface details and patterning as well as intricately composed superstructures. Durability is of secondary concern, since new Gęlędę and Ęfę masks can be commissioned for each yearly or biennial festival.

The choice of wood for the sacred images of the noctural mothers, Iyanla and Ęyę Ọrọ, is quite another matter. According to one Ọhọri sculptor (Olupọna 1975), all community "elders" are responsible for pro-

PLATE 165. This mask represents a misunderstanding. The artist mistakenly carved a female figure instead of a male priest of Ṣango, god of thunder and lightning, which the patron intended. Ilaro, 1978.

viding the wood, which is regarded as a "rare" type *(ọ̀wọ́n)*. One source identifies this "rare" wood as Chlorophora Excelsa *(iróкò),* an enormous tree that dominates the forest. Aside from its hardness and durability, which make it suitable for long-term use, in contrast to many Gẹlẹdẹ masks, *iroko* is believed to be the abode of spirits associated with the mothers and to serve as their nocturnal gathering place.

The wood, whether chosen for its physical or its spiritual properties, must meet another requirement: It should be green *(tutu),* freshly cut with the natural moisture present in the fibers. The tradition of working in moist wood seems to be widespread in Africa and contrasts with wood-carving procedures in Europe and elsewhere, where dried, seasoned wood is used. The Yoruba sculptor often soaks the wood in water to keep it moist throughout the carving period, explaining that it "makes the wood softer and the work easier." The moisture has a lubricating effect that makes the cutting easier and requires less-frequent blade sharpening. Working in green wood does not necessarily mean the piece will check or split when it dries out. Yoruba artists know and avoid the woods that tend to crack, and in the consistently high humidity, the slow drying process usually prevents splitting.

Fresh wood may also be preferred for spiritual reasons, since trees are living, growing entities. They possess vital force, or *aṣẹ*, of their own, which makes them useful in the preparation of various types of medicines and shrines. The sap is called *oje igi*, and runs red, like blood, just underneath the bark in the trees used for Gẹlẹdẹ masks. When a carver cuts into fresh wood and metaphorically "sheds" its blood, his action may be regarded as a sacrifice to the patron deity of carvers, Ogun. An explicit reference to the sap of the tree as sacrifice occurs in Ogun invocations (Olupọna 1975):

> Ogun of the blacksmith eats dog
> Ogun of the tattooer takes human blood
> Ogun of the carver consumes the sap of trees

Before the first cut of the axe or matchet pierces the bark of any tree, the carver must invoke the tree's spiritual residents (Ojo 1966:166–167). An abbreviated divination ritual carried out with kola nuts follows the invocations. The carver breaks a kola into quarters, throws the sections down at the foot of the tree, and "reads" their arrangement to determine positive or negative responses from its spiritual inhabitants. Sometimes special offerings of gin or palm oil are required. The carver takes a final reading to assure that the spirits have been assuaged and that he has gained permission to fell their abode. The way cleared, cutting begins. After felling the tree, the carver judges the amount of wood needed for his work—in the case of Gẹlẹdẹ masks, often enough for two identical headdresses. He cuts those portions from the trunk and takes them to his compound or farm shelter, if he is far from home, where he makes another sacrifice to Ogun, god of iron and patron of all who work with metal. He then commences carving.

Propitiations to Ogun, while sufficient for the carving of most Ẹfẹ and Gẹlẹdẹ headdresses, are not adequate for the image of the Great Mother. In this case, a much more elaborate and costly sacrificial ceremony must take place to ensure success in carving. In Ọhọri country, a goat, cock, dove—all completely white—oil, kola nuts, a large piece of white cloth and a substantial sum of money are offered. In Ketu similar gifts must be offered, and all the work must be done at night (Alaiye 1977). This last obligation is most appropriate since Our Mothers are abroad and most active during these hours. Thus, the covert activity evident in Iyanla's nocturnal appearance begins with the very creation of her image.

The Yoruba carver uses three types of tools: axes (*ăké, ẹdùn*) or matchets (*àdá);* adzes, both large-bladed (*àwọ́n*) and narrow-bladed (*iso);* and knives (*ọ̀bẹ́*) (cf. Drewal 1980). Carvers noted for their Gẹlẹdẹ masks with thin walls and deep, smoothly carved interiors use a special knife with a U-shaped blade for scooping out (*wọ̀*) the interior of the mask. To begin his work, the carver quickly removes the bark with a matchet or a wide-bladed adze in order to reveal flaws such as knots or cracks that might affect the final product. He then rotates the block, carefully surveying its idiosyncrasies in order to determine the position of the piece within the cylinder. He considers alignment and proportion—width vs. length vs. height, front, sides, projections, direction of wood grain. The artist must have a clear and detailed concept of the final work so that he can anticipate the placement of masses and voids in the form. He knows whether the mask will have a superstructure and whether it will be carved from a single block of wood (pls. 102–107, 166, 170) or carved separately and attached (pls. 82, 108, 144). All these considerations determine the ultimate composition of the work.

With the finished product in mind, the carver begins to cut the basic form, as he was taught by his instructor (cf. Drewal 1980). First he works on the bottom surface and interior of the headdress. He establishes the baseline by working around the circumference and toward the center of the cylinder, leveling the bottom to make it perpendicular to the vertical axis of the trunk. Maintaining straightness, and thus balance, from the outset facilitates the carver in developing bilateral symmetry. He tests his progress frequently by sighting along the bottom plane; placing the cylinder on a level surface, the ground or a board; surveying it from several perspectives; and rocking it to reveal uneven places. When he is satisfied that the base is properly aligned, he proceeds to the next important task, the interior.

The interior of a mask can often reveal as much about an artist's technique and style as the exterior. The shape, depth, and finish; the thinness of the walls; the way the walls are pierced for nostrils, eyes, and the insertion of ropes are all signs of an artist's "signature" or style. For example, the shape and smoothness of the interior of a fine mask at the Museum für Völkerkunde, Bern (pl. 167) helps to confirm the dating of a fragmentary Oluaiye mask from Ilaro, which is from the same hand (pl. 159). Kilani Ọlaniyan of Ọta (1981) praised the thinness (*fẹ́lẹ*) of a particular carver's masks, which he had remembered seeing when he himself was learning to carve. He rubbed his thumb and forefinger together to demonstrate the almost paper-thin walls of the headdresses sculpted by

PLATE 166. This large, entwined snake was carved from a single
block of wood. Museum für Völkerkunde, Berlin (III C 41127).

the Ọta master Dadaolọmọ. To a great extent, the dimensions of the
interior influence the shape of the exterior. Some of the most striking
regional style variations result from these interior/exterior relationships.
For example, Gẹlẹdẹ headdresses from extreme western Yoruba peoples,
especially the Ọhọri and Anago, tend to have broad, flattened heads with
shallow interiors (pls. 15, 34, 129), while masks from the Awori Yoruba,
made by the Ọta masters Onanẹyẹ, Olalẹyẹ, Ọlaniyan, and Ọlabimtan
and the Igbesa masters Kogbọdọku, Ọlamide, Akapo, and Nuru, have
tall heads with deep, smoothly cut interiors (pls. 69–72, 94, 96). These
variations may reflect aesthetic judgments as well as technical concerns,
for the Awori version requires greater skill in shaping and smoothing the
interior without puncturing or cracking the thin walls. The variety of
styles may also be in response to divergent costuming traditions. In
Ọhọri, Anago, and most other Gẹlẹdẹ areas, the headdress rests on top
of the performer's head, sometimes angled downward in front to cover

his forehead and eyes. Occasionally the dancer may use the nostril holes to see the ground, but most often he looks from below the lower rim of the mask and through the cloth or veil attached to this rim (pl. 168). It is only among Awori, and among Lagos Gẹlẹdẹ houses, which get many of their masks from Awori, that the headdress is a true helmet mask, i.e., one that fits over the head of the dancer, completely covers his face, and permits him to see through the pierced eyes of the mask (color plate 9, pls. 56, 63, 64, 69).

Hollowing out the interior is difficult and tedious. Using a strong stroke that ends with a twist of the blade, the carver loosens and separates the moist wood fibers of the heartwood. He works parallel to the grain first, breaking apart as well as cutting the wood. Then he sharply angles his stroke to cut across the vertical grain and removes chunks of wood. The interior, which begins as a V-shaped void, gradually widens and deepens, especially in the center and toward the back of the headdress, to form fairly vertical sides and back, while the front, the facial plane, remains at an angle. Care must be taken to leave the walls thick enough for the exterior sculpting yet not so thick that the mask is cumbersome for the wearer. The interior space should fit an average-sized head comfortably; too small and the headdress would cut into the wearer's head; too large and it would knock about and cause balance problems. The carver continually tests his work by trying it out on his own head. He checks weight distribution, alignments, surface texture, and shape. Patrons as

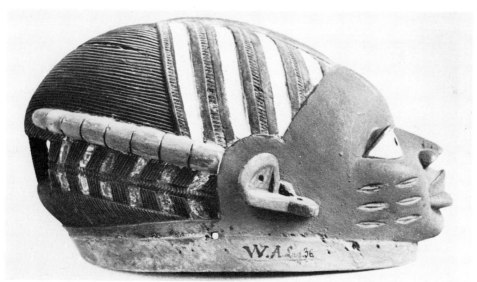

PLATE 167. The outer forms and the shape and smoothness of the interior of this mask confirm that it was carved by the same hand as another fragmentary mask documented in the field (pl. 159). Bernisches Historisches Museum (36).

PLATE 168. A masquerader wears a headdress on the top of his head and looks out from below its rim. Ilaro, 1978.

well as performers also test the headdress and may require the carver to make adjustments. If the interior is too large, a head wrap can fill the space. Tilted or wobbling masks are undesirable, and the fault may be attributed to the inexperienced dancer or to the carver or to both. The aesthetic ideal in the dance is balance and stability of the head in contrast to the active body, and a properly carved mask interior is essential to attaining this goal.

When the carver is satisfied with the interior, he turns to the outside. He must keep the inner dimensions in mind, for the finished headdress will, to a great extent, depend on them. With this awareness, the artist cuts into the cylindrical block, working quickly yet methodically, with strength, to remove the chunks of wood that stand between the uncut trunk and the finished work in his mind's eye. Such ability is associated with the gift of insight, which the Yoruba term *ojú inún* (literally "inner eye") (Abiọdun 1980a:14).

With successively smaller-bladed adzes, the carver refines his forms and rounds and smooths the surfaces. Then switching to his knives, he works on the surface details that determine the forms and the textures of the finished mask. One Awori master excelled in conveying the qualities of woven cloth (pl. 96), while Falọla of Idahin captured the texture of a woven mat (pl. 113). The carver can portray tightly braided coiffures (pls. 88, 89) and eyes staring between strong lids (pl. 89). Designs on sheaths received special attention from carvers in the Ẹtuọbẹ workshop (pls. 32, 33).

When the knifework is completed, the headdress is ready for painting. Sometimes the carver himself paints the mask, but often the client or some other person does so. In any case, once the mask is turned over to the client, it becomes his responsibility to repaint it before each Gẹlẹdẹ spectacle. In some areas the surface of the mask is sized with a thin latex coating from *iroko, ahun,* or *òro* trees to seal the pores of the wood and prevent them from absorbing the color, so the paint will adhere to the surface. Then the paints are prepared. Since at least the mid-nineteenth century, the Yoruba have imported enamel paints, but traditional pigments still continue to be preferred in some places (color plates 12, 13). The painter traditionally uses crushed mineral rock for various earth colors—red, brown, yellow, orange; charcoal, lampblack, or the bark of the *ebe* tree plus black soap *(ọṣẹ dúdu)* for black; indigo for blue; and snail shells, eggshells, kaolin, or chalk for white (Osubi 1971). The finely powdered pigments are then mixed with water or, in some cases, egg yolks to thicken them or egg whites to produce tempera with a slightly shiny quality.

Different kinds of applicators are used to paint the mask. Some painters prefer the pliable, fibrous end of a thin stick, similar to the

PLATE 169. The Ilaro style of
painting a band of contrasting
color to separate and delineate the
hairline and the forehead illustrates a local aesthetic preference.
1978.

common "chewing stick" used to clean the teeth. Others, known as *amuti*
(literally "the-holder-of-the-still-feather-of-the-bird," *a mu iti*), use a
brush made of birds' feathers (Murray n.d.). Still others use imported
paint brushes, cloths, or simply their fingers. The order of applying
colors varies considerably, but most often the artist begins with the lighter
hues and finishes with the darker ones. The reason is very practical: the
darker colors tend to bleed through the lighter ones. Thus, white for the
eyes, face, or mouth goes on first, followed by darker colors for eye lids,
hair, scarification marks, and so forth.

Lines where colors meet must be sharp to separate and differentiate
the various features. Painters juxtapose contrasting colors with precisely
rendered edges to produce this result; this technique is also evident in the
striking cloth patchwork facings on certain masquerades honoring the
ancestors (Drewal and Drewal 1978). The painter may even add a line of
a third color between two areas that are not sufficiently contrasting.
Ogunṣ̣eye of Ilaro separates the hairline and forehead with a single or
double band from ear to ear (pl. 169). All parts must be clearly distin-
guishable so that the viewer will be satisfied that the work is complete.

The choice of hues is based primarily on their visual effect in defining and separating parts. Verisimilitude in painting, although not very common, is a consideration for some. At Lagos, the Babalaṣẹ almost always paints hair black or indigo. Some faces are painted in different values of brown that closely resemble skin pigmentation (color plate 13). Other features may also require specific colors. For instance, masks depicting *orìṣa oko* worshippers have carved and painted lozenges in red and white on the forehead as the sign of their devotion. In most cases, however, the colors have only a general symbolic association with supernatural forces. White, the color of cool, covert deities, dominates masks representing the Great Mother and other "white deities" (pl. 170), while red, associated with hot and overtly aggressive forces, occurs at times on masks depicting Egungun masqueraders in the superstructures. The greater concern, however, is aesthetic: the actual choice of colors is not as important as their degree of contrast and how well they separate parts to make them visible from a distance, giving the mask a finished quality. Thus, most Ẹfẹ night masks have stark white faces, primarily for dramatic visual effect and only secondarily for symbolic reasons.

The creation and assembling of an Ẹfẹ or Gẹlẹdẹ masquerade represent the aesthetic ideal of completeness. Incising and painting the surface of the masks demonstrate the concern for accurate depiction of all important details. Carefully rendered details are essential for the dramatic illusion of masking, especially when some of the performances are conducted in the dark. Recognizable details attest to the thoroughness and the diligence of the artist.

The process of creation does not necessarily cease when an artist finishes carving and painting a mask. For art in Yoruba culture may continue to undergo alterations in response to the aesthetic preferences of its owners or caretakers, sometimes over several generations. Much Yoruba work, therefore, is really the product of many hands and continues to evolve over time.

Gẹlẹdẹ headdresses are changed primarily by the application of new layers of pigments and by the addition or alteration of attachments on the superstructures. Repainting is done before all performances, whether they are special funeral commemorations or annual festivals. Sometimes the sculptor is commissioned to do the refurbishing, but more often society officials in charge of the masks or the families of dancers will renew *(mura)* them. The availability of certain colors and types of paints, as well as the color preferences of the painters, can dramatically alter the appearance of the headdress. Changes in the forms usually occur in the attachments. Some Gẹlẹdẹ masks are constructed so that different items can be attached to the superstructure, such as different kinds of trays, containers, or products to depict specific roles within the broad category of marketwoman. And in some cases, a removable superstructure may be

PLATE 170. The whitewash and the snails evoke the "white deities," whose favorite sacrifices are snails. Museum für Völkerkunde, Basel (III 12681).

replaced by one that completely alters the subject matter of the headdress. For example, the ẹ̀kọ seller Gẹlẹdẹ by Ọduntan of Ṣawọnjo (pl. 111), reappeared some months later, newly painted and sporting a superstructure (probably by the same artist) honoring not a marketwoman but a priestess (color plate 10). These changes in iconography seem to reflect not only the continuing aesthetic input by the sculptor but also the evolution of the patron's perception of herself and how she wishes to be seen by the community, whether as an industrious marketwoman or as a religious leader.

The wishes and aesthetic sense of patrons and artists constitute some of the sources of diversity in the Gẹlẹdẹ masquerades. As both an artistic and a cultural phenomenon, Gẹlẹdẹ has undergone, and continues to undergo, dynamic changes while still anchored by certain fundamental beliefs about the spiritual powers of women and the means of channeling them for society's benefit. The phenomenon of Gẹlẹdẹ can be seen as an adaptive instrument with which society regulates individuals and, simultaneously, with which individuals effect change in society, creating and recreating it in a complex interactive system.

NOTES ON TEXT

1. Yoruba Spectacle

1. For another mention of opening and closing formulas in Yoruba verbal arts, see Ọlajuba (1978).

2. It is Pierre Verger (1964:15–19) who has given the most detailed account of the concept. See also Drewal and Drewal (1980).

3. Raymond Prince (1979:116) questions this interpretation because animals also are gagged during sacrifices. However, according to Yoruba thought, animals, speaking their own languages, are capable of uttering curses. Prince's alternative explanation, that the mouth of the sacrificial scapegoat is gagged to prevent the escape of the spiritual effluvia with which the victim has been infused, is also quite plausible. Both explanations support the broader notion of the victim's potential to emit destructive force through the breath.

4. Ayọade (1979:51) states further, "A name is the neatest encapsulation of a man's being. In a large number of cases it is believed that a man's name and the names of his parents are most essential to the control of the man because these names are regarded as the total summary of the person's being since they indicate his origin [iponri]. . . ." Bascom (1960:408) notes that knowledge of one's "history" (itan iponri), or praise names, "gives one the power to kill a person by summoning his ancestral guardian soul, and some informants hold that one will die if he even talks about his iponri." The importance of understanding the "instrumentality" of speech in African cultures has been argued convincingly by Benjamin Ray (1973).

5. The autonomous but equal segments of the whole are expressive of autonomous but equal forces operating in the universe, but they do not necessarily always invoke and activate those forces. Rather the seriate structure itself often symbolizes such a world order.

6. The concept of openings and closings has already been discussed. For other references to discontinuity, segmentation, and free rhythm in the arts, see Wolff (1962:48), Babalọla (1966:xx; 1973:81), Abimbọla (1976:64), H. J. Drewal (1977b:6–7), and Drewal and Drewal (1978).

7. The term ẹgbẹ́ in òrìsà ẹgbẹ́ (Gẹlẹdẹ) meaning "society" should not be confused with the term ẹlẹ́gbẹ́ associated with àbíkú, children "born to die," as has been confirmed by numerous Ẹgbado and Ketu Gẹlẹdẹ members. Àbíkú are also called eléèrè, (literally "person getting profit or advantage"), a reference to the special treatment accorded abiku in order to appease them (Abraham 1958:162). Circumstances of birth and inheritance make it possible for a family to have Araagbo (the tutelary deity of abiku/eleere) plus Gẹlẹdẹ, or any other combination of gods and/or spirits. Although Gẹlẹdẹ participants we have interviewed do not consider that Gẹlẹdẹ masqueraders represent abiku/ẹlẹgbẹ, Lawal (1978:68–69) suggests that they do.

8. See Idowu (1962:177–178) for a further discussion of ọmọ ar'aiye.

9. A second explanation often given is that the nighttime offers a private setting, since at that time the community is sleeping. However, it does not explain Ẹfẹ night performance, which the entire community is encouraged to attend. Finally, nighttime cere-

monies do not cut into the work day; but during festivals, all society or cult members are supposed to rest at home during the day in order to be on hand for festival events.

10. For a discussion of cooling or propitiatory rites, see Awolalu (1979:152–158).

11. For a discussion of Gẹlẹdẹ cult organization and the distribution of responsibilities for the various parts in Gẹlẹdẹ, see Drewal and Drewal (1975:38, 78).

2. Gẹlẹdẹ Performance

1. . . . *ere yin da gẹ́gẹ́ bí àṣẹ ti awọn àgbàlágbà ti ṣe kojá lo ti wọn pe gẹgẹ bí ẹ̀ṣọ̀ nitori wọn ko gbọdọ jo ni gbangba.*

2. The following description, based primarily on Ketu and Ketu-related Yoruba traditions, which are among the most elaborate and, we believe, the oldest, contains some elements from other western Yoruba groups. It is therefore a composite of Ẹfẹ and Gẹlẹdẹ spectacles, which serves as an introduction to this artistic phenomenon. This ritual complex is called simply Gẹlẹdẹ in the literature and by informants. Nevertheless the Yoruba clearly distinguish between Ẹfẹ and Gẹlẹdẹ ceremonies while recognizing their unity. Elderly informants claim "there can be no Ẹfẹ without Gẹlẹdẹ, and no Gẹlẹdẹ without Ẹfẹ."

3. An account of these preparations including consultations with the Yoruba oracle, Ifa, and sacrificial ceremony can be found in Drewal (1973:67–79).

4. The term *akijẹlẹ* may be related to the institution of *ajẹlẹ*, representatives of the Alaafin of Ọyọ charged with overseeing the activities of local rulers in areas subject to Ọyọ and with making reports to the king, functions somewhat analogous to Ọrọ Ẹfẹ's chorus. See Law (1977:110–113).

5. In some communities, elaborate precautions are taken to restrict or prevent certain people, especially women of childbearing age and children, from coming too close or seeing the Great Mother mask openly because of its alleged spiritual powers. See a discussion of these procedures of concealment in chapter 4.

6. It is significant that Ọrọ Ẹfẹ says he was "doing a task" for the *apá* and *iroko* trees, for they are believed to be the special abodes of the mothers (cf. Lucas 1948:284). This verse also confirms Ọrọ Ẹfẹ's role as servant of the mothers or, in other words, a "wizard" *(oṣo).*

3. Ẹfẹ Songs—Voicing Power

1. *Èfùfù* literally means "wind" and refers to the breath or vocal performance of diviners and Ẹfẹ singers. In this regard it is interesting to note that, according to Wande Abimbọla (1980), Ọrunmila, the deity presiding over Ifa divination, is said to "travel on the wind," a reference to oral transmission. William Bascom (1960:401) relates the Yoruba concept of breath *(ẹ̀mí)* to "man's vital force: it gives him life and makes him work."

2. Ulli Beier (1958:17) provides a graphic illustration when he writes that "It is Iyalashe who places the mask on the dancer's head, and even the great 'Efe' fully dressed . . . can still be impeded from coming out by Iyalashe. If at the moment when he is prepared to leave the hut Iyalashe tells him to stay 'he must go and sit down like a small boy'. . . ." Thompson (1972) reports that the *iyalaṣe* is the one who puts the mask on Ọrọ Ẹfẹ and that medicines are inserted in the headdress and costume to protect him.

3. These categories based on subject matter are our own and are used here simply for the analysis of texts. Yoruba may classify Ẹfẹ songs using other criteria, such as tempo or function. For example, Ọlabimtan, in his eagerly awaited book, *Akojopo Ọrọ Ẹfẹ,* deals with "Songs of Warning" (Orin Ikilo). See Aṣiwaju (1975:265, note 46).

4. The following discussion is based on a sample of 206 songs, 145 collected during interviews with cult elders, 30 recorded at Ẹfẹ performances in northern Egbado and Ketu areas, and the remainder taken from a variety of published sources (cf. Beier 1958; Ọlabimtan 1970; Harper 1970; Moulero 1970; Aṣiwaju 1975, 1976).

5. *Ijuba* are an essential part of all communications between the living and the supernatural forces as well as among different individuals and groups within society. They are a way of recognizing the distinctive potential of something or someone, honoring it, and as a result making that entity responsive to the concerns of the one reciting such homage. As a result, all rituals and sacrifices begin with *ijuba*.

6. The order of invoking the gods varies in different areas. At a Ketu Ẹfẹ ceremony, Ọbatala was called first; at Idahin, Orisa Oko, god of the hunt associated with "our mothers" (Ojo 1973) was called first. Ọlabimtan (1970) records Ogun as the first deity called in Abẹokuta, followed by Ẹṣu.

7. See also Prince (1961:796) for similar beliefs about burying secret substances under the earthen floor. According to informants, every "mother" must have a male *ọṣo* to carry out her work; she conceives the plan and he is her missive. Verger (1965:143) notes the same concept.

8. Sexual imagery is common in Ogun symbolism, as well as in that of other male deities and culture heroes, defining masculine, overt, vengeful characters (cf. Thompson 1971:ch.7/1–2 and Barnes 1980:29). Hoch-Smith (1978), by ignoring sexual themes and metaphors in ritual and symbolic representations of males and male deities, concludes erroneously that images of destruction and reproduction are peculiar to women in Yoruba society.

9. Ogun is known for his quick vengeance. This praise phrase mirrors reality, for in a sacrifice to Ogun the animal must literally be killed with one blow (cf. Barnes 1980:39) or it is not acceptable.

10. This example is only one part of a very long and elaborate *ijuba*. Shorter *ijuba* may occur at different points in Ọrọ Ẹfẹ's performance, but the initial one is usually very extensive. For an excellent example of an extensive *ijuba*, see Ọlabimtan (1970:201–207).

11. Ọlabimtan (1970:212) states that there are two types of Ẹfẹ songs based on tempo—the *mojáwéré* or *òlókó* (fast) and the *èwọ́* (slow). Descriptive language used to characterize song style is based on Lomax (1968:34–74).

12. Crowther (1852:54) records a praise song about the *àwòko* that states, "I sang 200 songs in the morning, 200 at noon and another 200 in the afternoon as my ordinary task as well as many other frolicsome notes for my own amusement." See also Ọlabimtan (1970:215, note 16).

13. See Prince (1961:796) and Verger (1967) for other medicines used as protection against the destructive mothers.

14. Agbojo is the first priest of Onidofoi, the deified ancestor of the Imala/Idofoi people in whose honor Gẹlẹdẹ is performed in that area.

15. For examples of Ẹfẹ songs used to comment on politics, see Aṣiwaju (1975).

4. The Masks and Costumes of Ẹfẹ Night

1. Moulero (1971:36–43) calls this mask Agbagba, to whom the audience sings praises in order to clear the way for the Gẹlẹdẹ festival.

2. In Ketu, the individual carrying fire is known as Agbena and is followed by a separate performer called Apana, "the Fire Extinguisher"; their entrance signals that all lights should be put out for the appearance of the Great Mother.

3. See, for example, the opening incantation *(ijuba)* presented by Ọrọ Ẹfẹ in chapter 3.

4. Some small communities of limited resources may not have night mother masks; however, in most cases a grove and/or shrine is maintained in her honor.

5. The following description is based on a corpus of twenty night mother masks: twelve photographed in the field, three from drawings by artist informants who carved the masks, two from verbal descriptions by specialist informants (priests and artists), two from published sources, and one from a museum collection.

6. Prince (1961:797) was given similar descriptions, such as "a white bird with long red beak and red claws" or "a brown bird like a bush fowl with long red beak."

7. Nocturnal mother masks, despite their central importance to the whole concept of Gẹlẹdẹ, have received only brief mention in an otherwise sizeable body of literature on the cult, perhaps because of their inaccessibility. For a review of this literature, see H. J. Drewal (1977a). Although the bearded mother mask has had brief mention, the bird mother mask is discussed here for the first time.

8. Prince (1960:67) notes the use of images, medicines, and words in the practice of curse and invocation.

9. Verger (1965:224–227) records a myth about the primordial mother, Odu, who prohibits anyone from seeing her "face." Odu's "face" refers to secret, powerful medicines kept in a closed container/calabash which, if seen, would cause instant blindness. The face also refers to the shrine, *ojubọ* (the face that receives offerings) or *oju orìṣa* (the face of the deity). It is the closed container placed on the shrine that serves as the focal point for prayers, divinations, and sacrifices and literally encloses the vital force of the deity.

10. Moulero (1970:53) received the same translation from elders in the Ketu area, while our own information comes from the Ọhọri area. It may be that instead of using a monosyllabic, action verb selected from the name of the potent ingredient, as in the case of chanting *ofọ*, the drummers activate the medicine by drumming double entendre. The name of the ingredient, then, is at the same time the verb phrase that activates it, so that in performance a double entendre may function both to invoke the essence of the ingredient and to set it into action.

11. Two variations should be noted. At Ijio, the mask is described as "black" (Harper 1970:75). That may be explained by its condition after a fire and by the fact that it no longer leaves the shrine. At Ohumbe, carver Lawani Olupọna (1975) states that it is not painted with any color, a condition that may in fact constitute "white."

12. At Sakete, this relationship between Ọrọ Ẹfẹ and Ogun is even more explicit, for the masquerader brings gifts for the deity and is formally greeted by the head of the Ogun worshippers, the Ologun (Beier 1958:15).

13. Harper (1970:78) received a similar explanation in Ijio.

14. Another documented by Carroll (1967:pl. 24) shows crosses, in all probability to identify the wearer as a Christian.

15. Besides providing rhythmic punctuation for his songs, leg rattles also suggest spiritual protective power. In form they are similar to those worn by an *abiku*, a child who is "born to die." The rattles are put on the child's ankles to frighten away spiritual forces that seek to destroy him. In another context, rattling iron bells on the herbalist's staff is said to prevent evil persons from approaching (cf. Thompson 1975:56).

5. The Dance

1. The term *ọkan*, usually translated as "heart," implies not simply emotions or feelings but rather "intellect," according to Rowland Abiọdun. Therefore, we have translated it as "mind."

2. The significance of these procedures is not entirely clear, but they imply procedures of protection that have parallels in hunter/Ogun masquerades and Egungun.

3. For a related analysis of doubling as an expression of the Yoruba philosophical concern with *syndesis*, see Armstrong (1981:72ff.).

4. The Ketu style analysis is based on observations in the towns of Ketu, Idahin, and Idofa. We wish to acknowledge the work of Forrestine Paulay, who viewed the Gẹlẹdẹ dance footage and prepared a dance profile for the Choreometrics project in 1972. This description benefits from discussions with her held at that time.

6. The Masks of Gẹlẹdẹ

1. Another example of mask upon mask is in the collection of the Santa Barbara Museum of Art.

2. Using Ifa literary sources, Rowland Abiọdun (1980b) provides a perceptive metaphor for the concept of art, whether verbal or visual; it is wisdom clothed or embellished in different ways.

3. Changes in proportion within a composition do not necessarily connote matters of hierarchy or social importance. Large central figures may simply be a means of focusing attention on a particular subject. Or they may be a solution to an artistic problem. For example, in a mask (pl. 122) showing a Muslim in a canoe, the teapots flanking the scene are in an entirely different scale, almost life-sized. The composition does not communicate relative importance through proportion. Such shifts in proportion (and perspective) are common in Yoruba art and appear to be expressions of a preference for seriate organization in which parts are separate and autonomous.

4. See the discussion of this subject in a mask from the Ketu/Idahin region in Drewal (1981:115).

5. This summary of myths is based on data collected from specialist informants in the northern Ẹgbado towns of Imala, Kẹsan Orile, Imaṣai, Iboro, Jọga Orile, and Igan Okoto, and in Idofoi and Aibo quarters, Aiyetoro. Similar accounts were also collected in Pobe and several Ọhọri Yoruba towns.

6. The same connotations for red parrot feathers were also collected at Ọwọ, in southeastern Yorubaland, 1975. See also Prince (1961:796).

7. The dots on Iju's face evoke the state of possession trance when goddess and priestess become one. The dots tend to diminish the volume and substance of the mask, giving it an ethereal, spiritual quality. At Ifẹ and Ila, dots are also painted on the faces of persons possessed by their gods.

8. Snakes, being nocturnal creatures, are associated with the mothers as well as with the qualities of patience and coolness. One elderly informant (Odu 1973) remarked that when you step on a snake, he does not react quickly, "He is cool" *(Onítútù)*. He also compared the snake's patience *(onísùúrù)* with that of his deified ancestor, Ondo.

9. The ancestral priestess masquerade seems to have survived among Yoruba descendants in Akutown, Sierra Leone. Two informants, whose grandparents were leaders of the Gẹlẹdẹ cult, described a special female masquerade known as Mama Sofi. She was said to represent one of the early female elders who was reputed to be very wise in the mysteries of the cult (Akinsulure and Frazer 1972). This masquerade shares certain traits with the mother masquerades of Ẹgbado. Appearing only on special occasions and performing alone, in contrast to other Gẹlẹdẹ, who dance in pairs, Mama Sofi comes at the conclusion of the ceremonies, moving slowly, bent over and leaning on a cane to depict her legendary age.

7. A Historical and Thematic Overview

1. The mothers are a primary concern in Ifa divination literature in non-Gẹlẹdẹ areas (Abimbọla 1976; Ọṣitọla 1982), although studies examining their place in the Yoruba world view are few. Drawing upon divination verses from eastern Yorubaland, Rowland Abiọdun (1976) documents the power of woman and the central role of the mothers in the Igogo festival at Ọwọ; and, based on Ifa verses collected at Oṣogbo, Pierre Verger in a lengthy monograph (1965) explicates the origins of women's spiritual power. With the exception of these three studies, little attention has been given in the literature on Yoruba cosmology to the role and place of the mothers.

The studies of the Atinga movement (Morton-Williams 1956) and of the Yoruba image of the witch (Prince 1961), which is based largely on mental patients' cases, highlight the negative dimensions of women's powers. And Hoch-Smith's study of radical sexuality (1978) implies that sexual images and a concern with reproductive processes in Yoruba ritual and symbolism are reserved for women. It thus provides a one-sided view by its omission of comparable male sexual images common in the ritual and symbolism of Ogun, Ṣango, Eṣu, and other male deities. This study perpetuates further an imbalanced picture of the mothers as negative, attacking "male-controlled society" (1978:249). From a Yoruba point of view, however, the mothers control society covertly and men simply act out their will. To put this into its proper perspective, it is perhaps more appropriate to focus on the mother-child bond rather than seek an explanation in the fact that women have achieved economic independence.

It is perhaps for similar reasons that the nocturnal mother masks have not been treated in the literature on Gẹlẹdẹ (cf. Drewal 1977a) and that concepts about women have not been examined sufficiently by scholars. In most contexts, the powers of the mothers are not generally discussed openly, yet they are central to virtually every Yoruba ritual. The probable reason for the secrecy surrounding this topic is that, unlike the deities and the ancestors who dwell in the otherworld and must be invoked to become manifest, the mothers are ever-present, and their influence and impact on ritual is covert. They inhabit the world and live in virtually every Yoruba household. Indeed, as we have seen, the mothers are the "owners of the world," the "gods of society," and to this extent, they mediate the power of the gods and the ancestors in "the world." Thus, the mothers and the gods and ancestors are "working hand-to-hand," as Yoruba often say. This applies as much to the cults of the ancestors (Egungun) and the deities as it does to Gẹlẹdẹ. Gẹlẹdẹ simply treats the subject of the mothers and their role in society more explicitly than do many other Yoruba cults, at least more explicitly than the literature on these cults presently acknowledges.

2. Aṣiwaju (1976:36–37, footnote 73) remarks that although there were connections between Old Ọyọ and Ketu, they "do not appear to have amounted to political control." Atanda (1973:11–12) suggests that an alliance may have existed whereby Old Ọyọ would protect Ketu from Dahomey in return for permission to control the trade route passing through Ketu territory.

3. Some intriguing data suggest historical and artistic interactions between the Gẹlẹdẹ world and the kingdom of Benin. Benin influence in Lagos may date from the late sixteenth century to the latter part of the eighteenth (Egharevba 1960:30–31; Norris 1789), and Benin is associated with Igbesa, Ado-Odo, and Badagri, all Awori or Anago towns (Aṣiwaju 1976:19). Using visual data, Thompson (1971:ch. 14/1) notes that formal ties linking Gẹlẹdẹ masks to Benin bronzes of the sixteenth and seventeenth centuries "suggest a firm foundation in Nigerian antiquity." The style of some Gẹlẹdẹ masks, more specifically those of Ọta, Awori, does show some similarities with Benin bronzes in pierced pupils and nostrils, and lenticular eye and lip shades. Yet these traits could be said to apply throughout most periods of Benin art, and the bronzes that mirror Yoruba Gẹlẹdẹ masks most closely are from the eighteenth and nineteenth centuries. The style of Ketu, Ẹgbado, and Ọhọri Gẹlẹdẹ masks is more closely related to other Yoruba styles than to Benin. The visual evidence remains inconclusive. Fagg (1978:21) illustrates two Ijẹbu Yoruba brass bell heads (*omo*) formerly in the possession of the king of Ketu. They indicate Ketu contacts with Ijẹbu (and perhaps Benin) but how early is uncertain since these brasses appear to be of nineteenth-century manufacture. Recurring references to brass, shells, and Olokun, an important Benin (and Yoruba) divinity of the sea, in songs and other oral testimony may also indicate some Gẹlẹdẹ world–Benin interactions, yet they cannot at present be dated. These same references may also be interpreted in other ways. For example, the mention of shells (*okoto*) may refer to cowries, which were im-

ported in great quantities by Europeans on the coast. Shells, brass, and the sea point as much to the wealth from Yoruba trading activities with Europeans at Porto Novo and Badagri as they do to Benin. A praise name, for example, for a renowned carver credited with starting Gẹlẹdẹ at Jọga is "Famous-Carver-Who-Uses-a-Brass-Knife-to-Carve" *(Afeju agúnwa li fi ọbẹ idẹ gbẹ'gi)*. The carver did not literally carve with a brass knife; rather the reference to brass is a way of praising his prosperity and thus his success as a carver.

4. In Agọsạsa and in the Ketu Gẹlẹdẹ society, Isalẹ Eko, Lagos, Gẹlẹdẹ is said to come from Ketu (Thompson 1971:ch. 14/1–2). Ilara, a Ketu Yoruba town on the Nigerian–Benin border, credits Ketu as the source of Gẹlẹdẹ (Onluiji 1971). Porto Novo in the south and Ṣabe north of Ketu say Gẹlẹdẹ came from Ketu at an undetermined time (Beier 1958:8; Bernolles 1966:23). According to Monserrat Palau-Marti (1980), Gẹlẹdẹ in Ṣabe seems to be a fairly recent introduction from Ketu. The towns of Iwoye in Ọhọri area, Imaṣai, and Pobe associate Gẹlẹdẹ origins with Ketu (field notes 1973). At Idofa, one cult official (Adeogun 1971) says that the first to do Gẹlẹdẹ was Iko, founder of the town, who is now regarded as a deity and honored at Gẹlẹdẹ festivals. He further states that his title, Aṣo Ẹfẹ, had in the past been held by a former king of Idofa named Alao Dudueko, a son of Alaketu Adio [Adiro, 1858–1867].

5. The Gẹlẹdẹ mask among Idofoi/Imala peoples depicts Muslims, and the first elder to hold the head Gẹlẹdẹ title in those areas was said to have dressed like a Muslim during his lifetime. See p. 176.

6. We wish to thank Fr. Thomas Moulero for permission to see and copy his handwritten manuscript, "Le Guèlèdè," in 1971. We dedicate this chapter to Fr. Moulero, who passed away in 1974.

7. In conversation with Moulero (1971), he admitted that some of his information was conflicting. He arrived at the designation of Ẹdun as Adebiya based on the recitation of the court herald (although he said this was not complete) and the tradition that attributes the start of Gẹlẹdẹ to the Mefu royal lineage (Adebiya's).

8. The Bale of Ilogun Quarter, Aiyetoro, stated (Bankọle 1971) that before there were masks people used calabashes. We observed a child wearing a painted calabash during a Gẹlẹdẹ performance in Ketu in 1971.

9. The Yoruba orthography is nonstandard, reflecting the Ketu dialect. Moulero's translations are not literal, but his interpretations are accurate. We have therefore kept close to a literal translation of the French into English. Note the remarkable similarity of this song with the one cited by Ogundipẹ at Ketu and by the king of Pobe. We collected the same song at Ọja Odan, where it is sung to greet the Gẹlẹdẹ and to encourage them to dance harder (Olowobese 1975).

10. We collected a similar praise name for Gẹlẹdẹ at Ilaro and Ọja Odan, but Olokun was replaced by Oluaiye ("Owner-of-the-World"), a reference to the mothers.

11. The following song includes "*atọkun*, Child of Ọjẹ, *egun* of the king," which seems to be a reference to the Egungun cult. Moulero does not attempt to explain this reference to Egungun in a song that is supposed to document the origin of Gẹlẹdẹ. It is interesting to note, however, that Parrinder (1967:100) lists an Alaketu named Ọjẹ, a name associated with the Egungun cult. Although it is not known which royal line he belonged to, one of the five Ketu royal families is Alapini, an important Egungun title. The song may suggest that somehow Gẹlẹdẹ derived from Egungun but we have no other evidence of that assertion. Another possibility is that certain of the royal lineages at Ketu owned both Gẹlẹdẹ and Egungun, a very common occurrence throughout western Yorubaland. Indeed, we witnessed the appearance of an Egungun masquerader before an afternoon Gẹlẹdẹ dance, which honored the anniversary of the death of an important member of both societies. The Egungun, however, did not approach the market where the Gẹlẹdẹ

spectacle took place. Thus, it is quite possible that the Ẹfẹ masquerader who offered this song was praising himself not only as a wonderful joker with reverberating leg rattles but also as a child of Ojẹ.

12. This date is recorded from an article in *Iwe Irohin,* a Yoruba newspaper, translated in *Church Missionary Intelligence,* 1860, Appendix, and quoted in Parrinder (1967:54–55).

13. In addition to Kẹsan and Ketu informants, people in the towns of Imaṣai, Itolu, and Ilaro also claim that Ijoun is the home of Bọrọmu.

14. Interviews with S. I. Adeṣina, Abepa of Jọga, and seven of his chiefs, April 2 and 12, 1971. The Ọba possesses a historical document dated 1921, probably a petition to the British Colonial administration.

15. Today Aibo is the central quarter of Aiyetoro, from which the kings are selected, and is recognized as the original settlement before Aiyetoro was established circa 1902. Because of its proximity to other towns on the former trade route and the local tradition that it was founded during the reign of Alaafin Abiọdun, it seems likely that it is the town Clapperton (1829) identifies as "Liabo."

16. Today Emado (Erinmado) is located within the town of Aiyetoro, but formerly it was on Erinmado stream, five miles south of Aiyetoro.

17. At Igan Okoto, two encounters with the Ẹgba are remembered. The first may have been the Owiwi War of 1832, fought between the Ẹgba and Ijẹbu on Ẹgbado soil. Biobaku's account (1957:20) mentions that after the Ijẹbu defeat, the Ẹgba warrior Apati "destroyed several Ẹgbado towns, notably Ijanna, and attacked Ilaro, the Ẹgbado capital." This route of reprisal would have passed very close to Igan Okoto, which may have been one of the towns attacked. The second encounter with the Ẹgba is clearly remembered as the Dado War (Ajibọla 1971). According to Biobaku (1957:22), the Ẹgba, in retaliation for attacks by Dado, a chief of Igan Okoto, "pursued Dado into the Egbado country, sacked many towns there and returned to Abeokuta." Biobaku gives a date of 1834 for these events.

18. Collected from Alapa Legbe, Babalawo and Ẹlẹfẹ, Emado Quarter, Aiyetoro, March 20, 1971. Jọga, it will be recalled, was founded circa 1790. The date 1825 is used here because it would have been at approximately this time that Jọga's founding forefather would have returned to Jọga after fighting the Fulani on behalf of Oyọ.

19. According to Morton-Williams (1964:40), trade was mainly through ports south of Little Ardrah in the eighteenth century, but by the late eighteenth century much of the trade had moved eastward to Badagri, the new route passing through a number of towns founded by sons of Alaafin Abiọdun. Then in 1784, apparently because the southern end of the route had grown too independent, the Alaafin allowed the Dahomeans to destroy Badagri. It was subsequently rebuilt, for it has been documented that F. da Souza, a slaver, had made a fortune there in 1818 (Dunglas 1957:ii, p. 41, cited in Morton-Williams 1964:34).

20. See note 18. According to tradition the founding forefather, Ọbalaju, returned from war with the Fulani and crowned the first king of Jọga. From that time until 1921, the date of Jọga documents, six kings reigned.

21. The Oniṣare was a non-Yoruba slave who served in the palace at Oyọ and was sent to Ijanna by the Alaafin to reassert Oyọ's control over the Ẹgbado province (cf. Law 1977:115–116).

22. It will be recalled that traditions about Ilaro tell of Oronna's journey down toward the coast in the company of a messenger who settled in Awori. Meanwhile Oronna returned northward to found Ilaro.

23. K. C. Murray (Nigerian Museum Archives) visited Iposuko Quarter, Badagri, at

least three times between 1942 and 1958. In 1942, he reports, a large number of Gẹlẹdẹ masks and other cult paraphernalia were stored in a shrine with a corrugated roof. The caretaker and head of the Gẹlẹdẹ society said his people brought Gẹlẹdẹ with them from Ilaro. From among eighty discarded masks, Murray selected a number for the Nigerian Museum collection (nos. 336–342). These masks were said to have been carved by Opere of Afarni, Dahomey, circa 1926. By 1946, when Murray revisited, the shrine had collapsed and the remaining masks were exposed to the open air. Finally, by 1958, the caretaker had died, and a relative said that Gẹlẹdẹ had not been performed since before 1945 because the drummers had died and many people had left Badagri.

24. We are grateful to K. C. Murray, who kindly provided us with information on Gẹlẹdẹ in 1971, including the letters from Beyioku (1943 and 1946). Burns (1929:42, 313) does not give dates for this reign but says the second king after Eṣinlokun reigned from 1836 to 1841. Using thirteen years as an average reign would corroborate Talbot's dates.

25. There are discrepancies in the literature about the history of Iṣeri people and their entry into Lagos. Losi (1967:11) places the foundation of Iṣeri at about 1699. Talbot (1969:81) gives circa 1660 for the Iṣeri colonization of Lagos and the first king, Aṣipa; however, he records only six reigns for Iṣeri kings before Eṣinlokun, who came to the throne in 1820. That would average out to 26⅔ years per reign, which is very unlikely. Burns (1929:38–40) suggests the end of the fifteenth century for the Iṣeri migration. Since his king list duplicates Talbot's, the length of reigns is even more unlikely. Finally, Ellis (1974:11) states that about 1807 "some of the Yorubas first pushed to the south and colonized Lagos. The first chief of Lagos was called Ashipa, and is said to have belonged to the family of the *Alafin*." Ellis does not cite his source, but his information corresponds more with our evidence that Iṣeri and their Gẹlẹdẹ are related to Ilaro. In Ilaro migration traditions, Oronna, the founding forefather, is said to have sojourned as far south as Ado Odo, Ilobi, and Awori country before returning to Ilaro. He was led by a messenger from Ọyọ, who was instructed by the Alaafin to settle on the coast, or where the sacrifice sank into the water. Oronna, son of the Alaafin, supposedly accompanied the messenger down to Awori country and then returned. If the foundation of Ilaro was late eighteenth century and if Iṣeri people are related to Ilaro, then Ellis's date seems more accurate. It would place the migration of Iṣeri people into Lagos after Benin influence was in decline, although Iṣeri apparently recognized Benin's authority as the first settlers (cf. Smith 1969:89–94 for a discussion of the same problem). The discrepancies in these historical accounts, like those of Ilaro, may result from the lack of distinction between earlier local authorities and those imposed by Ọyọ during the expansionist period of Alaafin Abiọdun. Another possible explanation is the political need of the various people to validate their authority in the area in order to maintain their chieftaincies in the face of British Colonial rule.

26. Scholars may have underestimated the extent and the rates of change in African art. Complex market and long distance trading networks assured widespread and rapid dispersal of goods as well as artistic ideas. For example, the elders at Jọga told us that traveling time to New Ọyọ was two days on foot through the town of Igbo Ora, and the Olu of Ilaro told Clapperton (1829:10) that a messenger could reach Lagos in a day. This rapid communication system together with the itinerancy of artists must have encouraged the rapid dissemination of artistic ideas.

27. Besides these Gẹlẹdẹ-related phenomena in Ijẹbu and Lagos, Gẹlẹdẹ itself is present in other Yoruba areas, notably Ijẹṣa, Ọyọ, and Ifẹ. This, however, is recent, primarily the result of a secularized form of dance theater. Nowadays, Gẹlẹdẹ troupes perform

throughout Yorubaland on social occasions such as births, marriages, and funerals, as do the Agbegijo masquerade companies, commercial traveling theaters derived from the ancestral Egungun cult.

28. However, Bastide (1978:256, citing Arthur Ramos) says that Our Lady of the Immaculate Conception of the Beach is syncretized with Yẹmọja, goddess of the sea.

29. We are indebted to Didi and Juana dos Santos for providing information on these masks during fieldwork in Brazil in 1974 and for permission to photograph them.

30. Although they were no longer worn, the masks were cared for by Iya Ọbabiyi of Aṣẹ Opo Afonja until her death and the rites performed on December 8, along with those for Onile and Apaoka, a tree divinity (dos Santos 1967:45). It will be recalled that the *apa* is one of the trees closely associated with the mothers.

31. This provenance is by no means certain, since there was much communication and travel between Bahia and West Africa in the second half of the nineteenth century. We have documented examples of cult objects being carved in West Africa and brought to Bahia for use, and one example of a form that crossed the Atlantic twice (Mimito 1974).

NOTES ON PLATES

Color Plates

1. Mask carved in the style of Mẹko (Ketu). See plate 134 for a detail and plate 11 for a mask by the same hand. Other masks from Mẹko appear in plates 48, 102, 108–109, 112, and 121.

2. Mask carved by Alaiya Adeiṣa Ẹtuọbẹ (died 1970) of Ita Ọba quarter, Ketu. Also see frontispiece, color plate 3, and plates 4, 5, 27, 29, 32, 33, and 60. Other masks by Ẹtuọbẹ are in the Musée de l'Homme (D 31/4.132, 133, 143, 155), collected in Dahomey for the Coloniale de Vincennes in 1931. According to Ẹtuọbẹ's grandson, Adegbọla, the family traditionally farmed near the Ẹgbado town of Igbogila. Thus, a number of Ẹtuọbẹ's works can be found in Igbogila and in the neighboring town of Ṣawonjo.

3. See color plate 2 and its note. In the headdress, cutlasses flank a representation of a rectangular leather panel (laba). The hunter's jerkin shows chevrons at the shoulders, inset mirrors, spirals, and appliquéd panels with motifs that probably derive ultimately from Islamic sources (Hausa).

4. Mask carved in Mẹko (Ketu) in use at Ilaro (Ẹgbado). Motif on top is a folded mat similar to the one illustrated in plate 113 from Idahin (Ketu).

5. Pair of masks carved by Falọla Ẹdun of Idahin (Ketu), who was born circa 1900. For other masks by this carver, see plate 113, Drewal and Drewal (1975:pl. 9), and Nigerian Museum (67.8.23); for a mask by his father, Fagbite, see plate 81; and, for a mask by Ẹdun's son, Sambilisi, see H. J. Drewal (1974b:pl. 18).

6. For a more complete view of the masquerader wearing this cloth, see plate 62.

7. Probably carved in the Ketu vicinity. The dancer is a visiting performer from Ketu. This mask and the one illustrated in plate 67 make a pair.

8. Carved by Fayomi Oduntan of Ṣawonjo (Ẹgbado), in the first quarter of the twentieth century, this mask depicts a Fulani-style hat worn over a turban, with a small parrot perched on top. Incorporated with the fabrics collected from the women are remnants of appliquéd panels transferred from older, worn-out costumes. For other works by the same hand, see plates 24 and 62, and, for works by Fayomi's father, Oduntan Aina, see color plates 10 and 11, and plates 101, 111, and 138.

9. Related in style to masks in plates 64 and 151.

10, 11. Carved by Oduntan Aina of Ṣawonjo, originally from Ijaka, in the late nineteenth century. Oduntan's father, Aina, reportedly migrated from Ikosi (Ọyọ) to Ijaka, where Oduntan was born. Oduntan then left Ijaka and spent some time in Oke Odan before settling at Ṣawonjo. The style of this mask indeed compares favorably with another from Ijaka (see plate 164). See masks in plates 101, 111, and 138, which were also carved by Oduntan. For works by Oduntan's son, Fayomi, see color plate 8 and plates 24 and 62. Other Gẹlẹdẹ masks by Oduntan Aina can be found in the Institute of African Studies, University of Ibadan (6712) and in Roy (1979:pl. 92), Armstrong (1981:pl. 5), and Fagg and Pemberton (1982:pl. 36).

13. Masks on a bed at Isalẹ Eko, Lagos, probably the work of various carvers at different times in Ọta (Awori). They are freshly painted and ready to be picked up by the dancers, who will wear them the same afternoon.

Black and White Plates

1. Although it was photographed in Isalẹ Eko quarter, Lagos, this Arabi Ajigbalẹ mask was probably carved by Ọlabimtan Odunlami (died ca. 1930) of Ijisu compound, Ijana quarter, Ọta (Awori), perhaps during the first quarter of this century. Also see plates 14 and 120 for works related to the same workshop. Other masks by the same hand are in the Pitt-Rivers Museum (1965.8.38) and in the Nigerian Museum (57.25.1c, 57.25.3, 48.33.53). Indeed, the first two examples from the Nigerian Museum were not used in Gẹlẹdẹ masquerades but were used by the Ekine society of the Ilaje Yoruba in Mahin, near Okitipupa, to represent water spirits. Another mask by this hand is illustrated in Thompson (1971:Ch. 14, color plate, right). Other examples of Ọta works are shown in plates 56, 63, 69, 88, 93, 96, 123, 124, and 165.

3. Spirit Bird headdress carved by James Akinde of Ilaro (Egbado), circa 1960, grandson of Onipaṣọnọbẹ, "The-One-who-Wields-a-Knife-Like-a-Whip." See plate 149.

4. Tetede mask by Alaiye Adeiṣa Ẹtuọbẹ of Ita Ọba quarter, Ketu (died ca. 1970), probably carved late in his career. See detail of the same mask in plate 29. For other examples of Ẹtuọbẹ's work, see frontispiece, color plate 3, and plates 5, 27, 29, 32, 33, and 60. Other masks by Ẹtuọbẹ are in the Musée de l'Homme (D 31/4. 132, 133, 143, 155), collected in Dahomey for the Coloniale de Vincennes in 1931.

5. Ọrọ Ẹfẹ mask carved by Alaiye Adeiṣa Ẹtuọbẹ of Ita Ọba quarter, Ketu, Benin. Also see frontispiece, color plates 2 and 3, and plates 4, 27, 29, 32, 33, and 60. See the note to plate 4 above.

6. Hyena (Koriko/Ikoko) mask carved circa 1944 by Omigbaro of Kẹsan Orile (Egbado), who held the title of Ajana in the Oro society and died at an advanced age during the 1970s. Other masks by Omigbaro are illustrated in plates 59 and 139.

7. Mask carved by an unknown Ilaro carver, probably late nineteenth century. A mask by the same hand, collected in Ilaro, is in the Institute of African Studies, University of Ibadan (6519); and another in a similar style and with the same motif is in the Art Museum, University of Ifẹ. See plate 144 for another example of this artist's work.

8. The mask in the foreground is closely related to the one shown in plate 7, but is probably from a more recent generation in the same Ilaro carving workshop.

9. Masks by Saibu Akinyemi of Agoṣaṣa (Anago), who spent three months carving them under a blacksmith's shed in Onọla quarter, Ilaro, circa 1974. See plates 53 and 82 for other examples of his work. For another Agoṣaṣa mask, possibly carved by Saibu's father, Akinyemi Akinlade, see plate 116.

10. Identical masks related to the work of an unnamed carver illustrated in plates 110 and 114 and in Carroll (1967:pl. 24), who photographed a mask in the town of Likimọn, near Ketu. Other illustrations of these masks are plate 57 and Drewal (1974:pl. 6).

11. In the style of the Mẹko vicinity. See plate 134 for another mask by the same hand, and plate 48 for another rendition of a warthog-attacking-snake motif.

12. Mask probably carved by Ogundare of Ṣawonjo (Egbado). For a detail of this mask, see plate 163.

13. Related to work attributed to Ogunwole of Oke Idọta quarter, Imaṣai (Egbado).

14. Amukoko mask probably carved by Ọlabimtan of Ijisu compound, Ijana quarter, Ọta (Awori), in the first quarter of the twentieth century. See plate 1 and note on plate 1 for details.

15. Headdress of the herald (Amukoko) reportedly carved by Laniba of Dagbe, Sakete (Anago), but possibly by his apprentice. See plate 34, by a different hand, but also attributed to Laniba. For another mask from the same vicinity, see plate 129.

16. According to Fagg (1968:pl. 117), this mask was collected in the village of Banigbe Poro-Poro, near Pobe (Anago).

17. Clouzot and Level (1926:pl. 38) give information on this mask as follows, "Daho-mean mask or headdress—height 60 mm.—Collection of Dr. Spire." Probably from the Ketu vicinity.

18. Attributed by the caretaker to Akinyele Ayefemi of Ile Ọlanle, Ṣawonjo (Ẹgbado), whose father migrated to Ṣawonjo from Sakete, in the late nineteenth century. See plate 163 for a work by a carver reportedly trained by Akinyele.

19. Possibly carved in the Anago area. Height: 241 mm., length: 700 mm. Traces of white pigment on the lower portion of the mask.

20. Carved by Ogunmọla of Ibaiyun (Ọhọri). For other masks with *oṣu*, although not so prominent, see plates 93, 100, 101, 159, and 163.

21. Probably carved between Pobe and Ketu.

22. The mask in foreground was carved about 1955 by Ṣegbe Osubi of Iwoye (Ọhọri); the one in the middle is by an unidentified forefather; and the one in the background was carved before the birth of Osubi, that is, before 1890.

23. Probably carved in the Ketu vicinity.

24. Spirit Bird mask attributed by the owner to Fayomi Oduntan of Ṣawonjo (Ẹgbado). Also see color plate 8 and plate 62. For works by Fayomi's father, Oduntan Aina, see color plates 10 and 11, and plates 101, 111, and 138.

25. Carver unknown, but mask probably made in Ibeṣe (Ẹgbado).

26. Surrounding the cloth-covered mother mask in the Odua shrine are ritual pots (*otun*), which hold water for libations.

27. Tetede mask by Alaiye Adeiṣa Ẹtuọbẹ of Ita Ọba quarter, Ketu. Also see frontis-piece, color plates 2 and 3, and plates 4, 5, 29, 32, 33, and 60. Other masks by Ẹtuọbẹ are in the Musée de l'Homme (D 31/4.132, 133, 143, 155), collected in Dahomey for the Coloniale de Vincennes of 1931.

28. Tetede mask probably from the Ketu vicinity.

29. Detail of mask in plate 4, carved by Alaiye Adeiṣa Ẹtuọbẹ of Ita Ọba quarter, Ketu. Also see frontispiece, color plates 2 and 3; plates 4, 5, 27, 32, 33, and 60; and note to plate 27 above.

30. Related to work attributed to Roye of Idọfa (Ketu) (cf. Nigerian Museum 59.33.74). This Tetede mask is said to have brought rain after a drought (PNM archives). The sign, which is unusual—although masks in Ẹgbado sometimes have writing on them (pls. 53 and 165)—may refer to the *agbe* tree, which has spherical fruit used for medicines. The Ẹgbe Kpokọn is probably the name of the Gẹlẹdẹ society that owned the headdress. A snake at the summit holds something in its mouth, and leaves cover the ears, as they usually do during ceremonies for those receiving titles.

31. In the style of Ẹgbado area. See also plate 44 for a mask in the same form, which follows this one in performance. Another Ẹfẹ mask of this type from Ilaro is in the Nigerian Museum (64.23.52), and one from Ọta (Awori) is illustrated in Thompson (1978:62, pl. 18). According to Murray's notes of 1940 (Nigerian Museum archives), the Ọta ensemble has a raffia costume.

32. Carved by Alaiye Adeiṣa Ẹtuọbẹ of Ita Ọba quarter, Ketu, in 1970. The birds are West African grey woodpeckers (*akoko*), the snake is a python, the animal at the top is a leopard (*ẹkun*), and the vertical blades at the sides are cutlass sheaths with designs remi-niscent of Islamic leatherwork. Also see frontispiece, color plates 2 and 3, and plates 4, 5, 27, 29, 33, and 60. Other masks by Ẹtuọbẹ are in the Musée de l'Homme (D 31/4.132, 133, 143, 155), collected in Dahomey for the Coloniale de Vincennes of 1931.

33. Carved by Alaiye Adeiṣa Ẹtuọbẹ of Ketu. Ọrọ Ẹfẹ headdress with turban wraps, cutlass sheaths, and birds in the superstructure. An arching snake is suspended over the face. Using basically the same repertoire of motifs, Ẹtuọbẹ alters their placement within

the composition. Compare this mask with the frontispiece, color plates 2 and 3, and plates 4, 5, 27, 29, 32, and 60.

34. Attributed to Kumuyi Laniba of Dagbe, Sakete (Anago). For another mask reportedly from the same workshop, possibly by his student, see plate 15, and, for a mask from the same vicinity, see plate 129.

35. Reportedly carved by Iwo Bawa of Agoṣaṣa and collected at Agoṣaṣa (Anago) before 1959. Although the catalog information (Nigerian Museum archives) identifies the animal as a lizard *(agilinti)*, it is probably a mongoose, as in plate 34.

36–38. Carved by Lawani Ojo of Ohumbe (Ọhọri-Ketu).

39. Probably carved in the vicinity north of Pobe.

40. Probably carved in the Ọhọri Ije area, north of Pobe. The masquerader apparently looks out under the face of the mask.

41. Carved before 1947 in Ọhọri Ije area.

42. Carved by Akindele Osubi of Iwoye (Ọhọri Ije), circa 1940. For a mask carved by Akindele's younger brother, Ṣegbe, see plate 22.

43. Carved by Koneṣe Ṣegbe, son of Ṣegbe Osubi, of Iwoye (Ọhọri Ije), ca. 1950. See also plates 22 and 42 for masks from the same workshop. For other examples of double-faced masks, see plates 149 and 150, Duerden (1968:pl. 23), Fagg and Pemberton (1982:pl. 36), and Institute of African Studies Museum, University of Ibadan (6287).

44. Carved by an Ẹgbado artist, possibly Ṣangolade of Ipahaiyi—see plate 149—and related to another mask collected in Ilaro (Nigerian Museum, 64.23.52). See also plate 31.

45. According to its caretakers, this mask was carved in 1918, probably in the Lagos vicinity. The workshop that produced it also carved for the Ejiwa society at Ijọra, Lagos (see pls. 77 and 154, and Nigerian Museum archives, 1940, neg. nos. 7.11.1, 7.14.11, 7.13.8, 7.14.10, 7.11.45, 7.12.2, and 7.12.3, photographed in the compound of the Oniru of Iru). This workshop is identifiable only by its style, which includes a very distinctive ear bisected by an exclamation mark form in relief. Other masks in this style are in the Wellcome Collection, British Museum (1954 Af 23.23, Af. 23.28—purchased 1932, Af 23.29—purchased 1924) and the Horniman Museum (neg. nos. 2292 and 2293).

46. Probably carved by Sunday Oloyede of Ibara Quarter, Abẹokuta. Also see plates 54, 79, 140, and 146.

47. Mask probably from Agoṣaṣa (Anago).

48. Mask with a wild boar attacking snake is from Mẹko and appears to be related to the Duga tradition. See plate 11 for a similar motif.

49. Old mask carved by Atọba of Ilu Ata quarter, Ilaro, originally of Ketu, who died circa 1940 (Chappel 1981). For other works by Atọba, see plate 117 and *African Arts* 7(4), 1974, inside front cover. Murray first documented work by Atọba in 1944 (cf. Nigerian Museum 44.1.1). The male instructor who accompanies masquerader is dressed in women's clothes.

50. Plump porcupine devouring corn probably carved by a Ṣawonjo carver. For another rendering of the porcupine, see pl. 136.

52. The facial plane and the position and construction of the superstructures suggest that these headdresses were carved in the vicinity of Agoṣaṣa (Anago). The mask in the background depicting a hunter with a sword and a gun is identical to some documented in Agoṣaṣa.

53. Carved by Saibu Akinyẹmi of Agoṣaṣa (Anago). See also plate 82. For masks by the same hand with a similar motif, see plate 9, and, for a mask possibly carved by Saibu's father, Akinyẹmi Akinlade, see plate 116. "Olori Agberu," painted on the forehead of the mask, refers to the titled elder in charge of the costumes. It is thus ironic that the figure

on the mask is shown without clothing. Likewise, the caretaker of the mask is a devotee of Ogun, god of iron. Plate 161 shows this mask and its mate on an Ogun shrine.

54. Mask in foreground carved by Sunday Oloyede of Ibara quarter, Abẹokuta (Ẹgbado), circa 1960–70s. Mask in background with a hunter's trap depicted on top was probably carved in northern Ẹgbado area.

56. Mask by an unknown carver, probably from Ọta (Awori).

57. Mask by an unnamed Ketu-area carver related to one documented by Carroll (1967:pl. 24) in the town of Likimọn. Other illustrations of these masks are plate 10 and Drewal (1974:pl. 6).

58. Headdress possibly carved in the Ketu vicinity. The breastplate consists of twin figures. The one on the left is carved in the style of the Ẹṣubiyi workshop at Abẹokuta, and the other is in a southern Ẹgbado style. For other works related to the Ẹṣubiyi workshop, see plates 79, 95, 146, and 150.

59. Mask and breasts probably carved by Omigbaro of Kẹsan (Ẹgbado)—see plates 6 and 139. Some elements, such as the ear form, relate Omigbaro's style to the Ọlabode workshop in Idofoi quarter, Aiyetoro (cf. pl. 133). Superstructure depicts a king flanked by policemen, with female in front. Loudspeakers are depicted on the sides of the mask. Reptiles and seated monkeys mount the breasts.

60. Probably carved by Alaiye Adeiṣa Ẹtuọbẹ of Ita Ọba quarter, Ketu. Also see frontispiece, color plates 2 and 3, and plates 4, 5, 27, 29, 32, and 33. Other masks by Ẹtuọbẹ are in the Musée de l'Homme (D 31/4.132, 133, 143, 155), collected in Dahomey for the Coloniale de Vincennes in 1931.

61. Probably carved in Ilaro, late nineteenth to early twentieth century. Compare with plate 168 for a mask by the same hand with the same motif, but painted differently.

62. Mask attributed to Fayomi Oduntan of Ṣawonjo (Ẹgbado), first quarter of the twentieth century. The prototype of this mask, by Oduntan Aina, Fayomi's father, has been recently acquired by the Nigerian Museum. According to the caretaker, it is surmounted by a representation of a *bayanni* for Oriṣa Oko, made of cowries (*owo eyo*) with a projection at the top (*ṣonṣo ori*). For another depiction of *owo eyo,* see plate 80. The dancer is wearing an embroidered and appliquéd wrapper. For a detail of the wrapper, see color plate 6. Other examples of Fayomi's work appear in color plate 8 and plates 24 and 62. For works by Fayomi's father, Oduntan Aina, see color plates 10 and 11, and plates 101, 111, and 138.

63. Carved by Kilani Ọlaniyan (born 1936) of Iga Igbein, Oruba quarter, Ọta (Awori), maternal grandson of Ọlaniyan, also a renowned carver. For other works by Kilari, see plates 88, 123, 124, and 165. Female hairstyle is called "shells" (*okoto*).

64. Mask probably carved somewhere in the Awori or Ijẹbu area, just north of Lagos. It is stylistically related to the masks in color plate 9 and plate 151, and is probably from the same workshop. Imported cloth is mixed with traditional strip cloth, and the head tie is realistically rendered, demonstrating the fashion of the period. The masquerader also wears sandals.

65. A detail of the mask worn by one of this pair appears in Drewal (1974:pl. 18), carved by Sambilisi Falọla of Idahin (Ketu).

66. A close-up of this masquerader appears in Drewal (1974:pl. 5). Mask by an unknown Idọfa artist.

67. Performer said to have come from Ketu. Carver unknown, but the mask, depicting a northerner, probably a Fulani, is closely related to Idahin work. See color plate 5; plates 75, 81, 107, 113; Drewal and Drewal (1975:pl. 9); and H. J. Drewal (1974b:pl. 18). Appliquéd panels include crossed keys, floral patterns, human head, and turtle motifs. Mate of the mask illustrated in color plate 7.

68. Mask with an *agogo* hairstyle, probably carved by an Agoṣaṣa/Ipokia artist (Anago). For other masks carved in Agoṣaṣa, see plates 89, 91, and 116.

69. The four pairs of masks shown here are by four different carvers, all probably from the Ọta vicinity (Awori), according to their style.

70. This mask appears in plate 69, third from the left.

71. This mask appears in plate 69, seventh from the left.

72. The same masquerader appears in plate 69, third from the left.

73. Because of its stylistic features, this mask is probably Anago.

74. Attributed in 1977 to Oduitan of Ijale Ketu by its caretakers.

75. Mask closely related to the work of Fagbite of Idahin (Ketu). Height: 38 cm. Compare it with the mask in plate 81, which was photographed in the hometown of the carver. Collected by Jäger in Ketu, 1967, for the Berlin Museum. For masks by Fagbite's son, Falọla Ẹdun, see color plate 5, plate 113, and Drewal and Drewal (1975:pl. 9); for a mask by his grandson, Sambilisi, see H. J. Drewal (1974b:pl. 18).

76. Collected by Harold Stewart Gladstone, who was D. C. at Warri before 1911. This mask and those shown in plates 99, 136, 141, and 145 were said to have formed a set used by traveling dancers. Fagg suggests that this group of masks is from Igbo Ora (Ibarapa) because the hornbill mask in the group (pl. 141) is identical to one Murray photographed in 1950 at Idere, near Igbo Ora (Ibarapa). The one illustrated in plate 141, however, was said to have been carved at Ketu, circa 1900. The problem is further complicated by the fact that we also photographed a mask by the same hand as one of the Gladstone pieces in the town of Ijado, near Ilaro (Ẹgbado), which the informant attributed to his grandfather. The Gladstone pieces are closely related to each other stylistically; however, field data, so far, have not firmly established the provenance of this collection, although they suggest the broad Ẹgbado/Ibarapa sector of Yorubaland.

77. This mask is either for Gẹlẹdẹ or for Ejiwa, a masquerade unique to Lagos. It is related to the mask illustrated in plate 45 and is by the same hand as that in plate 154. Also stylistically related to these are three in the British Museum (1954 Af 23.23, 28, and 29). The motifs on this mask include a woman, birds, a crescent moon and a star of Islam, a cactus plant, and a Benin-style *kola* box in the form of an antelope's head with its horns grasped by human hands.

78. According to Nigerian Museum documentation (1940), this mask was said to have been carved in Mẹko, circa 1880. It was first seen by K. C. Murray in the house of the carver, Ọlaniyan of Ọta, who was copying it for a Lagos chief from whom Murray eventually purchased it. The mask is painted with local pigments that have been mixed with egg.

79. Horse's head and mask attributed to Sunday Oloyede of Ibara quarter, Abẹokuta (Ẹgbado), who was trained by Ogunbayo Akiode of the Ẹṣubiyi workshop of Itoko quarter (cf. plate 150). Photographed and documented by T. J. H. Chappel, Ibara quarter, Abẹokuta, 1964. In 1978 at Oloyede's compound, we photographed a large animal mask by Sunday similar in form to the horse's head in Chappel's photograph. The mask representing a king, however, is closer to the style attributed to Akiode, Ogunbayo's father; that is, the style of the teacher of Sunday Oloyede's teacher. See plate 146 for a mask by Ogunbayo Akiode, Sunday's teacher. For other works related to the Ẹṣubiyi workshop, see plates 58, 95, 146, and 150.

80. Attributed by the caretakers to Otooro Oduṣina of Ketu, circa 1962. This mask represents a bride with a head wrap on which is placed a calabash tray, dishes, and a lid covered by a cloth (*ọja*) portrayed with hinged joints and topped by an *owo eyo* for the propitiation of one's inner head or destiny. For another view of this mask, see Drewal

(1974:pl. 12) and, for other examples of Otooro's work, see Carroll (1967:pls. 58, 100, 101, 102, 103, and 104). Painted brown, white, and blue with traces of red.

81. Head portion of this mask was carved by Fagbite of Idahin (Ketu), while the snake attachments were completed by his son, Falọla Ẹdun, in 1971. For masks by Falọla Ẹdun, see color plate 5, plate 113, and Drewal and Drewal (1975:pl. 9); for a mask by Fagbite's grandson, Sambilisi, see H. J. Drewal (1974b:pl. 18). Other works closely related to Fagbite's are in the Nigerian Museum (65.12.6); plates 75, 102, and 107; and the Harrison Eiteljorg Collection (E77.370).

82. Mask carved by Saibu Akinyẹmi of Agọsạsa (Anago). Also see plates 9 and 53. A mask possibly by Saibu's father is shown in plate 116.

83. Almost certainly carved in the Ọhọri area by the same hand as the masks in plates 128 and 166. This mask depicts a carpenter using a European saw in the Yoruba manner, i.e., with the cutting edge turned away from the body.

84. Carved in the vicinity of Isagba (Ọhọri). These body masks have traces of white. The one on the right depicts body marks *(kolo)* typical of the area. Masks such as this, which less frequently represent males, are typical of Ọhọri and Anago groups in Benin, although they have also turned up in Lagos. For other published examples of such torso masks, see Kerchache (1973:12, 24) and Huet (1978:pls. 80, 86).

85. Height: 607 mm. Body masks such as this can also be used with Egungun face masks in playful "miracle" displays *(p'idan)*, as we witnessed in Abẹokuta in 1978.

86. Probably carved in the vicinity of Dagbe, Benin, judging from correspondences with a Gẹlẹdẹ mask attributed to this town in the Musée Ethnographique, Porto Novo (61.2.11). Height: 44⅛ in. The mask depicts a priestess prepared for prayer, sacrifice, and dance at the shrine of a deity. Thus the head tie is appropriately removed from the head and draped over the shoulders. The masquerader sees through the hole cut in the figure's mid-section. While trunk masks representing humans appear to be fairly common among Anago Yoruba in Benin, trunk masks depicting female gorillas seem to be localized in Nigeria among northern Ẹgbado and Ibarapa groups. See plates 139 and 140.

87. Reportedly from a temple in G'boha, Benin. Fitte Collection, 1953. A pair of figures by the same hand, also in the Basel Museum (III 1276 and 1277), was collected in Danme Wokon in the area of the lower Weme River. Portrays the same theme as in plate 86. Holes under the breast allow the masquerader to peer out, and it also appears that the neck can be turned.

88. Mask carved by Kilani Ọlaniyan of Iga Igbein, Oruba quarter, Ọta (Awori). Also see plates 63, 123, 124, and 165.

89. Probably carved at Agọsạsa (Anago) and related to work attributed to Abidogun (cf. Thompson 1971:Ch. 14/pl. 13). Height: 22 cm.

90. Carved in the Ketu vicinity in the style of the Ẹtuọbẹ workshop. By a carver closely related to one whose work is illustrated in plate 103. Carved calabashes of medicine appear to be integrated into the coiffure. This mask is broken; however, a similar motif can be seen in plates 61 and 168, where snakes instead of ropes appear to connect the calabashes.

91. From the Ipokia/Agọsạsa vicinity. Related to the workshop of Kọlade Ọlabimtan of Agọsạsa. Height: 45 cm.

92. Probably from the vicinity of Ketu.

93. Entering the collection of the Musée de l'Homme in 1891, this mask was probably carved in Ọta (Awori). Other Gẹlẹdẹ masks by the same hand are also in the Musée de l'Homme (91.22.17), accessioned at the same time as this one, and in the Museum für Völkerkunde, Hamburg (a pair—34.59.2, 34.59.3), accessioned in 1934.

94. The mask on the left, wearing a cap with dog ears *(fila-abeti-aja)*, is attributed to Amosa Akapo of Igbe quarter, Igbesa, who died before 1964. The other, with a cloth cap *(ikori)*, is attributed to Ọlamide (died ca. 1943), a carver from a different workshop in Ogọna quarter, Igbesa. It seems likely, however, that the latter was carved by Amosa's father and teacher, Akapo, who died before 1911. See plate 100 for a mask also attributed to Akapo and plate 130 for another mask by Amosa. The name Akapo is given to a diviner and priest of Ifa.

95. Carved in the vicinity of Abẹokuta. This mask appears to be related to the Eṣubiyi workshop, whose origins are Ibara Orile, just west of Abẹokuta. For other works related to the Eṣubiyi workshop, see plates 58, 79, 146, and 150.

96. Attributed in 1940 to Idowu Olaleye or Onaneye, circa 1895, of Mabo Odu Quarter, Ọta (Awori). Onaneye reportedly died in 1906. The keloid mark on the forehead identifies this mask as a man of Egun or Popo origin.

97. Works by this hand have been documented in Aiyetoro (Ẹgbado) and in Idere and Idofin (Ibarapa). The Aiyetoro piece was said to have been carved by Ogunṣolu of Imala, late nineteenth to early twentieth century, while one of the Idere pieces was said to have been from Ketu. (See Nigerian Museum archives neg. nos. 14.27.15, 14.27.18, 14.29.26, and 14.30.31—all documented by Murray in 1950.) In addition, Thompson (1971:Ch. 13, pl. 29) illustrates a twin figure stylistically related to this piece, which he suggests is by Lawore (of Ile Alagbanka, Anko quarter, Eruwa), carved in 1947–48 (see also Nigerian Museum archives 48.9.13). As will be recalled, the Gẹlẹdẹ institution in a number of Ibarapa towns derives from Aiyetoro and Imala. Similarities in carving styles provide further evidence in support of this oral tradition. It is quite possible then that the carver of the mask illustrated here had family ties both in Imala and in the vicinity of Idere.

98. A twin figure by the same hand was attributed by the Balogun of Imala to his father, Ikuṣami, of Imala (Ẹgbado); however, in 1948 Murray (Nigerian Museum archives) photographed a mask by the same hand in Ibarapa—now in the Institute of African Studies, University of Ibadan (6287)—that was said to have been carved in Aiyetoro. Since the people of Imala and Idofoi quarters of Aiyetoro are related to those of Imala, it is quite possible that the carver of this mask is from Imala.

99. Height: 14.4 in. Collected by Harold Stewart Gladstone, who was D. C. at Warri before 1911. This mask and those shown in plates 76, 136, 141, and 145 were said to have formed a set used by traveling dancers. This mask is by the same hand as the one in plate 145. For more details, see the note on plate 76.

100. Attributed to Akapo of Igbe quarter, Igbesa (Awori), who died before 1911. Length: 11.4 in. See plates 94 and 130 for another mask by Akapo and two by his son Amosa. The name Akapo is given to a diviner and priest of Ifa. Depicted is an *ilari* hairstyle with a tuft of hair *(oṣu)* braided to the left.

101. Carved by Oduntan Aina of Ṣawonjo (Ẹgbado). Collected in Ẹgbado. Length: 17 cm. See also color plates 10 and 11 and plates 111 and 161.

102. Collected in Mẹko, but probably from Idahin (Ketu). See color plate 5 and plates 75, 81, 107, and 113. Height: 46.5 cm.

103. Carved in the vicinity of Ketu. Closely related in style to plate 90.

104. Collected in 1964 in Ilaro (Ẹgbado). It is related to Ketu-style works documented by us in Itolu, near Ilaro. Compare this mask with those from the Ketu town of Idahin (color pl. 5 and pls. 75, 81, and 113). It is also related to the mask shown in plate 107.

105. By the same hand as a mask in the American Museum of Natural History (90.2.81), said to be from Mẹko. Collected in Ilaro. Height: 28.5 cm.

106. Collected in Mẹko and probably carved in that area. Height: 40 cm.

107. Related to Ilaro-vicinity work, more specifically to work documented in Itolu. See plate 104 and its note.

108, 109. Purchased in Mẹkọ and probably carved by Samuel Laroye of Mẹkọ.

110. Probably from the Ketu vicinity. By the same hand as a mask illustrated in Carroll (1966:pl. 24), photographed in Likimọn, near Ketu; and also the one in plate 114. The masks in plates 10 and 57 are also stylistically related. Height: 38 cm.

111. Attributed to Oduntan Aina of Ṣawonjo, originally from Ijaka, last quarter of the nineteenth century. Other masks by Oduntan are illustrated in color plates 10 and 11 and plates 101 and 138. For works by Oduntan's son, Fayomi, see color plate 8 and plates 24 and 62.

112. Attributed to Tela, yet closely related to the style of Samuel Laroye, both of Mẹkọ.

113. Pair of masks carved about the middle of the twentieth century by Falọla Ẹdun of Idahin (Ketu), who was born circa 1900. The Musée de l'Homme (D31/4.156) owns a mask by this hand, collected in "Idigny" [probably Idahin] for the Coloniale de Vincennes of 1931. For other masks by this carver, see color plate 5 and Drewal and Drewal (1975:pl. 9); for a mask by his father, Fagbite, see plate 81; and for a mask by his grandson, Sambilisi, see H. J. Drewal (1974b:pl. 18).

114. Carved in the Ketu vicinity by the same artist as the mask in plate 110.

115. Attributed to Oguntade Iji of Ilara (Ketu) and carved before 1960.

116. Possibly carved by Akinyemi Akinlade of Agọṣaṣa (Anago) about 1940. For works of Akinyemi's son, Saibu, see plates 9, 53, and 82.

117. Carved by Atọba, a Ketu artist who settled in Iluata Quarter, Ilaro, and died circa 1940 (Chappel 1981). His works are found throughout Ẹgbado territory. For other works by Atọba, see plate 117 and *African Arts* 7 (4), 1974, inside front cover. Murray first documented work by Atọba in 1944 (cf. Nigerian Museum 44.1.1), which was said, at that time, to have been carved circa 1925.

118. Attributed to Moses Iji of Idọfa (Ketu).

119. Carved in Agọṣaṣa (Anago). A kneeling female figure, holding a bowl, and a male figure on horseback, called Wolewole ("Sanitary Inspector")—both by the same hand as this mask—are in the Museum für Völkerkunde, Hamburg (64.55.564 and 607), having been collected in Agọṣaṣa. The artist has carefully detailed the masqueraders, showing the netted veils in front of the faces, the layered panels of cloth, and the row of medicine containers over the face netting.

120. Both masks carved in Ọta (Awori) style, before 1887, perhaps by Ọlabimtan, who died circa 1930, or by his father, Odunlami, who was reportedly a very wealthy trader in addition to being a carver. These masks were presented to the British Museum by A. R. Elliott of Lagos in 1887. Heights: left—21 in.; right—23 in. The head on top of the mask on the right appears to be that of a twin figure from Ṣaki area with Ọyọ face marks. Works by the same hand can be found in the Museum für Völkerkunde, Berlin (III C 1231), acquired at Lagos in 1878, and the Reiss Museum, Mannheim (IV Af. 1558, 1559, 1562), collected before 1881.

121. Attributed to Duga of Mẹkọ (Ketu). A duplicate of this mask is in Ilaro. For examples of Duga's work, see Bascom (1973). See also Drewal (1974:pl. 10).

122. By the same hand as a mask now in the University of Ibadan's Institute of African Studies (6283), which was photographed by K. C. Murray in Pako quarter, Igbo Ora, and was reportedly carved by Adeleke of Lanlate, circa 1923.

123, 124. Carved by Kilani Ọlaniyan (born in 1936) of Iga Igbein, Oruba quarter, Ọta, and grandson of Ọlaniyan). Also see plates 63, 88, and 165.

125, 126. Attributed to Abegure Akere of Imala (Ẹgbado), who died before 1971. See also plate 122, which is stylistically related to this mask. The carving styles of Ibarapa and those of Aiyetoro and Imala are closely related, probably because of historical links.

127. Similar in style to work attributed to Seriki of Oto (Awori) in the British Museum (1959 Af 19.115).

128. Probably from the Ọhọri area. Height: 25.5 cm. Closely related in style to masks in plates 83 and 166.

129. Attributed to Kugbenu of Banigbe, Sakete, Dagbe (Anago). Other masks reportedly by Kugbenu in the Musée Ethnographique are nos. 55.9.43, 55.9.53, 55.9.54, and 55.9.63, although 55.9.53 actually appears to have been carved by another hand.

130. Carved by an Igbesa artist (Awori). Length: 12.8 in. Related to work attributed to Amosa Akapo. See plate 94.

131. Perhaps from Northern Ẹgbado. Height: 44 cm.

132. Possibly carved in Anago territory.

133. Probably carved by Michael Labode, son of Laleyẹ Labode, of Apesin Compound, Idofoi quarter, Aiyetoro (Ẹgbado). Another Gẹlẹdẹ mask by this hand is in the Art Museum, University of Ifẹ. For other masks by this workshop, see Nigerian Museum archives neg. nos. 46.5.C.1–4 and 46.5.C.5–6, all photographed in 1964 by T. J. H. Chappel.

134. In the style of Mẹkọ (Ketu). See color plate 1 for a full view of this masquerader.

135. Height: 440 mm. Compare this warthog mask with one in plate 138. For another published example, see Thompson (1974a:pl. 250).

136. Height: 18.6 in. Collected by Harold Stewart Gladstone, who was D. C. at Warri before 1911. This mask and those illustrated in plates 76, 99, 141, and 145 were said to have formed a set used by traveling dancers. For more details, see the note on plate 76.

137. Collected in Ketu by Jäger in 1967. A duplicate of this mask, perhaps its double, in the Musée de l'Homme (D31/4.151)—originally exhibited at the Coloniale de Vincennes, 1931—is attributed to "Fagbete" of Ketu.

138. Collected in Iganna, but probably carved in Ṣawonjo by Oduntan Aina in the last quarter of the nineteenth century. Length: 43.5 cm. See notes to color plates 10 and 11 and masks in plates 101 and 111, which were also carved by Oduntan. A similar mask attributed by family members to Oduntan's son, Fayomi, was photographed by us in Ṣawonjo in 1978. For other warthog masks, see plate 135 and Thompson (1974a:pl. 250).

139. Carved by Omigbaro of Kẹsan Orile (Ẹgbado) (died ca. 1975). See plates 6 and 59 for other masks carved by him.

140. Probably carved by Sunday Oloyede of Ibara quarter, Abẹokuta. See also Nigerian Museum archive neg. nos. 46.6.B.31, 46.6.B.29, and 46.5.B.7 for other versions of this mask from Abẹokuta.

141. Length 17.2 in. Collected by Harold Stewart Gladstone, who was D. C. at Warri before 1911. This mask and those shown in plates 76, 99, 136, and 145 were said to have formed a set used by traveling dancers. For more details, see the note on plate 76.

142. Carved before 1906 in the Lagos vicinity.

143. Length: 560 mm.

144. Mask by an unknown Ilaro carver. Height: 15 cm. For a mask by the same hand, see plate 7.

145. Collected by Harold Stewart Gladstone, who was D. C. at Warri before 1911. This mask and those shown in plates 76, 99, 136, and 141 were said to have formed a set used by traveling dancers. A mask by the same hand was photographed by us in Ijado, near Ilaro, in 1977 and attributed by its owner to his grandfather. For more details, see the note on plate 76.

146. Left, probably carved by Ogunbayo Akiode of Itoko quarter, Abẹokuta, of the Ẹṣubiyi workshop (see pl. 150). Right, the Ẹfẹ mask characteristic of Abẹokuta, painted

white and shown wearing a billed cap, was carved by Sunday Oloyede, Ogunbayo's former student. See plate 79 for another Abẹokuta-style Ẹfẹ mask in performance.

147. Mask carved by Faleye of Jọga (Jiga) (Ẹgbado). This photograph was taken in 1971, but by 1978 the mask had been replaced by one carved by Faleye's son Akinọla.

148. Closely related to the work of Saibu Akinyẹmi of Agọsạṣa. See plates 53 and 82 for examples of his work.

149. Mask in foreground carved by Ṣangolade Olege of Ipahaiyi, near Ilaro (Ẹgbado). For other examples of double-faced masks, see plates 43 and 150, Duerden (1968:pl. 23), Fagg and Pemberton (1982:pl. 36), and Institute of African Studies Museum, University of Ibadan (6287). In the background is a mask depicting a snake encircling the head, which was carved by Taiwo Onipaṣọnọbẹ of Ilaro before 1920. Another mask by Taiwo is in the Nigerian Museum (404), collected in 1944. For a work by Onipaṣọnọbẹ's grandson, James Akinde, see plate 3.

150. Attributed by the caretaker to Eṣubiyi, originally of Ibara Orile (Ẹgbado) (cf. Chappel 1972 for more details on this family). The tray on the head carries gin bottles used in ritual sacrifice. Head on the left has an *oṣu* hairstyle. See plates 93, 100, 101, 159, and 163 for other masks with *oṣu*. Other works related to the Eṣubiyi workshop are illustrated in plates 58, 79, 95, and 146. For other examples of double-faced masks, see plates 43 and 149, Duerden (1968:pl. 23), Fagg and Pemberton (1982:pl. 36), and Institute of African Studies Museum, University of Ibadan (6287).

151. Two Magbo masks for the Ekine society of Mahin, probably carved in the vicinity of Lagos. A more recent Gẹlẹdẹ mask from the same workshop, photographed in Isalẹ Eko quarter, Lagos, is illustrated in color plate 9. See also plate 64, photographed in 1945.

152. Probably carved in southern Ijẹbu area, possibly in the vicinity of Epe. Note the raffia mat costume attached to the rim of the mask and the use of palm fronds around the shoulders, both distinct from Gẹlẹdẹ traditions.

153. Probably carved in southwestern Ijẹbuland.

154. Same hand as in plate 77 and closely related to those in plates 45 and 154.

157. Compare this ear with those in plate 151.

158. For an Ẹfẹ mask by the same hand, see plate 44.

159. A mask by the same hand is illustrated in plate 167.

160. Same mask as in plate 68, while the twin figures are those illustrated in plate 158.

161. For one of these masks in performance, see plate 53. The Ogun shrine in the foreground shows signs of recent libations. The Gẹlẹdẹ masks are placed on cloth on the ground.

162. Carved by Raimi Ogundipẹ of Ilaro, originally from Pobẹ, in the 1970s.

163. Probably carved by Ogundare of Ṣawonjo, a student of Akinyele Ayefemi of Olanle compound. See plate 18 for a work attributed to Akinyele. For a portrait of the full masquerader in performance, see plate 12.

164. Reportedly carved at Ijaka-Orile (Ọhọri) and now used in Ẹgbado. Indeed the facial forms of this mask are related to the work of Oduntan Aina, originally of Ijaka. See color plates 10 and 11 and plates 101, 111, and 138.

165. Carved by Kilani Ọlaniyan of Ọta (Awori). Also see plates 63, 88, 123, and 124. Painted on the front is the phrase Ṣango Olukoso, a praise name meaning "The lord of Koso," where Ṣango's enemies say he hanged himself but where his supporters say he entered the ground and became a deity.

166. Said to be from Ketu, but almost certainly from Ọhọri area, south of Ketu. Same hand as in plates 83 and 128.

167. Gift from Mr. E. Barth, 1888, said to be from "Addo." See plate 159 for another mask by the same hand.

168. Probably carved in the Ilaro vicinity. See plate 61 for a mask by the same hand

painted differently. Another version of this motif is illustrated in plate 90, although a rope replaces a snake.

170. Collected in Sakete (Anago) and accessioned in 1953. Height: 28 cm. By the same hand as a mask in the Musée Ethnographique, Porto Novo (55.9.54) attributed to Kugbenu of Sakete; however, the mask in plate 129, also allegedly by Kugbenu, is clearly by a different hand. Large land snail shells in black scattered over the head, which is otherwise painted white, suggests a theme associated with the "white deities" *(orişa funfun).*

REFERENCES

Abimbọla, W. 1976. *Ifá: An Exposition of Ifá Literary Corpus.* Ibadan: Oxford University Press.

————. 1980. "Verbal and Visual Symbolism in Ifá Divination." Paper presented at the Conference on the Relations between Verbal and Visual Arts in Africa, Philadelphia, Pennsylvania, October 10–14.

Abiọdun, R. 1976. "The Concept of Women in Traditional Yoruba Religion and Art." Paper presented at the Conference on Nigerian Women and Development in Relation to Changing Family Structure, University of Ibadan, April 26–30.

————. 1980a. "Charactery in Yoruba Aesthetics." Paper presented at the 5th Triennial Symposium on African Art, Atlanta, Georgia, April 17.

————. 1980b. "Ritual Allusions in Yoruba Ritualistic Art: Ori-inu, Visual and Verbal Metaphor." Paper read at the Conference on the Relations between the Verbal and Visual Arts in Africa, Philadelphia, Pennsylvania, October 10–14.

————. 1981. "Some Religio-Aesthetic Aspects of Woman in Yoruba Society." Paper presented at the Seminar on Visual Art as Social Commentary, University of London, School of Oriental and African Studies, November 30–December 1.

————. 1982. Personal communication, January 2.

Abraham, R. C. 1958. *Dictionary of Modern Yoruba.* London: University of London Press.

Adamu, M. 1978. *The Hausa Factor in West African History.* Zaria: Ahmadu Bello University Press.

Adebowale, L. O., former Olobi of Ilobi. 1972. Letter to the authors, February 2.

Adegbolu, K., artist. 1971. Interview, Isede, May 19.

Adelẹyẹ, I. O., Amala of Imala. 1971. Interview, Imala, March 29.

Adepegba, Olori Ajo Gẹlẹdẹ. 1971. Interview, Aibo Quarter, Aiyetoro, April 3.

Adesina, A. S., Abepa. 1971. Interview, Jọga Orile, April 2 and 12.

Adewale, T. G. 1949. "The Ijanna Episode in Yoruba History." Proceedings of the Third International West African Conference, Ibadan, pp. 251–256. [Published in Lagos, 1956.]

Aibiro, R., Ajo Gẹlẹdẹ. 1973. Interview, Ibanko Quarter, Pobe, May 7.

Aimes, H. S. 1967 [1907]. *A History of Slavery in Cuba, 1511 to 1868.* New York: Octagon Books.

Ajayi, J. F. A., and R. Smith. 1964. *Yoruba Warfare in the Nineteenth Century.* Cambridge: Cambridge University Press.

Ajibọla, I., Otun Balogun. 1971. Interview, Igan Okoto, March 20.

Ajiṣafẹ, A. K. 1964. *History of Abẹokuta.* Rev. ed. Abẹokuta: M A. Ola.

Akinfẹnwa, S. 1978. Personal communication, March.

Akinjọgbin, I. A. 1965. "The Prelude to the Yoruba Civil Wars of the Nineteenth Century." *Odu* n.s. 1(2):24–46.

————. 1966a. "A Chronology of Yoruba History, 1789–1840." *Odu* n.s. 1(2):81–86.

————. 1966b. "The Oyo Empire in the Eighteenth Century—A Reassessment." *Journal of the Historical Society of Nigeria* 3(3):449–460.

Akinsulure, M., and E. Frazer. 1972. Interview, August 27.

Akinwole, A. O., Iyalaṣẹ Gẹlẹdẹ. 1971. Interview, Ketu Quarter, Aiyetoro, April 19.

Alaiye, A., artist. 1977. Interview, Igbogila, December 16.

Allison, P. 1950. Unpublished notes in the Nigerian Museum Archives, Lagos.

Armstrong, R. P. 1981. *The Powers of Presence: Consciousness, Myth, and Affecting Presence.* Philadelphia: University of Pennsylvania Press.

Asiwaju, A. I. 1975. "Ẹfẹ Poetry as a Source for Western Yoruba History." In *Yoruba Oral Tradition: Poetry in Music, Dance, and Drama.* Edited by W. Abimbọla. Ifẹ: University of Ifẹ, Department of African Languages and Literatures, pp. 199–266.

———. 1976. *Western Yorubaland under European Rule 1889–1945: A Comparative Analysis of French and British Colonialism.* Atlantic Highlands, N.J.: Humanities Press.

Atanda, J. A. 1973. *The New Ọyọ Empire: Indirect Rule and Change in Western Nigeria, 1894–1934.* New York: Humanities Press.

Awolalu, J. O. 1973. "Yoruba Sacrificial Practice." *Journal of Religion in Africa* 5(2):81–93.

———. 1979. *Yoruba Beliefs and Sacrificial Rites.* London: Longman Group Ltd.

Ayoade, J. A. A. 1979. "The Concept of Inner Essence in Yoruba Traditional Medicine." In *African Therapeutic Systems.* Edited by Z. A. Ademuwagun, J. A. A. Ayoade, I. E. Harrison, and D. M. Warren. Waltham, Mass.: Crossroads Press, pp. 49–55.

Ayodele, J., Akewe Ẹfẹ. 1971. Interview, Ketu Quarter, Aiyetoro, April 19.

Babalọla, I., Chief Onaka, Ọjẹtọla Compound. 1971. Interview, Idofin Quarter, Imaṣai, April 19.

Babalọla, S. A. 1966. *The Content and Form of Yorùbá Ìjálá.* London: Oxford University Press.

———. 1973. "'Rara' Chants in Yoruba Spoken Art." *African Literature Today* 6:79–92.

Bakare, A., king of Iboro. 1971. Interview, April 16.

Bankole, A. 1971. Interview, Onfolu Compound, Ilogun Quarter, Aiyetoro, April 3.

Barnes, S. T. 1980. *Ogun: An Old God for a New Age.* ISHI Occasional Papers in Social Change, #3. Philadelphia: I.S.H.I.

Bascom, W. 1951. "Social Status, Wealth, and Individual Differences among the Yoruba." *American Anthropologist* 53:490–505.

———. 1960. "Yoruba Concepts of the Soul." In *Men and Culture.* Edited by A. F. C. Wallace. Philadelphia: University of Pennsylvania Press, pp. 401–410.

———. 1969. *Ifa Divination: Communication between Gods and Men in West Africa.* Bloomington: Indiana University Press.

———. 1973. "A Yoruba Master Carver: Duga of Mẹkọ." In *The Traditional Artist in African Societies.* Edited by W. d'Azevedo. Bloomington: Indiana University Press, pp. 62–78.

Bastide, R. 1978. *The African Religions of Brazil: Towards a Sociology of the Interpenetration of Civilizations.* Translated by Helen Sebba. Baltimore: The Johns Hopkins University Press.

Bauman, R. 1977. *Verbal Art as Performance.* Rowley, Mass.: Newbury House Publishers.

Bay, E. 1974. Personal communication.

Beier, H. U. 1958. "Gelede Masks." *Odu* 6:5–23.

———. 1970. *Yoruba Poetry.* Cambridge: Cambridge University Press.

Ben-Amos, D., and K. Goldstein, eds. 1975. *Folklore: Performance and Communication.* The Hague: Mouton.

Bernolles, J. 1973. "Note sur les Masques de la Société Guèlèdè de Savé (Dahomey Central)." *Etudes Dahoméennes* n.s., numero special, 23–35.

Bertho, J. 1949. "La Parenté des Youruba aux peuplades de Dahomey et Togo." *Africa* 19:121–132.

Beyioku, A. F. 1943. Letter to His Excellency the Officer Administering the Government, Government House, Lagos. August 24.

———, Osunba, Ẹgbado Gẹlẹdẹ Cult, Lagos. 1946. Letter entitled "Historical and Moral Facts about the Gẹlẹdẹ Cult," January 16. Archives, Nigerian Museum, Lagos.

Biobaku, S. O. 1957. *The Egba and Their Neighbours, 1842–1872.* Oxford: Oxford University Press.

Burns, A. 1969 [1929]. *History of Nigeria.* London: George Allen and Unwin, Ltd.

Carneiro, E. 1954. *Candomblés da Bahia.* 2d rev. ed. Rio de Janeiro: Editorial e Andes.

Carroll, K. 1967. *Yoruba Religious Carving.* London: Geoffrey Chapman.

Chappel, T. J. H. 1972. "Critical Carvers: A Case Study," *Man* 7(2):296–307.

———. 1974. "The Yoruba Cult of Twins in Historical Perspective." *Africa* 44(3):250–265.

———. 1981. Personal communication.

Church Missionary Society. 1937. *A Dictionary of the Yoruba Language.* Oxford: Oxford University Press with the Church Missionary Society.

Clapperton, H. 1829. *Journal of a Second Expedition into the Interior of Africa, from the Bight of Benin to Soccatoo.* London: John Murray.

Clouzot, H., and A. Level. 1926. *Sculptures Africaines et Océaniennes.* Paris: Libraire de France.

Crowther, S. 1852. *A Vocabulary of the Yoruba Language.* London: Seeleys.

de la Burde, R. 1973. "The Ijebu-Ekine Cult." *African Arts* 7(1):28–32, 92.

Delano, I. O. 1966. *Owe L'esin Oro—Yoruba Proverbs: Their Meaning and Usage.* Ibadan: Oxford University Press.

Dennett, R. E. 1968 [1906]. *At the Back of the Black Man's Mind.* London: Cass.

dos Santos, C. M. (Mimito), artist. 1974. Interview, Salvador, Bahia, August 11.

dos Santos, D. M. 1967. "West African Sacred Art and Rituals in Brazil: A Comparative Study." Seminar Paper, Institute of African Studies, University of Ibadan, Ibadan, Nigeria.

dos Santos, J. E. 1976. *Os Nàgô e a Morte.* Petrópolis: Editora Vozes, Ltda.

Drewal, H. J. 1973. "Efe/Gelede: The Educative Role of the Arts in Traditional Yoruba Culture." Ph. D. diss., Columbia University.

———. 1974a. "Efe: Voiced Power and Pageantry." *African Arts* 7(2):26–29, 58–66.

———. 1974b. "Gelede Masquerade: Imagery and Motif." *African Arts* 7(4):8–19, 62–63, 95–96.

———. 1977a. "Art and the Perception of Women in Yorùbá Culture." *Cahiers d'études africaines* 17(4):545–567.

———. 1977b. *Traditional Art of the Nigerian Peoples.* Washington: Museum of African Art.

———. 1979. "Pageantry and Power in Yoruba Costuming." In *The Fabrics of Culture.* Edited by J. M. Cordwell and R. A. Schwarz. The Hague: Mouton Publishers, pp. 189–230.

———. 1980. *African Artistry: Technique and Aesthetics in Yoruba Sculpture.* Atlanta: The High Museum of Art.

———. 1981. "62. Mask (Gelede)." In *For Spirits and Kings: African Art from the Tishman Collection.* Edited by S. Vogel. New York: Metropolitan Museum of Art, pp. 114–116.

Drewal, M. T. 1975. "Symbols of Possession: A Study of Movement and Regalia in an Anago-Yoruba Ceremony." *Dance Research Journal* 7(2):15–24.

———. 1977. "Projections From the Top in Yoruba Art." *African Arts* 11(1):43–49, 91–92.

Drewal, M. T., and H. J. Drewal. 1975. "Gelede Dance of the Western Yoruba." *African Arts* 8(2):36–45, 78–79.

———. 1978. "More Powerful than Each Other: An Egbado Classification of Egungun." *African Arts* 11(3):28–39, 98.

———. 1980. "Composing Time and Space in Yoruba Art." Paper presented at the Conference on the Relations between Verbal and Visual Arts in Africa, Philadelphia, Pennsylvania, October 10–14.

Duerden, D. 1968. *African Art.* Feltham, Middlesex: Paul Hamlyn, Ltd.

Dunglas, E. 1957. "Contribution à l'histoire du Moyen-Dahomey." *Etudes Dahoméennes* 19–21.

Edun, A., Priestess of Are. 1975. Interview, Ilaro, November 5.

Egharevba, J. 1960. *A Short History of Benin.* Ibadan: Ibadan University Press.

Ellis, A. B. 1974 [1894]. *The Yoruba-Speaking Peoples of the Slave Coast of West Africa.* London: Curzon Press.

Fadipe, N. A. 1970 [1939]. *The Sociology of the Yoruba.* Ibadan: Ibadan University Press.

Fagg, W. B. 1951. "De l'Art des Youruba." *Présence Africaine* 10–11:103–135.

———. 1968. *African Tribal Images: The Katherine White Reswick Collection.* Cleveland: Cleveland Museum of Art.

———. 1978. Descriptive catalog entries in *Tribal Art* (Auction on Tuesday, October 24). London: Christie, Manson, & Woods.

Fagg, W., and J. Pemberton III. 1982. *Yoruba: Sculpture of West Africa.* New York: Alfred A. Knopf.

Folayan, K. 1967. "Egbado to 1832: The Birth of a Dilemma." *Journal of the Historical Society of Nigeria* 4(1):15–33.

Frobenius, L. 1913. *Voice of Africa,* vol. 2. London: Hutchinson.

Harper, P. 1970. "The Role of Dance in the Gèlèdé Ceremonies of the Village of Ìjìó." *Odu* n.s. 4:67–94.

Heathcote, D. 1976. *The Arts of the Hausa.* Kent: World of Islam Festival Publishing Co., Ltd.

Hoch-Smith, J. 1978. "Radical Yoruba Female Sexuality: The Witch and the Prostitute." In *Women in Ritual and Symbolic Roles.* Edited by J. Hoch-Smith and A. Spring. New York: Plenum Press, 1978, pp. 245–267.

Houlberg, M. H. 1973. "Ibeji Images of the Yoruba." *African Arts* 7(1):20–27, 90–92.

———. 1979. "Social Hair: Tradition and Change in Yoruba Hairstyles in Southwestern Nigeria." In *The Fabrics of Culture.* Edited by J. M. Cordwell and R. A. Schwarz. The Hague: Mouton Publishers, pp. 349–397.

Huet, M. 1978. *The Dance, Art and Ritual of Africa.* New York: Pantheon Books.

Idowu, D., Bale. 1971. Interview, Ofia, May.

Idowu, E. B. 1962. *Olodumare, God in Yoruba Belief.* London: Longmans.

Ikubatan, O., master potter. 1975. Interview, Ibaiyun, November 19.

Johnson, S. 1973 [1921]. *The History of the Yorubas.* Lagos: CMS Bookshops.

Kerchache, J. 1973. *Masques Yorouba, Afrique.* Paris: Galerie Jacques Kerchache.

Kilomoninse, B. F., Olori Elefe and Akewe Gelede. 1971. Interview, Idofoi Quarter, Aiyetoro, March 25.

Labat, J.-B. 1730. *Voyage du Chevalier des Marchais.* 4 vols. Paris.

Lagos *Daily Times.* 1972. September 27, p. 19.

Lamb, V. 1975. *West African Weaving.* London: Duckworth and Co.

Langer, S. K. 1953. *Feeling and Form: A Theory of Art.* New York: Charles Scribner's and Sons.

Laoye, I. 1959. "Yoruba Drums." *Odu* 7:5–14.

LaPin, D. 1977. "Story, Medium and Masque: The Idea and Art of Yoruba Storytelling." 3 vols. Ph.D. diss., University of Wisconsin.

———. 1980. "Picture and Design in Yoruba Narrative Art." Paper read at the Conference on the Relations between Verbal and Visual Arts in Africa, Philadelphia, Pennsylvania, October 10–14.

Law, R. 1968. "The Dynastic Chronology of Lagos." *Lagos Notes and Records* 2(2):46–54.

———. 1977. *The Oyo Empire c. 1600–1836.* Oxford: Clarendon Press.

Lawal, B. 1970. "Yoruba *Sango* Sculpture in Historical Retrospect." Ph.D. diss., Indiana University.

———. 1974. "Some Aspects of Yoruba Aesthetics." *British Journal of Aesthetics* 14(3):239–249.

———. 1978. "New Light on Gelede." *African Arts* 11(2):65–70, 94.

Legbe, O. A., Babalawo and Oro Efe. 1971. Interview, Emado Quarter, Aiyetoro, March 20.

Lindfors, B., and O. Owomoyela. 1973. *Yoruba Proverbs: Translation and Annotation.* Athens: Ohio University Center for International Studies.

Lloyd, P. C. 1963. "The Status of the Yoruba Wife." *Sudan Society* 2:35–42.

———. 1974. *Power and Independence.* London: Routledge & Kegan Paul.

Lomax A. 1968. *Folk Song Style and Culture.* Washington, D. C.: American Association for the Advancement of Science, Publication #88.

Losi, J. B. O. 1923. *The History of Abeokuta.* Lagos.

————. 1967 [1914]. *History of Lagos*. Lagos: African Education Press.

Lucas, J. O. 1948. *The Religion of the Yorubas*. Lagos: Church Missionary Society Bookshop.

MacLean, U. 1969. "Sickness Behavior among the Yoruba (Ibadan)." In *Witchcraft and Healing, Seminar Proceedings, February 14–15*. Edinburgh: Center for African Studies, pp. 29–42.

McLeod, J. 1820. *Voyage to Africa: With Some Account of the Manners and Customs of the Dahomian People*. London: Murray.

Marshall G. 1962. "The Marketing of Farm Produce: Some Patterns of Trade among Women in Western Nigeria." In *Proceedings of the 8th Conference of the Nigerian Institute of Social and Economic Research*, Ibadan, March, pp. 88–99.

Morton-Williams, P. 1956. "The Atinga Cult among the South Western Yoruba: A Sociological Analysis of a Witch-Finding Movement." *Bulletin de l'IFAN*. series B, 18(3–4):315–334.

————. 1960. "The Yoruba Ogboni Cult in Oyo." *Africa* 30:362–374.

————. 1964a. "The Oyo Yoruba and the Atlantic Trade, 1670–1830." *Journal of the Historical Society of Nigeria* 3(1):25–45.

————. 1964b. "Yoruba Responses to the Fear of Death." *Africa* 30(1):34–40.

————. 1969. "The Influence of Habitat and Trade on the Polities of Oyo and Ashanti." In *Man in Africa*. Edited by M. Douglas and P. M. Kaberry. London: Tavistock, pp. 79–89.

Moulero, T. 1970. "Le Guèlèdè." Manuscript. Porto Novo, Benin.

————, historian of Ketu and Sabe peoples. 1971. Interview, Ketu, May 15.

Murray, K. C. n.d.; 1936; 1940; 1942; 1946; 1948; 1950; 1960. Unpublished notes in the Nigerian Museum Archives, Lagos.

Norris, R. 1968 [1789]. *Memoires of the Reign of Bossa Ahadee, King of Dahomey*. London: Cass.

Nunley, J. 1981. "The Fancy and the Fierce." *African Arts* 14(2):52–58, 87–88.

Obajiwo, J., Olori Onigelede. 1978. Interview, Ibara Quarter, Abeokuta, April.

Odu, O., Oba of Pobe, Benin. 1973. Interview, Pobe, May 7.

Odugbesan, C. 1969. "Femininity in Yoruba Religious Art." In *Man in Africa*. Edited by M. Douglas and P. M. Kaberry. London: Tavistock, pp. 199–211.

Ogunbiyi, A., Oba of Ilobi. 1973. Interview, Ilobi, April 15.

Ogundipe, A. L., Oro Efe. 1971. Interview, Ketu, April 25.

Ogundipe, R., Babalawo and carver. 1975. Interview, Ilaro, November 18.

Oguntade, A., Bale. 1971. Interview, Kesan Orile, April 18.

Ojo, G. J. A. 1966. *Yoruba Culture: A Geographical Analysis*. London: University of London Press.

Ojo, J. R. O. 1973. "Orisa Oko, the Deity of the 'Farm and Agriculture' among the Ekiti." *African Notes* 7(2).

Oke, S. A. E., Bale. 1971. Interview, Igan Okoto, March 20.

Okesola, E. 1967. "The Agbo Festival in Agbowa." *Nigeria Magazine* 95:293–300.

Olabimtan, A. 1970. "An Introduction to Efe Poems of the Egbado Yoruba." *Staff Seminar Papers and Subsequent Discussions*, School of African and Asian Studies, University of Lagos, Lagos, Nigeria, pp. 192–216.

Olajubu, O. 1978. "Yoruba Verbal Artists and Their Work." *Journal of American Folklore* 91(360):675–690.

Olaniyan, K., carver. 1975. Interview, Iga Igbein, Oruba Quarter, Ota, October 18.

————, carver. 1981. Inverview, Iga Igbein, Oruba Quarter, Ota, April 23.

Olatibosun, E. A., Otun Bale. 1971. Interview, Igan Okoto, March 20.

Olowobese, E., Bale. 1975. Interview, Oja Odan, November 10.

Olupona, L., carver. 1975, Interview, Ohumbe, November 13.

Onluiji, Bale. 1971. Interview, Ilara, March 23.

Ortiz, F. 1906. *Hampa Afrocubana: Los Negros Bruyos*. Madrid: Editorial—Americana.

————. 1952. *Los instrumentos de la música afrocubana*. vol. 3. Havana: Ministerio de Cultura.

Ositola, K., Babalawo. 1982. Interview, Ijebu-Ode, May.

Osubi, S., Babalawo and carver. 1973. Interview, Iwoye, May 19.

Osun, A., Babalawo. 1971. Interview, Idofa, April 17.

Owoleye, Asipa. 1971. Interview, Igan Okoto, April 16.

Owomoyela, O. 1979. "A Fractioned Word in a Muted Mouth: The Pointed Subtlety of Yoruba Proverbs." Paper read at the Annual Meeting of the African Studies Association, Los Angeles, October 31–November 3.

Palau-Marti, M. 1964. *Essai sur la notion de roi chez les Yorubas et les Aja-Fon.* Paris: Berger-Levrault.

———. 1979. "Les Sabe—Opara (Hinterland de la Côte du Benin): Apport de Materiaux et Essai d'Interpretation." 3 vols. Thesis for the Doctorat d'Etat, Université de Paris V, Sciences Humaines, Sorbonne.

———. 1980. Personal communication, September 5.

Parrinder, G. 1967. *The Story of Ketu.* Ibadan: Ibadan University Press.

Peterson, J. 1979. *Province of Freedom: A History of Sierra Leone, 1787–1870.* London: Faber & Faber.

Petition from the Ilobi Tribes of Oke-Odan Districts, Ilaro Division, Abeokuta Province, Southern Nigeria to His Excellency the Governor in Council, Lagos. 1932. Lagos: Samadu Press.

Prince, R. 1960. "Curse, Invocation and Mental Health among the Yoruba." *Canadian Psychiatric Journal* 5:65–79.

———. 1961. "The Yoruba Image of the Witch." *Journal of Mental Science* 107(449):795–805.

———. 1979 [1975]. "Symbols and Psychotherapy: The Example of Yoruba Sacrificial Ritual." In *African Therapeutic Systems.* Edited by Z. A. Ademuwagun et al. Waltham, Mass.: Crossroads Press, pp. 114–119.

Quarcoo, A. K. 1972. *The Language of Adinkra Patterns.* Legon: Institute of African Studies, University of Ghana.

Ray, B. 1973. "'Performative Utterances' in African Rituals." *History of Religions* 13(1):16–35.

Robinson, A. 1971. Personal communication, November 13.

Roy, C. D. 1979. *African Sculpture: The Stanley Collection.* Iowa City: University of Iowa Museum of Art.

Schiltz, M. 1978. "Egungun Masquerades in Iganna." *African Arts* 11(3):48–55.

Smith, R. 1969. *Kingdoms of the Yoruba.* London: Methuen and Co., Ltd.

Snelgrave, W. 1971 [1734]. *A New Account of Some Parts of Guinea and the Slave-Trade.* London: Cass.

Speed, F. 1968. *Gelede: A Yoruba Masquerade.* Ile-Ife: Institute of African Studies, University of Ife. Sound film, 30 min., color.

Sudarkasa, N. 1973. *Where Women Work: A Study of Yoruba Women in the Marketplace and in the Home.* Anthropology Papers, Museum of Anthropology, #53. Ann Arbor: University of Michigan.

Taiwo, B. A. 1971. Interview, Ketu, April 25.

Talbot, P. A. 1969 [1926]. *The People of Southern Nigeria,* vol. 3. London: Frank Cass and Co., Ltd.

Thompson, R. F. 1970. "The Sign of the Divine King." *African Arts* 3(3):8–17, 74–80.

———. 1971. *Black Gods and Kings: Yoruba Art at UCLA.* Occasional Papers of the Museum and Laboratories of Ethnic Arts and Technology 2. Los Angeles: University of California Press. Reprint Bloomington: Indiana University Press, 1976.

———. 1972. Personal communication, April 20.

———. 1974a. *African Art in Motion.* Los Angeles: University of California Press.

———. 1974b. Personal communication.

———. 1975. "Icons of the Mind: Yoruba Herbalism Arts in Atlantic Perspective." *African Arts* 8(3):52–59, 89–90.

———. 1978. "Gelede Mask." In *Twenty-Five African Sculptures.* Edited by J. Fry. Ottawa: The National Galleries of Canada, pp. 58–65.

Turner, J. M. 1975. "Les Brésiliens—The Impact of Former Brazilian Slaves upon Dahomey." Ph.D. diss., Boston University.

Verger, P. 1954. "Rôle joué par l'état d'Hébétude au cours de l'initiation des novices aux Cultes des *Orisha* et *Vodun*." *Bulletin de l'IFAN*, series B, 16(3–4): 322–340.

———. 1957. "Notes sur le Culte des Orisa et Vodun à Bahia, la Baie de tous les Saints au Brésil et à l'Anciènne Côte des Esclaves en Afrique." *Mémoires de l'IFAN,* 51.

———. 1964a. "Le Tabac de Bahia et la Traite des Esclaves." *Cahiers d'études africaines* 4(3).

———. 1964b. "The Yoruba High God: A Review of the Sources." Paper prepared for the Conference on the High God in Africa, Ibadan, December 14–18.

———. 1965. "Grandeur et Décadence du Culte de *iyámi òṣòròngà* (ma mère la sorcière) chez les *yoruba*." *Journal de la société des africanistes* 35(1):141–243.

———. 1967. *Awon Ewe Osanyin: Yoruba Medicinal Leaves.* Ifẹ: Institute of African Studies, University of Ifẹ.

———. 1976. "The Use of Plants in Yoruba Traditional Medicine and Its Linguistic Approach." Seminar Paper, Department of African Languages and Literatures, University of Ifẹ, Ile-Ifẹ, Nigeria, October 25.

Warburton. 1837. *Missionary Register, February 28.* London: Church Missionary Society.

Wilkes, I. 1961. *The Northern Factor in Ashanti History.* Legon: Institute of African Studies, University College of Ghana.

Willett, F. 1967. *Ife in the History of West African Sculpture.* New York: McGraw-Hill.

———. 1971. *African Art: An Introduction.* New York: Praeger.

Wolff, H. 1962. "Rárà: A Yoruba Chant." *Journal of African Languages* 1(1):45 ff.

INDEX

300